CANADA'S
BEST
EMPLOYERS
FOR
WOMEN

CANADA'S BEST EMPLOYERS FOR WOMEN

A GUIDE FOR JOB HUNTERS, EMPLOYEES AND EMPLOYERS

Tema Frank

Frank Communications

This book is available at a discount when ordered in large quantities. For information, contact Frank Communications, 253 College Street, Suite 200, Toronto, Ontario, Canada, M5T 1R5, or fax (416) 591-7202.

Typeset by Computer Composition of Canada Inc., Whitby Ontario
Cover by Eskins Design, Toronto, Ontario
Printed by Edwards Brothers Inc., Ann Arbor, Michigan

Canadian Cataloguing in Publication Data

Frank, Tema, 1960–
    Canada's best employers for women: a guide for job hunters, employees and employers

    Includes bibliographical references and index.
    ISBN 0-9698737-0-0

    1. Women – Employment – Canada.   2. Sex discrimination in employment – Canada.   3. Corporations – Canada.
    I. Title.

    HD6099.F73 1994   331.4'0971   C94-932114-1

Acknowledgements

There are many people who helped and encouraged me as I wrote this book, but I am particularly grateful to John Shaw. His support, encouragement and editorial services were unwavering as the book moved from its conception in London, England, to its completion, two and a half years, many late nights and one baby later. My thanks also to Benedict, who gave me a first-hand appreciation of the challenges faced by working mothers.

Thanks also to my mother, Rheva, who drove me crazy when I was a child by interrupting my excited tales about what had happened in school that day to correct my grammar. I am so glad that she taught me how to speak and write properly.

My father, George, and my brothers, Albert and Murray, played the helpful role of devil's advocates. They forced me to question the popular wisdom and think through my assumptions. I hope the book reflects the critical thinking they tried to inspire.

Finally, my thanks to the Ontario Arts Council for its support; to my family members, who invested in the project when the initial publishing deal fell through; to Margaret Oldfield, for her editorial services; to the friends, family and colleagues (particularly Jane Cooney, of the Books for Business store) who offered editorial advice and helped with the proofreading; to Peter Scaggs, for his guidance through the production process; to Linda McKnight, for her moral support and advice; and to the Financial Post for providing a disk copy of its Top 500 list.

About the Author

Tema Frank is the President of *Frank Communications*, a consulting firm specializing in helping employers communicate their ideas and policies clearly to employees, customers, the public and governments. Ms. Frank, who is fluent in English and French, has an M.B.A. from the University of Toronto, a Bachelor of Commerce degree from the University of Alberta, and is a Fellow of the Institute of Canadian Bankers. Before opening Frank Communications, she worked in marketing, public affairs, and business-government relations. Her writing about business and marketing has appeared in national magazines.

Table of Contents

Why This Book?

If you are one of the millions of Canadian women looking for a good place to work or struggling to combine a job with a busy personal life, this book is for you. If you are an employer wanting a competitive edge as you head into the next century, this book is for you too. If you are a man looking for the best places to work, believe it or not, this book is for you too because most employers that are good for women are good for men too.

Unfortunately, the reverse is not always true. Some organizations in which men do well are hostile to women. Their male executives and managers think women should only hold clerical jobs, and they treat clerical staff like machines, not people. Other employers think of themselves as neutral, but they keep women out of the informal networks they need to be part of to get ahead. Finally, some organizations don't offer the flexibility that so many women need as they struggle to balance work and family commitments. Men like flexibility too, but the double burden of work and family still weighs most heavily on women.

I wrote this book because it is time to recognize employers that are making above average efforts to attract, retain and promote women. I want to help women discover which employers are most open to meeting their needs. I also want to give employers ideas on how to improve their organizations, to make them better places for women and men.

The Dual Role of Women in the Workforce

- 71% of couples with children under 19 were two-income families in 1990.
- In 1992, 64% of married women with children under 16 had paid employment (up from 49% in 1981).
- 57% of married women with children under age three were employed in 1992, up from 40% in 1981.
- Employed women spend four to five hours a day on domestic work; one to two hours a day more than men in the same domestic circumstances.
- In 52% of two-income families the wives do all the cooking and cleaning and in 28% they do most of the chores.
- Women are nearly twice as likely to report intensive elder care responsibilities than men.

Sources: Statistics Canada and The Canadian Aging Research Network.

The organizations in this book have different strengths and weaknesses. Some are wonderful places for people who want to combine work and family, but their female employees are still mainly in clerical jobs and junior management. Others are great places for women who want to get ahead, but those women must be totally dedicated to work. Still others are flexible and have satisfied employees, but little in the way of formal policies, so everything could change with a new chief executive officer.

The book is divided into five sections. **Part I** contains background information on how I chose the employers, where I found them, and a summary of trends I saw among the organizations I studied.

Part II describes each organization in detail. I compared employers to others within their own industries. I expected more of employers such as banks, that have long had a female-dominated workforce, than of employers in male-dominated industries like the energy sector. So it was harder, for example, for a hospital to get into the book than for a manufacturer.

The "best", especially in male-dominated industries, are sometimes organizations that are trying hard to become good employers for women and are headed in the right direction, but have not yet created wonderful working environments with lots of women in management and non-traditional jobs. I included them because they deserve credit for trying, and because women interested in those fields should know what "the best" means these days in such industries.

Part III looks at "The Best of the Best", including a top 10 listing and other handy reference lists of employers offering various types of benefits and facilities.

Part IV offers advice to employees and job hunters about how to make a workplace work for them.

Part V is mainly for employers. It explains why the employers in this book feel it is worthwhile to make special efforts to be a good employer for women, and offers advice about how to become one of the best.

If you want more details, have a look at the appendices. **Appendix A** is about alternative working arrangements (AWAs). It explains the different types of AWAs, and discusses the pros and cons of each. **Appendix B** summarizes federal and provincial laws on maternity and child care leaves. **Appendix C** elaborates on the methods I used to select Canada's best employers for women.

* * *

You may be tempted at this point to skip from here straight over to the employer entries in Part II. I think you'll find Part I interesting. It looks at issues like:

- why women in some organizations can't afford to let a soft, sensitive side show;
- the terrible waste of clerical talent in many organizations;
- the fact that some women (and men) are not senior executives because they don't want to be; and
- reasons why women still often earn less than men doing the same jobs in the same organizations.

In case you don't come back to it until later, though, I'd like to ask a favour of you now. This book is the result of a two-year search for the best employers for women, but there are undoubtedly some that I missed. **If you know of an employer that you think is as good as or better than those listed here, please complete and send in the suggestion form at the back of this book. I'd also love to hear what you thought about the book, and any ideas you have for the next edition.**

Part I:
Overview

How the Best Were Chosen

To decide which employers were Canada's best, I looked for a combination of:

- satisfied employees,
- numbers that showed women making good progress into senior management and non-traditional jobs, and
- policies and practices that help employees who are trying to combine work and busy personal lives.

Policies alone were not good enough to get an employer into the book; there had to be evidence that the commitment was real.

Over 700 organizations were sent a survey that asked about the following:

- the distribution of women and men in the organization,
- maternity leave provisions,
- support for child and elder care,
- flexible work options,
- career breaks other than maternity leave,
- recruitment and promotion policies,
- training programs,
- sexual harassment policies and practices, and
- other reasons why the employer felt it was good for women.

One hundred and thirty-two employers replied. They employ over half a million people full-time and 60,000 part-time. They each had to have at least 50 employees to qualify for the book.

I chose 70 organizations in which to do follow-up interviews. In total, I interviewed over 1,500 women. Some were in management, some were clerical workers, some worked in trades and technical jobs. Some had children, others did not.

The women I interviewed were guaranteed anonymity. When women are quoted by name in this book, it's because it would be obvious to their colleagues who had made the statement, so I got permission to quote them by name.

I would have liked to interview men, but it seemed unlikely that men would open up to a female interviewer writing a book on this topic. Professors Higgins, Duxbury and Lee had that experience when they studied work and family stress among Canadian employees.[1] When

---

[1] Duxbury, Linda, as reported at "The National Work & Family Challenge: Issues & Options" conference, The Conference Board of Canada and The Canadian Committee for the International Year of the Family 1994, March 22 & 23, 1994.

they had women interview men, the men claimed that they had no problems balancing work and family. The average interview length dropped from 40 minutes to 10. When they had men interview men, they discovered that men were experiencing the same sorts of stress as women. The average interview length became even longer than it had been when women interviewed women.

What is important for this book is how women *perceive* the attitudes of the men they work with; not what the men actually think. That's not to say that the views of men are unimportant: employers that want to improve the conditions for women in their organizations must learn what men and women think, and find ways to help them work together.

Where Are the Best?

Which industries are the best for women depends on the woman who is asking. Different industries and types of employers within an industry will appeal to different kinds of women.

The banks used to have women in the branches train young men fresh out of school to move into management jobs. Over time (and with prodding from employment equity legislation), most finally realized that it made more sense to have those women move into management jobs themselves. The financial services companies in this book have cultures that are generally good for women. They have, and are implementing, policies to make sure both that women are not held back, and to help female employees balance the many demands on their lives.

Governments, universities, and other public-sector employers can be wonderful for people who want to combine work and family, but not so good for entrepreneurial spirits, who may get frustrated with the bureaucracy.

The reverse is true in fast-growing companies. The opportunities are there as long as you are willing to put in long hours. Companies that are growing quickly don't care if a body is male or female as long as it can get the job done.

Want to do well in a company that's growing quickly? Don't be shy. You have to be able to spot and seize opportunities. Be prepared to argue your case if you want to do something out of the ordinary, like job-sharing or working a four-day week. Fast-growing companies have few policies or systems in place. In fact, most are not great places for combining work and family because everyone is rushing to keep up with the growth. The last thing they want to hear is that a valued employee wants to work fewer hours. They generally have fewer benefits than other employers, and are reluctant to spend time on training.

But, for the right sort of woman, the excitement and challenges they provide can more than make up for these drawbacks.

The manufacturing, resources, construction and transportation sectors are still tough for women. One manufacturer I interviewed had great policies on the books, but, during three hours of interviews, the women who worked there stressed that the policies only existed so that the company could bid on federal contracts; there was no commitment to them. Few resources or construction firms even bothered to answer the survey for the book.

Professional firms are surprisingly inflexible, especially considering that, for years now, many of the graduates of Canada's professional schools have been women. Part of the problem is that law, accounting and other professional firms are used to valuing people based on the hours they put in. Time is tracked almost to the minute. A woman who is considered a "part-time lawyer" at Tory Tory DesLauriers & Binnington works nine to five, Monday to Friday. Most professional firms will not even consider letting professionals work part-time. The result? They lose many of the brightest women. When Tory Tory advertised jobs for part-time lawyers it was flooded with applications from bright, competent women.

All organizations, even large ones, have an overriding corporate culture that can be good, bad or indifferent for women. The tone is set by the President and other top executives. But each employee's experience depends a lot on her immediate supervisors. You might get stuck with a bad supervisor even in the best of organizations. If you work in a large organization, as long as the overall culture isn't negative, you at least have a hope of being able to escape from a bad supervisor without having to quit. But you probably won't be happy if you hate bureaucracy.

The Largest of Canada's Best Employers For Women:

Bell Canada   41,000 full-time and 3,477 part-time employees

The Smallest of Canada's Best Employers For Women:

Freda's Originals   65 full-time and 13 part-time employees

Geographically, most of the best employers for women are found in Toronto, Montreal and Vancouver. That's partly because most Canadian companies are based in those cities, but also because the people who live and work there seem to be more open to career women. Smaller centres often have more stay-at-home wives, so employers aren't as used to dealing with career-oriented women. Also, women working in smaller centres often find that they don't dare get close to men who could mentor them because people would misinterpret the closeness.

Employers in Atlantic Canada tend to downplay their accomplishments, and most were reluctant to be considered for the book.

In fact, in all parts of the country, there were employers with good reputations that did not want to participate. Many claimed they were good places for women but wouldn't release the data that could help prove it. One has to wonder if, in some cases, their good reputations have more to do with their public relations skills than with solid achievements. Other employers may be strong in one area, like flexible working hours, but know that they are not as good overall.

Many companies that have good reputations in the United States either wouldn't participate or didn't look as good here as they are reputed to be there. Canadian law requires much more of employers than does American law. Many companies that are leading-edge in the United States just do what the law requires here.

Other organizations worried about an internal backlash if they appeared in this book. That view was common among universities, many of which look wonderful compared to private sector employers but can't do enough to meet the high expectations of their employees. "Staff complain that we *only* have four day care centres," said one university's employment equity officer, in a typical comment.

Life in the Boy's Club

When an employer first becomes aware of the concerns of female employees and starts trying to address them, there will still be a lot of internal resistance. This is the first stage of becoming a good employer for women.

Women who work at organizations in the first stage have to be tougher than women in more advanced organizations. They must perform much better than their male colleagues to have a hope of advancing. They have to play by the 'boys club' rules. They dare not act 'feminine'.

It is in those organizations (or those that haven't even reached the first stage) that support staff complain that women are not good bosses; say that they prefer working for men. Why? Because the few female managers are so rushed and stressed in their effort to outperform the men that they don't have time for socializing. They need their support staff to work constantly in order to keep up. Many such women are also trying to be more masculine than the men; they don't dare let a softer side show.

There's no point in telling women in such organizations that they should be more feminine. As Catherine Ford at the Calgary Herald noted, "In order to succeed in this business I suppose I took a naturally aggressive, domineering personality and sharpened it to a fine point. Nobody should have to be this aggressive in order to be successful." She started in the business when there were few women. The reality was that she *had* to be aggressive!

The blue-collar areas of most employers are still in the first stage, even if the organization as a whole has moved beyond it. Surprisingly, the blue-collar women I interviewed were some of the most content workers I met. They knew they were trail-blazers; understood that they had to be tough and not be offended by vulgar language. Once they had proven themselves, they were accepted. They were glad to be allowed to do the work and to be paid well for doing it. Many enjoyed the physical side. Those who had previously been clerical workers often commented that they had more freedom and autonomy in their new jobs. Women who are not tough and determined do not last in blue-collar jobs.

Office workers, on the other hand, tended to expect more of the men they worked with, and were often offended by subtle slights that would barely have been noticed by their blue-collar counterparts. As a result, white-collar workers often perceived their situation as worse.

The Special Case of Support Staff

Technology is changing the role of white-collar support staff. With computers on almost every desk, it now seems reasonable for managers to do most of their own typing. As more data is stored electronically, the need for filing is fading away. Many secretaries, though, feel that managers should also be doing their own faxing, photocopying and coffee-fetching. Many managers disagree, arguing that a manager's time is more expensive and should be devoted to work that only the manager can do. If managers type their thoughts straight into a computer rather than writing them out long-hand and passing the scribbles to a secretary, the organization saves time. No time is saved, however, when managers do tasks like faxing and photocopying — the same task is done, but by different hands.

Most employers that talk about empowering their staff have not figured out how to empower their support staff and still get the menial work done. Support staff feel that they are being asked to assume new responsibilities on top of their old ones without more help or pay.

Clerical and management women can have very different needs and perceptions. For example, benefits tend to be more important to clerical women because benefits often make up a greater share of their compensation. Clerical women may also be less likely to be married to men with generous benefit packages.

We tend to overlook important similarities between clerical and management women though. It was clear from the interviews I did for the book that both groups want to be respected, to have challenging work, and to have opportunities for education and advancement.

There is a terrible waste of clerical talent in Canadian organizations. Increasingly, employers are focusing on academic credentials at the expense of experience, ability and a willingness to learn. I met many women who had joined their organizations as clerical workers in the 1970s or early 1980s and are now doing well as managers. Every one of them said that it would be nearly impossible to make that transition today.

Not Everyone Wants to be a Senior Manager

One of the most surprising findings was the number of women ready to enter senior management who said they didn't want to do so. The time pressure that goes with senior management jobs is the main deterrent. Women still bear most of the responsibility for household and family care, so it's harder for them to put in as many hours as do ambitious men.

Even with good support systems in place, some women found that once they had children their priorities changed. They still wanted interesting, challenging paid work, but there were limits to how much of it they were willing to do at that stage in their lives. They weren't slackers; most still worked a solid eight to ten hours a day in the office and spent another hour or so working from home once their children were asleep. However, they weren't willing to put in the 60 to 80 hour week that is typical of senior managers. Commented one such women at Union Gas, "I no longer want to be a V.P. It involves too much time and too much responsibility."

Another deterrent to entering senior management is that many women prefer work with a people orientation. These women commented that as managers moved higher in the organization they got further removed from clients and staff, and focused more on paper. An assistant store manager at Ben Moss Jewellers was typical of this line of thinking. "I prefer being an assistant manager because I like to sell and to be involved," she said. "I don't want the bottom-line responsibility of budgeting."

I was also struck by how many women I met with strong technical backgrounds who, after several years in technical jobs switched into "softer" areas like human resources. Their employers didn't pressure them to make the move; they wanted to.

Many of them said that the change was temporary, but it was rare to find any who had made the transition back. A manager at NOVA explained, "After eight years in a previous company and eight years here, I still had not made it into management. I decided to make a change. I applied for a management job in a softer skills area. I wanted to manage staff; I wanted to work with people. It was wonderful. . . . Now [five years later] I've been told that I've demonstrated good leadership skills, but when I try to combine the two, they say that I no longer have the technical skills."

Technology can be a blessing and a curse in helping women to cope with the time demands of their work. It gives them the flexibility to work from home when, for example, a child is sick, but it is becoming an intrusion on family time. Managers in several organizations noted that they are now expected to check their electronic mail from home and to stay in touch electronically during vacations. Men who used to go out for drinks after work are now going home, having dinner with the family and then hooking up with the boys on computer while their wives get the children to bed and clean the house.

Why Women Earn Less Than Men in Similar Jobs

The ratio of female to male earnings is increasing as women get the training and experience to move into jobs traditionally held by men, and as employers learn to consider women for such jobs. In 1992, women earned 71.8 cents for every dollar earned by men, up from 69.6 cents a year earlier. But the fact that most women still earn less than most men traps women in a vicious circle. If one spouse has to make a career sacrifice, it will usually be the woman because she earns less. By making that career sacrifice she perpetuates the view that women are less committed to their careers, so she (and other women) are less likely to get promotions. Without the promotions, they will continue to earn less than men.

Women are still often paid less than men who hold the same types of jobs in the same organization. During one focus group interview the management women talked about how much they enjoyed their work, how much time they devoted to it and how wonderful the opportunities were for advancement. When I asked them about pay, the mood changed abruptly. "The men at the same level earn much more," said one, to a chorus of nodding heads. "It's a sore point," said another. Added a third, "It wouldn't be so bad if everybody was poorly paid."

Why do they accept lower pay? First, women are more likely to have moved up internally. If an employee started at a junior level and is promoted to a much more senior job, both she and her employer are likely to focus their attention (and negotiations) on the amount of the pay *increase* rather than on what the employer would have to pay to hire an outsider to fill the senior job.

Second, many women interviewed seemed willing to accept lower pay in exchange for challenge and opportunity. It may be that women are more risk averse than men when it comes to their jobs and thus less willing to threaten to quit if they don't get the salary they want. More likely, the actual risks they face are greater. I wanted to include more employers in this book, but I couldn't, because there are still so many organizations in which women's opportunities are more limited than those of men. If women quit, they may not be able to find better jobs.

Third, most management women don't have as much time to socialize as the men, so they are probably less aware of what their colleagues earn. As any negotiator knows, the more information you have, the stronger your bargaining power.

Fourth, many women work in lower paying, people-oriented industries, like hospitality, health care, retail and other services. As a result, they are used to lower rates of pay. Even if they cross over to work in a higher paying industry, they will likely not expect to earn as much as a man who has always worked in the higher paying industry.

What Makes an Employer Good for Women?

There are four elements that go into making an organization good for women:
- it provides good opportunities for advancement and career development;
- it is flexible in meeting the needs of its employees;
- it supports them in their child and elder care responsibilities;
- it has a friendly, tolerant working environment.

What are the best employers doing in these areas?

1. *Advancement and Career Development Opportunities*

There is a myth afloat that an employer that's good for women must somehow be bad for men, that this is a zero-sum game. That just isn't true.

Not one of the organizations I surveyed uses quotas to guarantee positions for women. Many set targets, just as they do for other business objectives, but all recognize that promoting incompetent women just to "get the numbers up" will harm them in the long run. Good men have nothing to fear from working in an organization that wants to give equal opportunities to equally good women.

Instead, the best employers are using one or all of the following approaches to get more women into senior and non-traditional jobs:

(a) *Better use of in-house talent:* They are taking a closer look at the abilities of the women on staff and finding better ways to use them. They have stopped making career-limiting assumptions, for example, women will not return to work once they have had babies (the Bank of Montreal found that 98% do return) or women will not accept jobs that involve travel, night-time work, or relocation.

   They have reviewed their systems and practices to make it easier for women to take on new challenges. Some employers, like the Canada Mortgage and Housing Corporation, will pay for babysitters when no family member is available to look after children during work-related travel or evening functions. Others, like Union Gas, help spouses find new jobs when an employee is asked to relocate.

   The best employers have also looked at unintentional, or systemic, barriers to the advancement of women and tried to overcome those barriers with things like mentoring programs. (See Part III for a list of organizations with formal mentoring programs).

   Some, like the Calgary Board of Education and American Express, now have performance evaluations done by peers, subordinates, and customers as well as immediate superiors. This gives a more balanced view of the employee's performance and can help employees get around unsupportive supervisors.

(b) *Finding new sources of outside talent:* The best are taking new approaches to recruiting. These employers now work directly with groups in the communities that are under-represented among their employees to try to find qualified candidates who might never have considered working for them in the past. If an employer is in an industry that has a reputation for being bad for women, it may take this kind of effort to overcome the stereotype and get talented women to apply.

   Some employers take the process a step further back, trying to increase the number of women who have the needed qualifications. Many companies in the energy sector, for example, support programs that encourage girls to study science and engineering. Wood Gundy, an investment banker, speaks to women in first-year Masters of Business Administration (M.B.A.) classes to encourage them to study finance.

(c) *Special training programs:* When there is a clear need, usually in trades and technical jobs, some employers offer programs designed specially to help women move into areas where they are under-represented. The City of Toronto's "BRIDGES" program was one of the first and has been used as a model by many other employers. Loto-Québec set up an internship program to help female employees become sales representatives. The program was so successful that by the third year Loto-Québec had overcome its shortage of women in the sales force. Managers were pleased with the training it provided, so the internship program was opened to male employees too. As the Loto-Québec example shows, a commitment to education and training benefits all employees.

In addition to the "bridging" courses, some employers surveyed offer occasional courses or seminars just for women (such as self-defence courses at the Toronto Transit Commission and a Women's Health Day at Credit Valley Hospital). None of the employers surveyed, however, have budgets that are weighted unreasonably in favour of women. They almost all reported that men and women take training in proportion to their numbers in the organization's workforce.

2. *Flexibility in Meeting Employee Needs*

Flexibility can be formal or informal. Formal flexibility includes alternative working arrangements (AWAs): policies that let employees vary the standard nine to five work day, both in terms of when and where the work gets done. (For more information about AWAs and their advantages and drawbacks, see Appendix A). AWAs must be endorsed formally to be meaningful, except in small organizations. When AWAs are not endorsed formally most supervisors are afraid to risk allowing anything out of the ordinary.

Even more important to most employees is the informal flexibility they can get from a good supervisor. A bad supervisor can keep them from using the best of policies; a good supervisor can be flexible even when the policies are not.

Flexibility is important to men too. The Bank of Montreal found that 40% of the users of its flexible work arrangements are men. Even child care leaves are starting to be used by men, especially men in non-managerial jobs. Canadian National Railways reports that during a recent

18-month period, 40% of its employees on parental leave were men.[2] Though they did not have data, staff at the Canadian Broadcasting Corporation also commented that a lot of men in technical jobs now take parental leave.

3. *Support for Child and Elder Care*

Child care responsibilities still fall mainly on women. A steadily increasing number of those women are in the workforce. Care of aging parents is also a growing concern to employees.

Even among the best employers, few have on-site day care centres. (For a list of those who do, see Part III). Employer-based day care tends to be top quality, but it is expensive to build and run and it only meets the needs of a handful of employees. In large cities many employees find that commuting with a young child is more trouble than it is worth. Even on-site day care centres are not usually open long enough to accommodate overtime or shift work.

Instead, a growing number of employers are hiring outside companies to provide computerized child and elder care referral services to their employees (see list in Part III). Most services report on the licensed care options available in the employee's (or elderly parent's) neighbourhood. They give details about the type of care, the cost, and space availability.

VanCity has also experimented with a development fund to create new child care spaces by giving seed money to in-home day care centres to help them get licensed.

Some employers are also considering ways to help parents deal with children after school and during school holidays. They are looking at options like summer camps for children of employees, and on-site activities when the schools are closed for "professional development days". Some professional firms, like Price Waterhouse, will consider a "part-time" work option where employees work full or even overtime hours during busy seasons, but can take the summer off to be with their children.

Care of sick children is a problem for most working parents. Many employers, such as York University, now let employees use some or all of their sick time toward the care of ill dependents. Employees are relieved that they no longer have to lie and pretend that they were the ones who were sick, but, as many of them said, three or five days vanish quickly when you have more than one pre-schooler. The rest of the time

---

[2] Abramowitz, Fran, quoted in "Family Ties", Report on Business Magazine, March, 1993.

they need to look after sick family members comes from their own vacation time. Unfortunately, that means that some parents of young children have no sick time or vacation time left for themselves, so they may be more likely to become run down or ill.

The Bank of Montreal trusts its employees not to abuse what it calls "People Care Days". Employees may take as many days as they need to deal with sick dependents or even to attend to personal matters. The Bank has found that the people abusing the system are the same ones who abused the old system. On average, employees take two or three People Care Days a year. Some actually take fewer days off than they used to. In the past they would pretend to be sick in order to run an errand that only needed a couple of hours. Since they were pretending to be sick, they felt they could not come in once the errand had been done. Now they will.

4. *Positive work environment*

Almost every employer surveyed has a sexual or personal harassment policy. Some are more effective than others. The best employers make it clear through actions and words that they will not tolerate sexual harassment or sexist behaviour.

If an employer gets to the point where it has to take strong disciplinary action or even fire an employee for harassment, it's a good idea to be open with staff about why the action was taken. In companies like Petro Canada, where someone was fired for harassment and the company was open about it, the women were absolutely confident that they did not have to tolerate harassment and that, if they reported it, their complaint would be taken seriously.

It is equally important to educate employees about what the rules mean while cracking down on inappropriate behaviour. A lot of men are, as one woman said, "walking on glass". They need reassurance and guidance about what is appropriate behaviour.

All employees should be taught about what is appropriate, not just managers. That is especially important in parts of the organization that have a history of being "macho cultures".

Most women find that confronting the harasser directly ends the problem, but they can't always risk doing so. Human resources policies shouldn't force them to.

Maritime Life has two particularly good options to help deal with sexual harassment. First, employees can call a confidential advice line run by an outside company that will not release any information to Maritime Life unless the employee allows it. The advisors may be able to suggest ways to solve the problem before it explodes. The advice line is also available to people who have been accused of harassing, to help them understand why the problem has arisen and to suggest ways to deal with it. Maritime Life also provides a mediation service that can be used to try to resolve problems before formal complaints are laid.

Sexual harassment from clients seems to be an even bigger problem than harassment by co-workers. Women in sales are especially vulnerable. Many men seem to think that behaviour they know is not acceptable within their own organizations is fine when someone wants their business.

Successful salespeople find ways to deal with sexist customers, but they appreciate knowing that their employer will stand behind them if there is a problem. Staff at the Calgary Herald, for example, were reassured when the publisher intervened after learning that one of his salespeople was being harassed. He made it clear to the client that he was prepared to lose the business if necessary.

How to use Part II: Reading Between the Lines

In Part II, you will discover what each employer is doing for women. Many of the employers' policies apply to others in the so-called "designated groups" too: visible minorities, people with disabilities, and aboriginal people. I have not dealt separately with the concerns of women who are members of other "designated groups". What I found was that in the good organizations, such women also commented on being treated well. At problem places, their problems were magnified.

A few words of caution in interpreting the charts that accompany each listing:

1. *Numbers.* Employers were surveyed between May and December 1993. A few were able to update the data they had on the numbers and distribution of employees to early 1994 figures before this book went to press, but most of the numbers provided are from year-end 1992 or sometime in 1993.

   The total numbers of full-time employees do not always add up to the same total in the job category breakdown (which is normally based on the number of full-time employees). They often come from different internal sources and may have been collected by the organization at different times. Some employers couldn't separate part-time from full-time employees. Some also included temporary or casual employees in one listing or the other.

2. *Who is an "upper level manager"?* Look at the percentage of full-time

employees that are considered "upper level managers" to get an idea of how tightly or loosely the term was defined. The broadest definition was used by Ben Moss Jewellers, which defined 26.06% of its full-time employees as upper level managers. The narrowest was the Toronto Transit Commission, where only 0.07% were defined that way. Employers were given less credit for having lots of female upper level managers if they defined the term loosely.

3. *Use of the word "manager".* For the sake of simplicity, I have used the term "manager" to refer to all management and "professional" employees, whether or not they supervise staff. Other office workers are generally referred to as support staff or clerical workers, many of whom pointed out that they, too, are "professionals" — often a sore point in legal and accounting firms.

4. *Commitment.* If the person responsible for workplace equality reports to the president or chief executive officer, the commitment to women is more likely to be serious and effective. (For a list of such organizations, see Part III).

5. *Top-up of U.I.C. during maternity leave.* Employees who have worked long enough to qualify for unemployment insurance commission benefits (UIC) during their maternity leaves face a two-week waiting period, during which they will have no income unless their employer chooses to pay them something. Many employers pay nothing during the waiting period, but there are several that do pay up to 95% of the employee's normal salary. After the two weeks, UIC normally pays up to 55% of insurable earnings (to a maximum benefit amount of $429 per week) for 15 weeks of maternity leave and 10 weeks of parental leave. Several employers "top-up" those payments for some or all of the period covered by UIC, to help bring the employee's income closer to her regular earnings.

In the charts that accompany each entry, I have listed as **"generous"** those employers that top-up the benefits paid by UIC to cover more than 90% of the employee's regular salary for longer than six weeks, including the two-week waiting period. **"Good"** are those that top-up the UIC benefits to over 90% of salary for six weeks, including the waiting period, or that have a lower top-up but for a much longer period. **"Average"** includes all other employers offering a top-up. The top-up may have conditions applied to it, and/or there may be no salary for the waiting period. Remember, though, that this is "average" among Canada's best employers for women; my research suggests that most Canadian employers provide no top-up.

6. Employment equity policy. Starting in September, 1994, all Ontario employers with 50 or more employees must develop employment equity plans. As a result, every Ontario-based employer in this book that does not already have an employment equity program is developing one. The charts only list them as having a plan only if one was already in place at the end of December, 1993.

A final comment on the charts. The employers in this book gave me detailed information on a wide range of benefits and policies. It is difficult to summarize and compare that information due to its complexity. Subtle differences can have a big impact on the employees. For example, two employers may each have an educational assistance program under which they pay for the full cost of approved night school courses taken by employees. One may pay the tuition fees in advance, and expect reimbursement from the employees if they fail. The other may not pay until the employees can prove they've passed the courses. Some also pay for books and other course-related fees. One single mother I interviewed commented that she could never have taken the courses she needed if the employer had not paid in advance. She didn't have the cash.

The information can also be difficult to compare because some employers provided more detail than did others. For example, when discussing the benefits available to part-time staff, some simply said "prorated", whereas others gave much more detail. Likewise, some employers may not have thought to mention some of the "noteworthy benefits" that are listed for others, even though they also offer them. The charts are included as a convenience; they don't tell you everything.

Part II:
The Best Employers

COMMUNICATIONS AND TECHNOLOGY

BC TEL

BC TEL is the second largest telecommunications company in Canada, providing basic telephone service to virtually the entire population of British Columbia. It is also involved in other voice and data-related activities, such as information management, consulting, equipment maintenance and manufacturing.

"This is a great place to work. You can change your life every three years without having to leave the company," said a woman who had worked at the company since 1978 in jobs ranging from serving customers to climbing poles. The latter "wasn't really a job I had considered," she said, even though she had taken night school classes to qualify for work in the traditionally male "craft" areas of the firm. Craft workers are technical employees who support and mantain the telephone equipment, but this employee did not, at first, have a very clear idea of what sort of work that involved. "I had thought I'd do more of a clerical-type of craft job. But I went for the interview and the crew seemed really nice. So I took it and they were great. Really helpful. I was the first woman in that job and I had no technical background *at all*, so how I passed the electricity course I have no idea . . . but I ran into no problems. There was the odd outside installer who gawked at the idea; thought I was clerical. But other than that, I was treated just the same."

That employee was planning to start a family soon, and hoping to persuade the union to permit job-sharing in her area. "The kind of job that I'm doing is perfect for job-sharing because you share the job among the crew anyway, so if you're off one day someone else can do the job," she said.

Job-sharing was a big topic of conversation in the summer of 1993 as the company had just begun a pilot job-share project for clerical employees in the union. Job-sharing had already been available to management employees and non-union clerical staff for about three years. While some parts of the union were still cool to the idea, for fear that in the end it could result in job losses or jobs being designated part-time, the response to the pilot project was overwhelming. A central registry was set up within the bargaining unit and it was flooded with over 100 applicants.

Not all of the applicants were women with young children. Some, for instance, saw job-sharing as a way to ease into retirement. However, there were concerns about the implications job-sharing would have on pensions, which are based on each employee's final years' earnings. Management and the union were looking at ways to change the pension structure to adapt to job-sharing, and it looked likely that a formal job-sharing plan would be approved during 1994.

Many areas of the company permit flex time for non-union employees. Official starting times can be anywhere from seven to nine in the morning. Trials with compressed work weeks have also begun.

Another initiative which sets BC TEL apart is its encouragement of women going into traditionally male areas. Counselling is available for female employees considering a move from a non-craft to a craft position. Employees without a technical background can take a qualifying test after having done basic training, in order to transfer into a craft job. The collective agreement allows two of every six vacancies to be filled by employees who are new to craft jobs but have passed the test.

Men have mixed reactions to women making the move. "I had a hard time with the men," said one woman who had worked in a variety of male-dominated jobs. Once the men got past their initial concerns, though, even the most hesitant of them recognized that they could benefit from having women doing the same jobs. Many of the jobs have relied on brute strength in the past, but once women entered the field new ways were found to get the work done. For example, the company used to pack ringers in 96-pound boxes. Explained one woman, "They didn't look like large boxes, but they were extremely heavy. *Everybody* had problems lifting them; men and women. So I said, 'Why don't we pack them in smaller boxes?' We did, and everybody was happier." She felt that the men would not have been comfortable making such a suggestion for fear of how they would be perceived by their male co-workers. "When they brought women into the warehouse," said another woman, "one of the things that happened was that they had fewer injuries. The men didn't have to prove themselves. They didn't have to be so macho. They were moving things *smart*, not strong."

Women working in management, professional and clerical jobs also found that the attitudes of male co-workers could be a problem. "We are getting there," said one, "but there is still a lot of old thinking." Another, who had worked at BC TEL for nearly two decades, noted that "some of the younger men are afraid.... There are still a lot of areas in BC TEL where women do not get into senior positions." Part of the problem, she felt, was the double-standard often applied to women's behaviour. "You have to be persistent, but then you get looked at as being mouthy."

To try to change such attitudes workshops on "managing human rights" have been made available to managers and the company has recently started offering an anti-harassment training program to all employees.

Staff felt that pay and benefits were generally good compared to other companies in the province. Employees who want to build up their muscles can do so in the head-office fitness centre and those who want to focus on their brains may take up to four years educational leave. There is no day care centre, but the company does provide a referral service for employees with child or elder-care needs.

BC TEL seems to be aware of the issues of concern to female employees and, slowly but steadily, is doing what it can to ensure equal opportunities for all staff.

BC TEL
3777 Kingsway, Burnaby, BC, V5H 3Z7
Telephone: (604) 432-2151

	Total	No. of Women	% Women
Full-time employees	12,676	5,592	44%
Part-time employees	268	266	99%
Board members	11	2	18%

Job category (figures based on full-time employees, unless noted otherwise):

Upper level managers	45	4	9%
Middle or other managers	941	297	32%
Professionals	838	232	28%
Semi-professionals & technicians	987	146	15%
Supervisors	303	230	76%
Foremen/women	395	22	6%
Clerical workers	3,522	3,304	94%
Sales workers	1,046	918	88%
Service workers	23	5	22%
Skilled crafts & trades workers	3,990	204	5%
Semi-skilled manual workers	277	86	31%
Other manual workers	309	144	47%

Percentage of full-time employees considered upper level managers:	0.36%
Top-up of U.I.C. during maternity leave:	good
On-site daycare centre?	no
Child/elder care referral service?	yes
Employment equity rep. reports to CEO/President?	no
Target numbers for women in management?	yes
Pay equity policy?	yes
Employment equity policy?	yes
Mentoring program?	no

Noteworthy benefits:
- flexible benefits program
- computer purchase plan
- share purchase plan
- educational assistance
- generous extended leave options

Part-time employee benefits:
- pro-rated to hours worked

Bell Canada

Bell Canada, a wholly owned subsidiary of BCE Inc., is Canada's largest supplier of telecommunications services. It serves more than seven million business and residential customers in Quebec and Ontario. Its operations are regulated by the Canadian Radio-television and Telecommunications Commission (CRTC).

"Ma Bell" is known as a cradle-to-grave employer and has prided itself on being a good place to work. In recent years, the changing nature of the telecommunications industry and the way it is regulated are eroding Bell's dominant place in the market. As a result it is struggling to become more efficient and competitive while maintaining the loyalty of its workforce.

Rather than undertaking massive layoffs, Bell has tried the unusual approach of encouraging employees to either work a four-day week for a year or take a leave of absence. The types of leave offered in late 1993 varied from a 10-week unpaid leave to educational leaves of up to four years, during which the employees would still be paid 25% of their salary. A similar subsidy was available to employees taking leave to work for a non-profit organization. Unpaid personal leaves of up to two years and early retirement packages were also offered.

Not all parts of the company were eligible for the reduced work arrangements, but in the clerical workforce, for example, approximately 90% of the staff opted to participate. By early 1994 the company had decided that it would not have to resort to involuntary measures.

The main drawback to this alternative to layoffs is that Bell still has overhead costs for the employees working reduced hours or on leave. The big advantages, though, are that the employees are still loyal and they bring more energy to their work than would five-day-a-week employees struggling to cope with the gaps left by laid-off staff.

Bell managers were already used to dealing with staff on varied schedules. Bell was one of the first companies in Canada to introduce flextime, which it did in 1974. Compressed work weeks have been available for years, and are widely used. Long-term leaves are also relatively common. Bell has been at the forefront of developing telecommuting options for employees, starting with a policy on home use of company equipment in 1985. In 1990 it began letting service workers take Bell vehicles home so that they need not waste time every day going to and from a central location simply to pick up and return a truck. Some sales staff joined the telecommuting trend in 1992, and in January 1994, when over 2,000 employees were already telecommuting for part or all of their job, the company opened its first "telecommuting centre", in Kingston, Ontario.

The centre has fully equipped work stations that can be reserved for a day or weeks at a time by home-based employees to use when they need more equipment than is available at home. It can also be used by employees who are travelling in the area. Joy Vokey, the manager who organized the Kingston centre, explained in the Bell newspaper, "I work out of my home office several days a week but book this office so I can have part-time access to the company's mail system, photocopiers and desk-top video-conferencing facilities." Telecommuting centres offer the prospect of being able to hire employees who live far from their supervisors, which could be a real boon to recruitment and could make it easier for two-career couples to manage both careers.

Bell employees appreciate the company's fair and flexible atmosphere and its concern for their welfare. One woman told of a series of illnesses she and her child experienced during several years, which had forced her to take repeated long leaves. "Not once was my job in jeopardy," she marvelled, and when she returned to work "They took the time with me to make sure I was okay."

As in any large organization, some managers are more flexible than others, but employees who are unhappy or want a new challenge can move internally.

The company, in cooperation with the unions, developed a "Qualifications Development Program" in 1991 to help female employees move into non-traditional jobs. The program included a day-long field visit to give women contemplating applying for a non-traditional job a better idea of what the job would involve. Those entering the program got six-months of classroom and/or on-the-job training, after which their skills were evaluated in the same way as other new craft and services employees, and they could apply for permanent placements as jobs became available. The program is not being run at the moment, as there are currently many trained employees, male and female, and few positions for them to fill.

Climbing up the career ladder is more difficult than moving laterally since not all jobs are posted and the organization is streamlining. As in many companies, it is now rare to enter management without a university degree. This did not seem to disturb the non-management employees interviewed at Bell: they did not want to get into management. "Empowerment" has become a buzz-word for the 1990s, and clerical staff commented that they have more responsibility and variety than they did in the past. They felt challenged enough in the support stream without the hassles of management.

One long-time clerical employee who had turned down several opportunities to move into management explained: "I came to Bell right out of school because Bell was the only company that would hire people without experience. I figured I'd get a year's experience, and then move on. . . . Twenty-five years later, I'm still here and I'm still experiencing!" A secretary who had been with the company for 16 years felt the same way. "I had been approached about going into management, but it didn't appeal to me. There is not much respect for your personal life if you are a manager."

Managers reluctantly agreed. For example, many now feel that they have to log on to their electronic mail from home, even when they are on vacation. At first they did so because they wanted to, said some, but now they are expected to. They feel trapped between old and new expectations. "Senior management says, yes, we have to set new priorities and cut the workload," explained one manager, "but there are still layers of mid-management that can't change their thinking. They cut people but add to the workload. We have to change our way of thinking. For example, every time someone calls in because her kid is sick, we panic. Why don't we *plan* for it?" They worry that the company is sending contradictory signals and that, as one manager put it, "We'll end up with a lot of pissed-off employees".

New ways of thinking have not fully caught on when it comes to pregnancy. While some managers have had good reactions to the news of their pregnancies, and even been promoted afterwards, others find management less supportive and fear being viewed as being on a "baby track" rather than a "career track", especially if they cut back at all on their hours. Said one manager, in her area, "You don't get sick and neither do your kids. You are expected to be on the job all the time."

Nevertheless, the managers, like the non-managers, feel tremendous pride in working for Bell and devotion to the company. They hold the firm to a high standard and get angry when it does something they consider unfair, but they get even angrier when anyone from outside dares to criticize it.

Bell Canada
1050 Beaver Hall Hill, Montreal, PQ, H2Z 1S4
Telephone: (514) 870-2955

	Total	No. of Women	% Women
Full-time employees	41,000	20,783	51%
Part-time employees	3,477	2,431	70%
Board members	17	1	6%

Job category (figures based on full-time employees, unless noted otherwise):

Upper level managers	80	11	14%
Middle or other managers	8,802	3,375	38%
Professionals	1,208	373	31%
Semi-professionals & technicians	91	69	76%
Supervisors	0	0	0%
Foremen/women	0	0	0%
Clerical workers	19,824	18,455	93%
Sales workers	766	375	49%
Service workers	22	17	77%
Skilled crafts & trades workers	12,127	410	3%
Semi-skilled manual workers	1,386	76	5%
Other manual workers	171	53	31%

Percentage of full-time employees considered upper level managers:	0.20%
Top-up of U.I.C. during maternity leave:	average
On-site daycare centre?	no
Child/elder care referral service?	no
Employment equity rep. reports to CEO/President?	no
Target numbers for women in management?	no
Pay equity policy?	yes
Employment equity policy?	yes
Mentoring program?	no

Noteworthy benefits:
- share purchase plan
- discounted rates on personal telephone calls
- educational assistance
- scholarships for children of Bell employees
- generous extended leave options

Part-time employee benefits:
- most the same as full-time; some pro-rated to salary level

Canadian Satellite Communications Inc. (Cancom)

Cancom delivers television and radio signals to cable systems from St. John's in the east to Tofino in the west and Inuvik in the north. Its mandate is to make broadcast signals accessible to small or remote communities. It also provides satellite-related services to businesses and users of private satellite dishes. Cancom is 99.4% Canadian-owned. Its executive offices are in Mississauga, Ontario, and it has regional offices in Halifax, Montreal, Ottawa, Saskatoon, Edmonton and Vancouver.

Cancom's annual report is full of pictures of women and men working together, but the women are not just there for show. The pictures are of the company's nine senior executives and, at the time of the photos, the President, the Vice President Finance and the Vice President Regulatory, Corporate and Native Affairs were women.

Sheelagh Whittaker, the President, moved on to another company late in 1993, but she had a tremendous impact while she was at the helm. Even with her gone, female staff are convinced that "it is too late to turn back the clock". Women flourished under her influence. "My career took off when she came in," said Louise Tremblay, the V.P. Finance and Chief Financial Officer. "She let me do what I wanted to do; to take the initiative."

Under Ms. Whittaker's leadership the company instituted a policy requiring that at least two women be interviewed for any job vacancy and that the president interview the top male and female candidates for senior positions. The company also gives a $500 bonus to any employee who suggests a female or minority candidate who ends up being hired.

There is a friendly, team-oriented atmosphere at Cancom. A quiet, non-management employee commented that the senior executives know everybody's name, and "they'll chat with you. You feel part of the team; that the work you do is genuinely appreciated. It makes me want to work that much harder to do my best for the company." She felt that the company had built up her self-esteem. "I'm a lot more outgoing and self-confident than I used to be, because of the environment here," she said. "I've held a half dozen jobs because my husband kept getting transferred, and no other company even comes close."

Everyone, from the woman in the mail room on up, feels that their work is appreciated and their opinions and ideas valued. One employee commented on how impressed she was that "they had the sensitivity to include the other clerical person I'd be working with in the interview."

Staff appreciation is also enhanced by sharing perks, such as baseball tickets, with employees at all levels, and an annual "play day", when the office closes down and everybody is bussed out to a resort for a day of fun.

Benefits are good for an organization with relatively few employees, and include matching staff members' contributions to their RRSPs, annual bonuses based on individual objectives and the company's overall performance, and a continuation of all benefits at the employer's expense during maternity leaves.

Combining motherhood with work was also role-modelled by Ms. Whittaker, who has six children, the last of whom was born while she was president. "When the president got pregnant, it gave me a real sense of pride," said an employee who had found the company extremely accommodating of her maternity leaves, even though she worked in a male-dominated area. "They were all young and unsexist; they also had family responsibilities. They assumed I'd be returning," she said. "I had to extend my latest leave because I couldn't get a sitter. . . . The reaction was fine; it was taken in stride." Finance V.P. Tremblay explained the company's philosophy: "We have outstanding employees, so we want them back."

The company is open to part-time work and job-sharing, although such options have not become widely used. One non-management employee was working a four-day week so that she could spend one day a week at university. Another woman was grateful for the company's flexibility in accommodating her during a prolonged illness of her child. For more than two years since the end of her maternity leave she has been working part-time, coming in at night or whenever she can to get her job done, while spending most of her time at the hospital. She commented that she is one of the few mothers at the hospital who has not lost her job. The company plans to reinstate her to a job equivalent to the one she held before the child's illness, once she is able to return to full-time work.

Staff appreciate the flexibility, but also wish the company had some standard policies. In particular, they would like to have regular performance reviews and a system of internal job postings. "We shouldn't prejudge if people would be interested in or have the background for a job," said one employee. "The people here don't necessarily know what else I've done before working here." It is frustrating to discover that a job has been filled when most employees did not even know that it was available.

With the lack of job posting it is especially important that staff make their interests and aspirations known to management. The company promotes from within whenever possible. One woman who is now a senior manager started as a secretary in a branch office. She displays the self-confidence that is typical of the women in this organization. A non-management employee commented that "the women in this company are very secure, and they have not lost their femininity." There are still some male employees with traditional attitudes, but the impact of those attitudes is negligible. One employee described Cancom this way: "Young, aggressive, highly intelligent people work here. . . . The departments co-operate, and you don't run into any sexist typecasting."

Canadian Satellite Communications Inc. (Cancom)
50 Burnhamthorpe Rd. W., #1000, Mississauga, ON, L5B 3C2
Telephone: (905) 272-4960

	Total	No. of Women	% Women
Full-time employees	116	45	39%
Part-time employees	11	9	82%
Board members	13	1	8%

Job category (figures based on full-time employees, unless noted otherwise):

Upper level managers	9	2	22%
Middle or other managers	21	3	14%
Professionals	14	3	21%
Semi-prof & technicians	19	2	11%
Supervisors	1	1	100%
Foremen/women	0	0	0%
Clerical workers	33	29	88%
Sales workers	13	3	23%
Service workers	0	0	0%
Skilled crafts & trades workers	6	1	17%
Semi-skilled manual workers	0	0	0%
Other manual workers	0	0	0%

Percentage of full-time employees considered upper level managers:	7.76%
Top-up of U.I.C. during maternity leave:	none
On-site daycare centre?	no
Child/elder care referral service?	no
Employment equity rep. reports to CEO/President?	yes
Target numbers for women in management?	no
Pay equity policy?	yes
Employment equity policy?	yes
Mentoring program?	no

Noteworthy benefits:
- company matches employee contributions (up to 5% of salary) to an RRSP in employee's name; employee gets tax receipt for full amount
- group RRSP also available
- all benefits continue at employer's expense during maternity leave

Part-time employee benefits:
- pay in lieu of benefits

GE Hamilton Technology Services

GE Hamilton Technology Services grew out of a 1993 merger between Hamilton Computer Sales and Rentals and General Electric Capital Corporation. The company sells, leases, rents, and services new and used computer equipment to medium- to large-sized corporations and government agencies. It sells products made by Apple, AST, Compaq, Digital, Hewlett Packard, IBM and Toshiba, and operating systems and software such as Novell, OS/2, VMS and Microsoft. The company has branch offices in Vancouver, Edmonton, Calgary, Winnipeg, London, Toronto, Ottawa, Montreal and Quebec City.

GE Hamilton has grown quickly ever since it entered the computer sales and rental business 15 years ago. In the early days, when it could barely keep up with the demand for its services, the company actively recruited the best people it could find. It was a time of stiff competition for computer people so the company was certainly not about to limit its options by neglecting female talent.

Pat Nielsen, who was one of the first people hired, started as a sales representative and quickly worked her way up to the position of General Manager, which she was offered when she was $7^1/_2$ months pregnant. She held that position for six years, but about two years ago she approached the President asking for a new challenge because the company was maturing and she preferred the entrepreneurial side. She now heads a new business unit, still serves on the Board of Directors and is a key member of the executive team.

Ms. Nielsen has been an important role model and mentor for other women at the firm. "That's one of the things I found really good about Hamilton," said one young employee, "there's no shortage of strong female role models. That was really good to see when I first started. There are women mangers who've done really well in this company, and that's very encouraging."

The company has many women in areas which are male-dominated in most other firms in the computer industry; areas like technical support, programming, purchasing and sales. Why are there more women here? "I think they see the edge we have," said one. "When they saw that the first women were successful, that paved the road." Those early women not only gave management the confidence to hire more, they also actively recruited other women and brought them to management's attention.

"I was hired really green," said a woman who is now a sales manager. "I had no sales background, nor any computer background. I was just out of university and working in the fitness industry. I wasn't terribly qualified, but they gave me a chance. The woman who was National Sales Manager at the time sort of took me under her wing. She was a member of the fitness club where I worked. She got me in the door, and they hired me." She assumes that she was hired for her attitude, enthusiasm and stamina — in other words, her potential — and the company was willing to take the chance of training her on the technical side.

The women interviewed did not perceive a glass ceiling for capable women but, like the men, they must be willing and able to put in extremely long hours. "This is a very big overtime company," said one. "It is expected. Nobody pays you for it; it's an unspoken law. You have work to do, you stay and you do it; everybody in the company does. That's why they hired us: we're producers."

They agree that the workload really demands long hours but as a result, "it would be difficult to have kids in this job," said one employee. Another, who does not yet have children, felt she could accept the hours better if the company would "build us the tools", like support for day care and after-hours care.

There seems to be corporate ambivalence about flexible working arrangements. There are no formal policies supporting them but the company has been willing to meet many of the employees' requests for job changes to accommodate outside time commitments. Several now work part-time or a combination of days in the office and at home. One, whose job involves shift work, said the company agreed to adjust her evening schedule so that she could make regular child care arrangements.

Another employee with young children was allowed to switch to part-time work but only after she made it clear that she would quit otherwise. "This sounds kind of arrogant, but I have ten years experience here and I know a lot. Their alternative was to let me go over three days. I think that would have been crazy. I still have a lot to offer."

"At the beginning I think they really thought that part-time was almost like a temporary help sort of thing," said one employee. "Part-time people are looked at as if they have the best of all worlds. *We* [the company] are being very gracious in allowing you to do this. To some degree that may be true, but the work we are doing is still valuable."

The company recently extended full benefits to part-timers, which many saw as a signal that it is beginning to understand and accept that part-time employees are committed to the organization.

The organization shows its commitment to the employees by seeking and valuing their opinions. One employee cited a "lunch 'n learn" session which had been held about the company's approach to training. The feedback staff gave at that session was quickly worked into a vastly improved introductory information package now given to newly hired employees. A dispatcher also noted that "the 'lunch 'n learns' are for everybody" — no one is looked down on because of their gender or job.

Management's confidence in its employees is also appreciated when it comes to dealing with clients, who can still be reluctant to deal with women in computer sales and service. One young woman in technical support noted that the "customers sometimes think we are too young, but our supervisor always backs us up".

The women in sales commented that sales in the computer industry has a long "work hard; play hard" tradition which can sometimes pose a challenge for female sales representatives. "In our business there is a lot of entertaining of clients. As a woman I tend to go for a lunch because I've got a purpose, not because I want to chew the fat. I think guys do that more. Or they'll go for a beer after work. If I called my husband and said, 'I'm going to be late because I'm going for a beer with a bunch of guys', well. . . . You almost have to avoid those kind of situations because drinking and men don't mesh well." For the same reason women at sales meetings feel they have to be more restrained than men at the evening activities. That restraint does not make them any less effective. "There is no feeling that you have to drink to fit in here," said one employee. Said another, "they quickly accept you as one of the group."

The women at GE Hamilton are an assertive, intelligent group. They are there because all employees, male or female, are given good opportunities for growth. "If you seem to excel or prove yourself," said one, "they'll give you more opportunities; more ways to advance."

GE Hamilton Technology Services Inc.
5985 McLaughlin Rd, Mississauga, ON, L5R 1B8
Telephone: (905) 568-4111

	Total	No. of Women	% Women
Full-time employees	400	200	50%
Part-time employees	12	6	50%
Board members	9	1	11%

Job category (figures based on full-time employees, unless noted otherwise):

Upper level managers	6	1	17%
Middle or other managers	43	19	44%
Professionals	25	21	84%
Semi-professionals & technicians	71	5	7%
Supervisors	5	5	100%
Foremen/women	4	0	0%
Clerical workers	107	77	72%
Sales workers	73	25	34%
Service workers	0	0	0%
Skilled crafts & trades workers	0	0	0%
Semi-skilled manual workers	0	0	0%
Other manual workers	0	0	0%

Percentage of full-time employees considered upper level managers:	1.50%
Top-up of U.I.C. during maternity leave:	none
On-site daycare centre?	no
Child/elder care referral service?	no
Employment equity rep. reports to CEO/President?	no
Target numbers for women in management?	no
Pay equity policy?	yes
Employment equity policy?	yes
Mentoring program?	no

Noteworthy benefits:
- fitness fund: $200/year; can be used towards purchase of equipment for home use or towards fitness club membership

Part-time employee benefits:
- same as full-time (*not* pro-rated), except not eligible for the fitness fund

EDUCATION

Calgary Board of Education

The Calgary Board of Education is the public school board in Calgary. It is responsible for teaching over 96,000 students from early childhood services through to high school and another 64,000 continuing education students, in 213 schools. Most of the employees are unionized. Sixty-eight per cent of the staff are teachers; the other 32% include support staff such as secretaries, technicians, and maintenance staff.

Alberta public schools are facing increasing competition from private schools, and the Government has announced plans to set up "charter schools" which would also compete for funding and students. As a result, said a teacher, "we will have to re-think the way we do things." Some of that "re-thinking" is being done by an Inquiry on Opportunities for Women set up by the Calgary Board of Education in 1989.

The Inquiry had a five-year mandate to study and monitor the promotional opportunities for women within the board. It sparked a wide range of initiatives including:

- eliminating all-male interview panels;
- creating mentoring and professional development programs for female teachers and support staff;
- hiring a half-time Special Advisor on Women's Issues;
- eliminating gender-linked words from job titles;
- holding seminars about gender issues for staff and students.

These efforts have had mixed results. More women than ever before are in administrative positions (principals, vice-principals, department heads and other academic leadership roles). Between November 1990 and November 1992 the percentage of women in school-based administrative positions increased from 39% to 43%. However, progress was mainly at elementary schools, where the vast majority of teachers are women. There was actually a drop in the percentage of women holding senior high school assistant principal jobs, and the percentages were stagnant in most other junior and senior high school administrative positions.

The Opportunities for Women panel, in its June 1993 annual report, suggested that part of the problem was that the board has not taken into account the impact of its downsizing and re-structuring efforts on women. Many of the positions being cut are those where women are well represented. It recommended that the board look at equity issues not only when recruiting, but also when reducing staff. Teacher lay-offs are currently based on seniority, but the board has started collecting data on the gender of those being laid off.

Senior administrators are trying to spot talented women and encourage them to apply for more senior jobs. "A lot of people that I don't know, know my name," said one teacher. The associate superintendents have been touring the schools asking women in junior high schools why they are not applying for administrative jobs. The answer seems to be that at the junior and senior high school level the route to the principal's job is through the assistant principal's, and the assistant principals are expected to be disciplinarians. That role "puts a lot of women off," according to a woman who had been a high school assistant principal. "At the high school level the focus is on specialists, so everybody thinks that somebody should be a specialist in discipline." That somebody is the assistant principal.

Lack of support from principals has also held some women back. As the board moves to a more collaborative style of operation, the traditional attitudes of some principals are changing. The board has revamped its approach to promotion, to speed that process and to help people get around unsupportive principals. In September of 1993 it announced an "extended assessment program" for people wanting to become principals or assistant principals.

Interested teachers must first do a self-assessment, comparing their knowledge, skills and attitudes to those the board has identified as being important for leadership roles. If they feel ready to apply, they then provide input on their strengths and weaknesses from past or present peers, subordinates and supervisors as well as their current principal. Next, each candidate makes an oral presentation of his or her views on the educational system to a panel of students, parents, teachers and administrators. Those who are accepted into the program take part in events designed to prepare them for more senior positions. The Administrative Staffing Committee reviews their progress yearly and recommends them for vacancies as they occur.

Not everybody wants to be an administrator. Many teachers are drawn to the profession because it can be combined nicely with raising a family. This is one of the few careers in which parents can have the same basic holiday schedule as their children, and similar hours. Teachers are generally at the school before and after the students, but at least one principal lets them bring their children in to play with the children of other staff before and after classes.

Many support staff are also drawn to the school system to have holiday schedules that coincide with their children's. All twelve-month support staff (i.e. mainly those who are not in the schools) work an extra 15 minutes a day all year long in exchange for having eight Fridays off during the summer. Working in a school can also offer the advantage of working close to home, if a school nearby has an opening.

Job-sharing is starting to be available to teachers, but it is still rare among support staff. It is not easy for them to find partners and they need administration approval to job-share. (Teachers typically advertise for job-sharing partners in the board's weekly employee newspaper and on electronic mail.)

The Calgary Board of Education is one of the few organizations that seems acutely aware of the concerns of its support staff when it looks at women's initiatives. It developed a two-year program called Archways to help support staff develop personally and professionally. Weekly meetings were held half on board time and half on the employee's time, and after the first year the meetings were run by the support staff themselves. "Archways was great," said one secretary. "You could see the growth in people." Unfortunately, after four years its funding was cut.

There are limited career paths for people without education degrees, as school boards generally assume that teachers are the best people to administer the activities of other teachers. At a time when there are many unemployed teachers, it is natural to hire them rather than to promote from within the non-teaching staff. This issue has been looked at by the Opportunities for Women group, which is pilot-testing a career-track booklet for support staff in the finance division.

School-based support staff say they like the people-orientation of the work. Even in single-secretary schools, where the hours are long and inflexible because there is no back-up, they enjoy their pivotal role which involves working with teachers, administrators, children and parents.

Many of the support staff commented on having been mentored and nurtured; encouraged to develop their skills. Because the system is large, they can move within it to suit changing needs or interests.

The Calgary Board of Education is clearly interested in the career development of its women, be they support staff, teachers or administrators. It is still grappling with how to encourage that development when funding is tight.

Calgary Board of Education
515 Macleod Trail S.E., Calgary, AB, T2G 2L9
Telephone: (403) 294-8631

	Total	No. of Women	% Women
Full-time employees	7,077[a]	4,153	59%
Part-time employees	0	0	0%
Board members	7	6	86%

Job category (figures based on full-time employees, unless noted otherwise):

Upper level managers	28	11	39%
Middle or other managers	219	50	23%
Professionals	5,279	3,379	64%
Semi-professionals & technicians	0	0	0%
Supervisors	0	0	0%
Foremen/women	0	0	0%
Clerical workers	780	682	87%
Sales workers	0	0	0%
Service workers	525	31	6%
Skilled crafts & trades workers	151	0	0%
Semi-skilled manual workers	95	0	0%
Other manual workers	0	0	0%

Percentage of full-time employees considered upper level managers:	0.40%
Top-up of U.I.C. during maternity leave:	generous
On-site daycare centre?	no
Child/elder care referral service?	no
Employment equity rep. reports to CEO/President?	yes
Target numbers for women in management?	yes
Pay equity policy?	no
Employment equity policy?	no
Mentoring program?	no

Noteworthy benefits:
- maternity leave can be extended to total 18 months
- retired employees benefits package
- teachers retirement fund

Part-time employee benefits:
- same as full-time (*not* pro-rated); teachers must work at least 30% of full-time to qualify; support staff must work at least half-time to qualify

Notes: (a) includes permanent part-time staff, on a full-time equivalent basis

North York Board of Education

The North York Board of Education is responsible for teaching nearly 63,000 day-time students and almost as many continuing education students in 129 schools in the City of North York, which is in the greater Toronto area. Approximately 95% of the employees are covered by one of five unions and two teachers' federations. Sixty-five per cent of the staff are teachers.

The provincial Minister of Education issued a challenge to school boards in Ontario in 1975 to increase their representation of women in leadership positions. Charlie McCaffery, who was the head of the North York Board of Education at the time, called together a handful of promising women who worked for the board. They met over lunch and he told them about the minister's challenge and asked what they planned to do about it.

The women, who got nicknamed "Charlie's Angels", sprang into action. By 1979 the board had approved an affirmative action policy and hired one of those "angels", Veronica Lacey, as the first affirmative action officer. She is now the board's Director of Education, its most senior person. The number two spot is held by Marguerite Jackson, another of "Charlie's Angels".

The group set up an effective affirmative action office which still exists and is credited by staff as being a positive force for women at the board. The office was backed up by clear policy statements from the top and supported by employee training programs.

The women in that founding group actively sought others who they felt had potential. They would invite them for lunch and give them career guidance. They also lobbied key men in the system to ensure that the support would be there for those women as they started applying for more senior positions.

One of the most important things they did was found a group called "Women In Leadership" (WIL), the main goal of which was to get women so well prepared to fill leadership roles that their applications could not possibly be rejected. WIL, which was founded by about a dozen women in 1980, grew to over 400 at its peak. Its members met monthly to hear from women who had made it into senior positions and to participate in workshops doling out advice on how to get ahead. The women would be advised to get further education, such as masters' degrees, and given individual counselling. They would also take part in mock job interviews which were videotaped and analyzed, so that

"When those women went into the interviews, they'd be shining, especially compared to the men, who hadn't done any preparation," said one of the participants.

The results were dramatic:

- in 1979, 3.5% of the supervisory officers (who oversee the teaching in the schools), 2.5% of the principals and 15.6% of the vice-principals were women;
- by September of 1992, those figures had increased to 52% of the supervisory officers, 43% of the principals and 48% of the vice-principals;
- even at the secondary school level, where the tradition of male principals and vice-principals is strong in most school boards, 40% of the principals and 37% of the vice-principals were women, as of September, 1992.

The progress was given added impetus by the board's setting of numerical targets in 1984, which stated that by 1994, 50% of each of those positions should be held by women.

Not surprisingly, such a dramatic change has caused some hard feelings among male teachers, but the backlash has been minor compared with other organizations that have seen such rapid shifts. Senior women feel there are two factors that have helped minimize the backlash. First, the women were so clearly qualified and have performed so well in their jobs that it would be hard to believe that they had been promoted for reasons other than merit. As one woman explained, "We are doing so well because typically we've had far more experience than the men who have been promoted to senior levels." Second, successful women have since mentored men as well as women.

Mentoring is central to the culture of the North York Board of Education. It was mentioned by staff at every level, in nearly every type of job. Commented one senior administrator, "Early in my career another woman said to me, 'When you get where you're going, don't pull the ladder up behind you.' That is the prevalent attitude here."

A lot of mentoring happens naturally, and the board has also added a formal mentoring component to the administrative internship program pursued by teachers wanting to become vice-principals.

The results have been less dramatic in the business and operations side of the organization. The provincial Ministry of Education has said that school boards should have 30% of non-traditional and managerial positions filled by women by the year 2000. The North York Board is implementing goals and timelines to increase the representation of women in Facilities and Transportation Services. As of December 1992,

15% of the caretaking staff and 22% of the transportation department employees were women.

The board has exceeded the Ministry's goal for managerial positions, but it is working to increase the proportion of those women who are in the upper levels of management. As of 1992, only 24% of them were in the upper half of supervisory and management jobs.

It created bridging positions to try to help secretaries and clerical workers move into management. One former clerk who benefited from the bridging program said, "I had a wonderful female boss who came into my office one day and plunked a briefcase down on my desk. She said, 'You're a bright woman, you've got a lot of talent, but you need more education. Here's a briefcase; take it and go back to school.'" The woman got her degree, moved into management, and says, "I'm a different woman than I was ten years ago."

Others got stalled as funding tightened and fewer jobs were available. "Bridging positions took people to the middle of the bridge, but then we couldn't get off," said one administrative assistant who had worked for the board for 22 years. No thought was given to where those bridging positions would lead. Here, as in other school boards, it is difficult to progress without at least a bachelor's degree, preferably a degree in education. Staff are frustrated when they see the board hiring young people with degrees rather than promoting from within.

The board supports further education and professional development, and is receptive to hearing about people's career goals and trying to meet them. It has traditionally been well funded, so for a long time "you just had to go to the administration and say this is what I'd like to do, and they'd help you do it," said one employee. Although financial constraints mean that the board can no longer offer as many opportunities as it once did, it is still open to new ideas and creative thinking; an attitude that staff appreciate. "They are willing to try new things, to jump in with both feet and be the leaders," said one teacher who had turned several ideas into programs for the board.

The openness to new ideas extends to part-time work and job-sharing, which have started to happen despite the lack of formal policies on alternative working arrangements. There is still some resistance though. A woman who tried working three days a week found that she was expected to produce as much as she had when she worked full-time. She switched back to full-time after six months. She found that "people forget about you if you work part-time." Meetings were often scheduled on her days off, for example.

Job-sharing is happening mainly in the schools, but some principals complain when their secretaries do it because of the communication problems inherent in managing two people instead of one, and many parents object if two teachers try to share one class.

The first principal to get pregnant did so in 1990, but, given the number of women becoming principals, it seems to be only a matter of time before pregnancy no longer raises eyebrows.

The North York Board of Education is full of impressive role models. "What's really nice," said one woman, "is the variety of personalities of our female leaders. If you take Marguerite and Veronica, there you have, on a pedestal, two very powerful people, two very different people, but the end product is still impressive. That has been a positive thing for the assertive, aggressive women and the soft-spoken, competent women. You've got the models up there, and they are respected by everyone."

North York Board of Education
5050 Yonge St., North York, ON, M2N 5N8
Telephone: (416) 395-8376

	Total	No. of Women	% Women
Full-time employees	6,502	4,024	62%
Part-time employees	0[a]	0	0%
Board members	14	9	64%

Job category (figures based on full-time employees, unless noted otherwise):

Upper level managers	21	11	52%
Middle or other managers	148	58	39%
Professionals	4,348[b]	2,831	65%
Semi-professionals & technicians	0	0	0%
Supervisors	0	0	0%
Foremen/women	0	0	0%
Clerical workers	1,100	1,000	91%
Sales workers	0	0	0%
Service workers	0	0	0%
Skilled crafts & trades workers	885[c]	124	14%
Semi-skilled manual workers			
Other manual workers			

Percentage of full-time employees considered upper level managers:	0.32%
Top-up of U.I.C. during maternity leave:	average
On-site daycare centre?	no
Child/elder care referral service?	yes
Employment equity rep. reports to CEO/President?	yes
Target numbers for women in management?	yes
Pay equity policy?	yes
Employment equity policy?	no
Mentoring program?	yes

Noteworthy benefits:
 • generous extended leave options

Part-time employee benefits:
 • permanent part-timers get pro-rated benefits if work at least 17.5 hours/week (half-time); casual or temporary part-timers get pay in lieu of benefits

Notes: (a) part-time numbers not available
  (b) consists of:
    teachers: 4,082 total, of which 2,700 are women (66%)
    academic administrators (principals & v.p.s.): 266 total, of which 131 are women (49%)
  (c) includes: caretakers, bus drivers and trades workers (seasonal and permanent)

York University

With 52,700 students, York University is the third largest univer-sity in Canada. It has two campuses in the Toronto area, one of which offers a French-language undergraduate program. York University's research and teaching has a liberal arts focus, and it offers programs at the undergraduate, masters and doctorate levels. Approximately 83% of the full-time employees are unionized. Ac-ademic faculty members account for approximately 52% of the staff, support staff (clerical, technical and blue-collar) another 37%, with the balance being administrators.

Many university employees have never worked anywhere else, which may explain why they hold their employers to an idealistic standard. universities that were far ahead of most private sector employers in terms of the facilities and flexibility they offered to their staff felt they could not participate in this book because they were "not good enough". York University employees also talked a lot about what the university could do to make itself better but those who had worked elsewhere felt that York was one of the best. Said one, in a typical comment, "A lot of things have to change at York . . . but compared to the outside world it is wonderful!"

The needs, interests and attitudes of faculty members, administrators (managers) and support staff can be quite different but they all agreed that "there is a genuine consensus and commitment to women at York University". The commitment is so ingrained that, as one professor put it, "Even the sexists keep quiet now."

There are sexists at York, as anywhere else, but the university has many systems in place to weed out problems. It has had an Advisor on the Status of Women for nearly two decades, it has an active women's centre, and four women's studies programs (one for daytime under-graduates, one evening program for mature students, a French program and a graduate program). York was the first Canadian university to set up a Sexual Harassment Education and Complaints Centre, which opened during the 1984/85 academic year. The centre's role is largely educational and advisory but it will mediate disputes and has some legal clout to use if necessary. The special problems faced by visible minority women are addressed by a Centre for Race and Ethnic Rela-tions.

York University has had a female president since 1992, but she upset many female academics by suggesting that tenure decisions should value research and publication more highly than teaching. Women can get trapped in a vicious circle when it comes to splitting their time among teaching, committee work and research. Many of them are good at the people-oriented tasks of teaching and committee work, so they get asked to take on more and more such duties. That takes them away from the all-important research and writing, but, as several noted, "How do you say no to the people who will be deciding whether you get tenure?" The university tries to ensure that there are women on all committees, but since only 30% of the full-time faculty members are women they inevitably end up carrying a heavier load of committee work than their male colleagues.

Many of them also find that, as role models, they spend a lot of time counselling students, many of whom are not even in their classes. And those who have a reputation for being good teachers end up with larger classes. "I spend three to four weeks at the beginning of term just turning down students," said one. Noted a graduate student, "We are flocking to the few female faculty that there are, and we're watching them burn out."

The situation is difficult for the women who were part-way through the multi-year process of qualifying for tenure when the president's new approach to tenure decisions was announced, but even they say York is one of the best universities for women. The proportion of female academics is good compared with many other universities. In departments where fewer than 35% of the full-time faculty are women, a committee reviews recommended appointments to ensure that the position is offered to the woman if two candidates are "relatively or substantially equally qualified".

A similar rule applies to women, visible minorities, people with disabilities and aboriginal people being hired from outside for non-academic jobs. Targets have been set in areas of management where women are under-represented and progress is measured annually.

York is a comfortable place to combine work and family. Academics, by the nature of their jobs, have a lot of flexibility. Many do their writing at home and they are free to come and go as they choose when they are not teaching or in committee meetings. One woman even scheduled breast-feeding breaks for her newborn daughter during her interviews for a position at York, and once she got the job she kept her baby in her office for the first nine months.

Non-academic staff commented that they were given a lot of flexibility to deal with sick children or elderly parents. Unionized employees are allowed to use as much of their own sick time as necessary to care for ill dependents, and professional and management employees have five paid and 15 unpaid days specifically to care for sick family members. Many supervisors let staff do what work they can from home when their children are ill rather than having to use up family care days. One employee commented that York bought her a modem so that she could also work from home when bad weather made the roads treacherous.

The university has two day care centres. One is run as a cooperative, so parents are expected to contribute either time or money on top of their registration fees. The staff association's collective agreement allows members to spend up to four hours a week working at the day care centre during business hours, as long as that time is made up for at a time agreeable to their supervisor. There is also a drop-in day care centre used mainly by students when they are attending classes or studying, but also available to employees when their regular child care arrangements fail.

There are no formal policies on reduced or compressed work weeks or job sharing, and only a handful of support staff work part-time. Almost twice as many academic staff work part-time as full-time, but not always by choice. Part-time jobs are often the only ones available. During the slower summer months of July and August the university closes one hour earlier on Fridays.

Many staff are allowed to take university courses during the day and almost all the employees interviewed said how much they appreciated the tuition fee waivers for themselves and their families. An administrative assistant, who had started as a secretary 23 years earlier, said, "All my family did degrees here; myself, my husband and my two kids".

Pay and benefits are good, especially for support staff. Some of them complained that it made it difficult to move into management or professional positions because they would have to take a cut in pay. Nevertheless, staff often do move from support to management and professional jobs, although they note that "the further up the administrative ladder you go, the cooler the climate gets for women."

For most employees, though, the climate is a comfortable one. The experiences of a woman who came to York University 26 years ago show that the attitudes that make it a good place for women are not new: "I came to do a special project for two weeks. They approached me to stay on permanently, but I had three small children at the time, so I said I couldn't. The person said to me, 'If you take this job, you take off whatever time you need for your kids.'. . . . I had never worked anywhere where they had the attitude to staff that York did".

York University
10 East Office Building, 4700 Keele St., North York, ON, M3J 1P3
Telephone: (416) 736-2100

	Total	No. of Women	% Women
Full-time employees	3,308[a]	1,694	51%
Part-time employees	2,320[b]	1,067	46%
Board members	28	6	21%

Job category (figures based on full-time employees, unless noted otherwise):

Upper level managers	13	3	23%
Middle or other managers	227	124	55%
Professionals	126	46	37%
Semi-professionals & technicians	136	69	51%
Supervisors	164	150	91%
Foremen/women	0	0	0%
Clerical workers	929	809	87%
Sales workers	2	1	50%
Service workers	73	27	37%
Skilled crafts & trades workers	124	6	5%
Semi-skilled manual workers	8	1	13%
Other manual workers	267	84	31%

Percentage of full-time employees considered upper level managers:	0.39%
Top-up of U.I.C. during maternity leave:	generous
On-site daycare centre?	yes
Child/elder care referral service?	no
Employment equity rep. reports to CEO/President?	no
Target numbers for women in management?	yes
Pay equity policy?	yes
Employment equity policy?	yes
Mentoring program?	no

Noteworthy benefits:
- free tuition for family members

Part-time employee benefits:
- if work 24+ hours/week: full medical coverage, other benefits pro-rated
- no benefits if work less than 24 hours per week

Notes: (a)   of these, full-time academic staff account for 1,239 employees, of whom 374 are women (30%)

   (b)   of these, 2,295 are academic staff

   (c)   York also has approximately 2,000 "casual" staff, of which 60% were women in 1990 (the other employee numbers are as of mid-1992)

NOVA Corporation of Alberta

Calgary-based NOVA has four main divisions. Its Alberta Gas Transmission Division carries more than 15% of the natural gas produced annually in North America. NOVA Gas Services is responsible for gas gathering, processing, storage and sales, and is Canada's largest exporter of gas. Novacorp International sells NOVA's natural gas services overseas, and Novacor Chemicals makes petrochemical products.

NOVA is in the midst of a bold experiment of forced change. As one senior woman explained it: "To affect change we swung the pendulum completely out. Now we will try to find the right balance." The pendulum is still swinging, with the result that the company is full of contradictions and it is not clear how things will settle.

Some companies have focused their employment equity efforts on changing attitudes toward women. They believe that once attitudes improve women will find it easier to climb the corporate ladder. NOVA has taken the opposite approach. It has put women into leadership positions first, confident that once men see how they lead, good attitudes will follow.

NOVA was concerned that its old system valued technical skills at the expense of people skills, and felt that a radical shift to a people-oriented style of management was needed. The traditional way was to promote people with superb technical skills out of hands-on technical work and into management. NOVA decided that it made more sense to team them up with good managers who might or might not have much technical background. The managers were to be called team leaders and would be responsible for the effective management of the group. The senior technical staff member, however, could still earn more money, in recognition of the value of the technical expertise and to avoid losing technical experts to competitors.

Women with good people skills were actively encouraged to apply for the team leader positions and were prepared for the challenges ahead of them. Those challenges included not only trying to manage a group of technically oriented men who would doubtless question their authority at first, but also, for many of them, switching from an urban to a rural environment.

"We deliberately positioned women into the most traditional parts of the organization," explained one of the women who implemented the change. "We offered them an informal network, but they didn't need it; they wanted to work it through themselves." However it did implement a buddy system, pairing them up with other team leaders in the same region who had stronger technical backgrounds.

There were fears among female employees that the women were being set up to fail, but it does not seem to have turned out that way. The company was careful in who it chose, where it put them, how they were introduced into the group, and in ensuring that they had access to good back-up support through the buddy system. About two years into the project, most of the women were still in their jobs or had been promoted. What many had found hardest was not being women in a male culture, nor the lack of technical expertise (many just acknowledged this gap and found that the men were happy to teach them), but getting used to living in a rural setting.

To a certain extent NOVA's move-'em-into-the-trenches approach has worked. There has been a backlash, but, according to one manager, "the men who complained weren't actually working for a woman." Nevertheless, attitudes are very much in transition and women's experiences in the company vary widely. "I think we've neglected the men," said one manager. "We have not given them an improved understanding of women's management and communication styles." That is clear even in how staff describe the new approach to management. "There has been quite a change in the skills that are valued in the past three or four years," said one manager. "Now we value people skills and nurturing. . . . Although if a man were in this room I'd call those skills coaching and mentoring!"

The mixed messages go beyond words and into behaviour. Women struggle to be seen as team players, but, as one put it, "Even if you did go to the hockey game with a man, how would it be perceived? People gossip about men who spend time with women." One women told the story of a female colleague who was the only woman at an out-of-town meeting. When she got home from the meeting her manager scolded her for having had drinks in the bar with her male colleagues. "Did you say the same thing to the guys I was drinking with?" she asked. He had not. Her experience was not unusual.

This makes it difficult to get the mentoring that is needed to succeed. The company is considering implementing a formal mentoring program that might overcome this dilemma. In the meantime, most successful women have found mentors. Explained one: "I watched to see who I thought were the natural influencers within the organization. I'd make the first move. I'd ask them for help or simply ask them out for lunch." A newer staff member took an even more direct approach. "Ask questions," she advised. "I'll even ask people whose careers are going well how they do it, what organizations they belong to, . . . I've asked people to mentor me."

The conflicting attitudes are also seen in things like the company's approach to alternative working arrangements. They are available and starting to be used, but women using them find that they are no longer seen as committed to their careers. One woman who had been working part-time since the birth of her first child five years earlier said, "It's great . . . but part-time is career-limiting. . . . I had an excellent performance evaluation but they wrote on it that I will not be considered for promotion until I return to full-time work." Another woman, who is job-sharing, said, "My department was very supportive in setting up the job-sharing, but my manager has trouble coping with it when he's stressed out."

With such turbulent changes within the past few years, stress is an issue. The company recognized that many employees were having trouble coping and made "stress leaves" available to them. One woman, who had been on two stress leaves, said: "After my last one I told them I couldn't return to that job. They supported me. They gave me career counselling, and let me test out a new job." Ironically, she enjoyed the new job but it was about to be phased out. She was confident, though, that she would have other good opportunities.

It will be interesting to watch the opportunities unfold for other women as NOVA's experiment continues.

NOVA Corporation of Alberta
801-7th Ave. S.W., Box 2535, Station M, Calgary, AB, T2P 2N6
Telephone: (403) 290-7503

	Total	No. of Women	% Women
Full-time employees	5,802	1,522	26%
Part-time employees	237	165	70%
Board members	17	1	6%

Job category (figures based on full-time employees, unless noted otherwise):

	Total	No. of Women	% Women
Upper level managers	144	10[a]	7%
Middle or other managers	143	15	10%
Professionals	1,275	310	24%
Semi-professionals & technicians	456	209	46%
Supervisors	495	50	10%
Foremen/women	0	0	0%
Clerical workers	926	792	86%
Sales workers	23	4	17%
Service workers	0	0	0%
Skilled crafts & trades workers	1,200	86	7%
Semi-skilled manual workers	635	8	1%
Other manual workers	55	3	5%

Percentage of full-time employees considered upper level managers:	2.48%
Top-up of U.I.C. during maternity leave:	good
On-site daycare centre?	no
Child/elder care referral service?	no
Employment equity rep. reports to CEO/President?	no
Target numbers for women in management?	no
Pay equity policy?	no
Employment equity policy?	yes
Mentoring program?	no

Noteworthy benefits:
  • flexible benefits program
Part-time employee benefits:
  • same as full-time employees, if work 20+ hours/week (i.e. half-time)
Notes: (a) consists of two vice-presidents (V.P. People and V.P. Community) and eight managers

Nova Scotia Power

Nova Scotia Power is a utility company which generates electricity and delivers it to customers throughout Nova Scotia. It was a crown corporation until 1991, when it was privatized. The company is one of the largest employers in the province. Fifty-three per cent of its employees are unionized. These employees comprise most of the operations staff and some office workers.

One of the most interesting efforts at Nova Scotia Power has been its work with the International Brotherhood of Electrical Workers and the Halifax YWCA to increase the numbers of women working in trades, technology and operations.

The Halifax YWCA runs a program called YW-NOW, which works on several levels:

- First, it helps organizations spot barriers which might be keeping women out of non-traditional jobs. Some barriers are easy to fix, like making job titles gender neutral. For example, N.S. Power now refers to a maintenance journeyman as a maintenance person (certified). Other barriers can be more challenging, like changing the way the company recruits, hires and promotes staff.
- Second, YW-NOW goes into the workplace to run seminars to help change attitudes, like stereotyped ideas of what is "men's work" and what is "women's work".
- Third, the program helps prepare women who are considering working in non-traditional fields by training them in both the technical and personal skills they will need as trail-blazers.

The women who have been through the program are given first crack at term appointments whenever possible so that they can try out working in non-traditional areas.

One woman who had spent several years as a word processing operator is now thoroughly enjoying a term appointment as a utility worker. "The plant manager here wanted more women working in the plant, so he offered jobs to the women who participated in YW-NOW," she said. "At first it was kind of hard trying to fit in . . . but YW-NOW trained us for this type of work."

The women were given sessions on stress management, self-esteem, risk-taking and other related topics. Most helpful, according to this employee, were the role playing sessions in which they learned ways to handle the tricky situations that inevitably arise when women start to work in non-traditional areas.

Most of the women who tried working in non-traditional areas found they enjoyed the physical element of the work, and felt that they were given greater autonomy and respect than they had been in their desk jobs. They also found the men they worked with very supportive once they were over any initial misgivings.

"When I started, the guys were all paranoid about swearing," said one woman. "I told them I didn't really care. Now they are comfortable again." When it came to what she saw as the important issues, like how she was treated, she had no problems. She was treated fairly and with respect. She quickly became a fully accepted member of the team, and was surprised to find that the men would sit and talk to her about their children and their family lives in the same way that the women in the office had.

And while the language may still be crude, the men have mellowed since her arrival. One of them told her how much he appreciated the way the behaviour of his co-workers had changed; they were more polite in their dealings with one another than they had been before she joined.

Another woman, who went from a clerical position to a term appointment testing protective equipment, also found that she had been given suitable training to overcome the men's initial scepticism. She had taken courses in electricity so she would understand the equipment, learned how to drive a forklift, and done weight training because the job involved lifting loads of 50 or 60 pounds at a time. "Once they saw we could do it, there was no problem. In fact, the guys were very supportive; we all worked well together."

The company is also changing in other ways that it hopes will make it more accommodating to women. Workplace flexibility is encouraged officially, with the employee handbook stating that wherever possible employees should have some control over their work hours and suggesting compressed work weeks, flexible hours and job sharing.

The formal sanctioning of job-sharing made it possible for two women who had proposed it, had their proposal rejected a year before the new policies were announced, and, afterward, were allowed to job-share. Once it became a formal option, they found the company wonderfully accommodating.

"They left it to us to decide how to work it out," said one of the participants. "They bent over backward in accommodating me and my job-share partner." She started job-sharing in 1991, and after two years in one job-sharing position was able to switch to another one, which was advertised as a job-share position.

The person who initiates the request to job-share is allowed to post the position internally once she (or he) has her (or his) supervisor's approval, and to participate in all the interviews for a partner. The initiator and the supervisor have the ultimate say in who is selected, although the personnel department will advise them and help them focus on the special challenges of making the right match.

The firm has committed itself to an employment equity policy that states explicitly that, when there are equally qualified candidates, preference will be given to women, visible minorities, persons with disabilities and aboriginal people. One woman who, over 16 years, had consistently beat out male candidates for jobs in a variety of engineering and computer-related areas, said that at first she was angry about the employment equity policy. "I figured everyone should earn their way up the way I did. But I've since realized that you have to have a program like that, otherwise it won't happen. Now guys have to work harder to get ahead; it won't just happen because of who they know."

She got her foot in the door by having technical expertise that the men who were applying for the job lacked. She moved up steadily through a combination of technical ability, good leadership skills and mentors, some of whom she worked for and others she found by networking. She used the fact that she was typically the only woman to her advantage. "Because I was different, I'd stand out in a conference room. People would come and talk to me." When she met senior staff, she would be sure to follow up with them. "I'd always make sure I had a specific business thing to discuss with them. An idea, or a solution to a problem." She also increased her profile by getting involved in community events which were of interest to the senior management, like the Terry Fox Run, and by volunteering to work on high-profile internal committees and task forces, like the values-change program.

That program, which ran week-long courses for senior and mid-management and a shortened version for other managers and supervisors, grew out of the company's desire to operate in a more flexible, team-oriented way. Unfortunately, it has not yet had a major impact on attitudes. One woman felt that part of the problem was that "they talk about change, but they have not given us the tools to change". Despite the values-change courses and more recent employment equity seminars, what she referred to as the "white, male, 50, syndrome" still exists. "All his life he's been rewarded for behaving one way and all of a sudden he's told he has to change his behaviour." Managerial pay and promotion are not linked to efforts to recruit, develop or promote women and no hiring targets have been set, so managers have little direct incentive to change.

However, senior management was recently reorganized. Many employees think that the men who are now in charge have a different, more modern approach to human resources; one which may end up increasing the opportunities for women in management.

Nova Scotia Power Corporation
P.O. Box 910, Scotia Square, Halifax, NS, B3J 2W5
Telephone: (902) 428-6221

	Total	No. of Women	% Women
Full-time employees	2,224	363	16%
Part-time employees	250	69	28%
Board members	11	2	18%

Job category (figures based on full-time employees, unless noted otherwise):

	Total	No. of Women	% Women
Upper level managers	18	1	6%
Middle or other managers	145	10	7%
Professionals	258	37	14%
Semi-professionals & technicians	229	24	10%
Supervisors	32	16	50%
Foremen/women	144	0	0%
Clerical workers	432	326	75%
Sales workers	1	0	0%
Service workers	7	0	0%
Skilled crafts & trades workers	830	2	0%
Semi-skilled manual workers	226	8	4%
Other manual workers	47	1	2%

Percentage of full-time employees considered upper level managers:	0.81%
Top-up of U.I.C. during maternity leave:	none
On-site daycare centre?	no
Child/elder care referral service?	no
Employment equity rep. reports to CEO/President?	no
Target numbers for women in management?	no
Pay equity policy?	yes
Employment equity policy?	yes
Mentoring program?	no

Noteworthy benefits:
 • group RRSP
Part-time employee benefits:
 • pro-rated; premium cost shared

Ontario Hydro

Ontario Hydro is a crown corporation that generates and supplies electricity throughout the province. Ontario Hydro employees, 91% of whom are unionized, operate hydro-electric, nuclear, and fossil-fuelled generating stations and an extensive transmission and distribution system.

These are turbulent times at Ontario Hydro. Long accustomed to growing steadily and being able to offer generous programs to its employees, it is now faced with a declining demand for electricity, so it has had to start slashing costs and closing stations. In the months leading up to the interviews for this book, thousands of jobs had been eliminated, the whole corporation had been reorganized and a new chairman had taken over. There was a lot of uncertainty among the employees.

Despite that uncertainty, most of the policies and practices that established Ontario Hydro's reputation as a leader in human resources are still in place:

- flexible work arrangements are widespread, particularly for office workers, and they are increasing in popularity as the company looks for ways to pare costs;
- support for education is excellent;
- increasing numbers of women work in non-traditional areas;
- benefits are generous.

Ontario Hydro was one of the first major employers to take employment equity seriously. Its employment equity unit was set up in 1984. Since that time it has been working to ease the entry of women into the organization and up the career ladder. It has also been active in outreach and other programs to increase the numbers of women working in non-traditional areas, such as technical jobs in the power plants.

The number of women in all but clerical ranks still looks small compared with other industries, but within its industry, Ontario Hydro is the leader. As an engineering-based company, the pool of qualified women from which it can recruit is still relatively small, although growing. Compared with most other utilities, a significantly larger proportion of Ontario Hydro's total workforce is female, and it has had far more success at getting women into trades, technical, management and professional jobs, even at the senior levels.

For example, in 1984 only 1.4% of the "executive salary roll" (senior managers) were women. By the end of 1993 the figure had increased ten-fold, to 10.9%. In 1984 women only accounted for 6.8% of the "management and professional" staff; a figure which had more than doubled by the end of 1993, to 14.1%. The percentage of trades and technical jobs filled by women increased from 2.2% to 6.5% during the same period. The total number of employees, however, which had increased significantly between 1984 and 1992, actually ended 1993 slightly lower than in 1984.

An unfortunate side-effect has been a strong backlash from men at Hydro. Many seem convinced that "you have to wear a skirt to get ahead". A survey of the female engineers on staff done in late 1991 revealed that they perceived the employment equity initiatives as a two-edged sword: on the one hand, they had made managers more willing to hire women and consider them for advancement, on the other hand they had created a perception that the women were hired because of their sex rather than their abilities.

"It takes twice as long for supervisors to believe that we know our jobs," said one woman who worked in a technical job, "and God help you if you make a mistake!" Female engineers "never feel part of the club", said one, noting that it has disproportionately been women who have taken advantage of the voluntary severance packages. Another, and perhaps more significant, reason why so many women have taken the package is that many of them were hired more recently than the men, so if the company has to lay off more staff they would be among the first to go. It seemed safer to take the voluntary severance package while it was available.

Despite the backlash, many managers, both male and female, have taken the equity initiatives to heart and have gone out of their way to encourage the development of their female staff. "I've had a lot of support, especially since '86 or '87 when our old manager retired," said one woman who had moved from an entry level clerical position nine years ago to a supervisory role in an area that has not traditionally had many female staff. "Since the new manager took over there have been a lot more women on our staff, and he is also very supportive when we apply for jobs elsewhere in the company. Once he pulled us all together and asked why none of us had applied for a meter reader position that had opened up. The next meter reader hired was a woman from our office. None of us had ever really thought of applying for a job like that before."

Switching to gender-neutral job titles also had an impact. "When I was first at Bruce [nuclear station]," said one woman, "it was unthinkable that a woman would be in a handyman job. It only started to happen after they changed the name to handyperson."

The women entering technical and trades areas find that they are met with growing acceptance. One of the first female generating station operators hired noted that "new operators are hired in mixed groups now, so they have fewer hang-ups about women once they get into the field."

Finding suitable day care is a big challenge for shift workers who have young children. Ontario Hydro has day care centres near its Pickering plant, at the Kipling Research Centre in Etobicoke and at head office in downtown Toronto. The facilities are top-quality but cannot accommodate evening, night or weekend shifts. On the other hand, some of the flexible working arrangements have been applied creatively even in the plants. At one plant, for example, there is a team of operators who job-share by alternating five-week shift cycles. Thus, rather than having to work a mixture of day and night shifts each week, one works days only for five weeks while the other works nights only. At the end of five weeks they switch.

Other flexible working arrangements include recent experiments with staff working from home. One woman, who lived far away from her office and was caring for a husband with Alzheimer's Disease, had such an arrangement offered to her. "There was an opportunity for a promotion. I told my manager I'd love it, but that I couldn't take it. He said I might as well apply. I got the job and we instituted an electronic office in my home. For two years I worked in Toronto two days a week, at home two days a week, and had one day off." When her husband was placed in a nursing home in another city she returned to working a five-day week, but two of the days were still from home. "It gave me time to be with him and to work. The company made a very big difference in enabling me to be strong."

The company's support for education has also helped many women get ahead. Not only are courses funded, employees may be promoted while they are still pursuing their degrees. One woman who had started as a clerical worker 20 years ago was promised and got a promotion once she was half-way through her degree.

The staff cutbacks have also led to new opportunities for many of the employees. Entire departments have been reorganized and almost everyone has assumed new responsibilities. The workload has increased, but so has the interest level for some employees.

There are many examples of women who have progressed from clerical to management or technical ranks. All jobs are posted so employees are aware of new opportunities, and many of the clerical staff hired already have university degrees. They have been willing to start in clerical positions because the pay, benefits and opportunities at Ontario Hydro have been good. The recent job cuts eliminated the job security that Ontario Hydro employees once had, but for those who remain the pay, benefits and opportunities are still good.

Ontario Hydro
700 University Avenue, Toronto, ON, M5G 1X6
Telephone: (416) 592-5111

	Total	No. of Women	% Women
Full-time employees	22,590	4,480	20%
Part-time employees	0[a]	0	0%
Board members	22	5	23%

Job category (figures based on full-time employees, unless noted otherwise):

Upper level managers	18[b]	3	17%
Middle or other managers	503[c]	54	11%
Professionals	6,070[d]	857	14%
Semi-professionals & technicians	5,132[e]	397	8%
Supervisors	536	69	13%
Foremen/women	0	0	0%
Clerical workers	3,197	2,696	84%
Sales workers	0	0	0%
Service workers	0	0	0%
Skilled crafts & trades workers	7,134	404	6%
Semi-skilled manual workers	0	0	0%
Other manual workers	0	0	0%

Percentage of full-time employees considered upper level managers:	0.08%
Top-up of U.I.C. during maternity leave:	generous
On-site daycare centre?	yes
Child/elder care referral service?	no
Employment equity rep. reports to CEO/President?	no
Target numbers for women in management?	yes
Pay equity policy?	yes
Employment equity policy?	yes
Mentoring program?	no

Noteworthy benefits:
  • some post-retirement benefits
Part-time employee benefits:
  • pro-rated
Notes: (a) data not available
        (b) vice-president/general manager level and above
        (c) others in executive salary roll
        (d) the remaining management and professional staff
        (e) technical workers

Petro-Canada

Petro-Canada is the largest Canadian-owned oil and gas company. It has two operating divisions: the Resources Division, which explores for, produces and markets crude oil, natural gas, natural gas liquids and sulphur; and the Products Division, which refines crude oil and sells petroleum products to motorists, businesses and homes throughout Canada. Its corporate headquarters are in Calgary.

Petro-Canada won a Merit Award under the Federal Contractor's Program in 1993 for its efforts to make the company a good place for women and other members of under-represented groups. Those efforts began with an equal employment opportunities policy in 1984, two years before the federal Employment Equity legislation was passed.

Like many companies, Petro-Canada has cut staff dramatically in recent years, but it developed a "staffing for diversity" process to ensure that women and other members of under-represented groups would not be disproportionately affected by the cuts. As a result, while the number of staff has fallen from nearly 10,000 in 1986 to just over 5,000 today, representation of women in professional jobs has increased from 16% to nearly 28%, and in mid-management from six to nine percent. The company has also hired graduates of Montreal-based College Maissonneuve, which has a refinery operations program in which 25% of the students are female. This recruiting initiative is helping it increase the number of women in trades.

Parents who work at Petro Canada's head office in Calgary appreciate the 60-space, on-site day care centre which opened in 1988. One engineer, who has two children in the day care centre, finds it the perfect way to combine motherhood and professional life. "With my second child I could have taken up to six months off work, but I chose not to because I was too bored at home. But I really appreciate that I can spend my lunch times with the children."

The company also hired an outside contractor to provide a child and elder care referral service to employees across the country. The service is used heavily. Last year, for the first time, it was used even more for elder care referrals than for child care.

Some managers have shown tremendous flexibility in adapting to individual circumstances. For example, one woman in technical sales was able to work mornings in the office and afternoons at home while she was pregnant with twins. "My boss was very sensitive. . . . He took on a fatherly role," she said. She had trouble getting a nanny, so she asked for, and got, an extension of her leave for a further two months. When she returned to work her old job no longer existed, but she worked on special projects for a month and then got a promotion to a job two levels higher than her old one.

Professional women are starting to find it easier to combine work and family. Several of them are working part-time or job-sharing. So are some clerical staff, although the number of them doing so seems to be dwindling. One secretary who has been job-sharing for the past eight years knew of two other job-share teams that had been broken up because "their boss said, 'I can't take having two different faces to see in the morning'."

Clerical staff are expected to work fixed hours but they appreciate having access to up to 12 flex days a year. "The flex days are a tremendous boost for those of us who have sick kids all the time," said the mother of a two-and-a-half year old. Others use flex days for attending to personal commitments like dental appointments.

Management employees have a lot of flexibility in their days, which helps to compensate for long hours. They can take time out to attend to personal matters when they need to. "As a senior employee I'm expected to manage my own time," said one.

Sexual harassment is a subject most companies shy away from, but Petro-Canada has tackled it head on. The company fired a senior employee for harassment and made no attempt to cover up the reasons for his firing. That sent a strong message that such behaviour would not be tolerated. As a result, said one secretary, "it has made it easier for people to talk about it". It has also changed the way people behave. "A lot of the young staff have completely different attitudes about working with women than the older school . . . They automatically don't touch, and that sort of thing . . ."

Petro-Canada recognizes that its biggest challenge is in changing employee attitudes, so that is where its diversity efforts are focused now. Staff surveys are used to help improve policies and practices. Employees are given the survey results and feel that their comments do have an impact.

One initiative that grew out of employee comments was Petro-Canada's half-day seminars called the "Gender Connection". There are separate seminars for women and men and their objective is to help employees understand each other's behaviour and attitudes better so that they can work together more effectively.

The seminars were pilot-tested with a group of male vice-presidents and directors, including the five most senior men in the company. By the summer of 1993 the Gender Connection had been taken by about 70 men and 60 women. The company's goal is to have all employees take the seminars eventually.

The company has also developed a follow-up course called "Building Better Business Relationships", which focuses on the differences in male and female communication styles. Again, the objective is to have all employees take the course.

"Valuing Diversity Teams" that consist of men and women from all parts of the company were established three years ago to champion change. They sponsor and deliver awareness sessions, work to identify systemic barriers in the organization and recommend ways to eliminate those barriers.

Despite its efforts the company still has a long way to go in changing the attitudes and management styles of its male employees. "There are some women being moved through," said one manager, "but after a certain level they either stop moving or quit." Part of the problem, she feels, is that women "are not part of the networking loop. Things like playing squash with the boys become more important at the senior levels". Others agreed. "The problem," said one, "is getting to know the internal politics. That happens at informal meetings, like over lunch. We are not included in the spur-of-the-moment chats, the 'let's grab a coffee' chats. You miss a lot of stuff. It doesn't hinder the job you are doing, but it does hinder your movement within the company." Said another, "They respect you, but they don't include you."

The informal networking is particularly important because not all jobs are posted internally; particularly not senior jobs. And while external recruiters are instructed to present at least one female candidate for every job opening, not much external hiring is taking place. The result is a shortage of mentors and female role models.

Petro Canada is still struggling to find the best way to manage clerical staff. It is nearly impossible to move from clerical to management ranks, and it is even difficult to have much mobility within the clerical sector.

There are still weak spots but, as one female engineer put it, "We have improved dramatically in the 10 years I've been here." Human resources staff are determined to ensure that the improvement continues.

Petro-Canada
150-6th Ave. S.W., P.O. Box 2844, Calgary, AB, T2P 3E3
Telephone: (403) 296-8000

	Total	No. of Women	% Women
Full-time employees	5,249	1,239	24%
Part-time employees	60	42	70%
Board members	11	2	18%

Job category (figures based on full-time employees, unless noted otherwise):

Upper level managers	158	12	8%
Middle or other managers	348	30	9%
Professionals	1,603	444	28%
Semi-professionals & technicians	163	32	20%
Supervisors	134	43	32%
Foremen/women	258	4	2%
Clerical workers	832	617	74%
Sales workers	27	22	81%
Service workers	16	2	13%
Skilled crafts & trades workers	1,710[a]	29	2%
Semi-skilled manual workers			
Other manual workers			

Percentage of full-time employees considered upper level managers:	3.01%
Top-up of U.I.C. during maternity leave:	good
On-site daycare centre?	yes
Child/elder care referral service?	yes
Employment equity rep. reports to CEO/President?	yes
Target numbers for women in management?	yes
Pay equity policy?	no
Employment equity policy?	yes
Mentoring program?	no

Noteworthy benefits:
- 12 flex days
- fitness facilities available at Calgary head office and at North York Civil Centre (Toronto); for other locations company subsidies fitness club memberships
- educational assistance
- scholarship program for children of Petro-Canada employees
- capital accumulation plan: company matches up to 5% of basic monthly earnings which employee may invest in cash, bond, equity or balanced funds

Part-time employee benefits:
- pro-rated to hours worked

Notes: (a) includes semi-skilled manual workers and other manual workers

Syncrude Canada Ltd.

Syncrude is the largest synthetic crude oil operation in the world, and Canada's second largest oil producer. Its head office is in Fort McMurray, Alberta, and its plant, where most of the employees are based, is at Mildred Lake, 40 kilometres away. It also has a 125-person research centre in Edmonton. Syncrude is a joint venture owned by a consortium of oil and gas companies and the Alberta Government.

"When I started as a fire fighter," said a woman who was originally a secretary at Syncrude, "the fire chief told me I was being hired because he had no choice and he was convinced that I'd fail in six months and he'd never have to hire a woman again." Six months later she was still there but the fire chief was gone.

"Syncrude is a company that truly cares about the progress and treatment of women, and it is not being done to gain contracts, through coercion or because somebody told us to," said Human Resources Advisor, Pat Atkins. "The company thinks it is important to get the best talent available," and one way to do that is to make sure that it develops the full potential of its existing staff and recruits and promotes a good share of the limited supply of women with education or experience in engineering, refining and mining.

Attracting good employees to work in a northern community where the temperatures are well below zero for much of the year and the nearest large city is several hours drive away can be a challenge, although, as some employees point out, Fort McMurray is no longer the tiny frontier community it was in the late seventies when Syncrude was getting rolling, and it is a comfortable community in which to raise a family.

Even so, Syncrude knows it has to be a place where people want to work if it is going to get its share of the best, and has come to realize that it can't afford to waste female talent. Syncrude uses a three-pronged approach to keep its employees satisfied.

First, it listens to its staff. Even non-management staff say that the President, Eric Newell, is approachable and open-minded. "It is a pretty progressive company when it comes to the involvement of its employees," said an employee who had worked her way from an entry level clerical job to one of the firm's few management positions (only about two percent of the staff are managers).

A "Pipeline" system lets employees raise concerns with executives anonymously. When the "Pipeline" coordinator gets a question or comment, the name of the person submitting it is removed and it is passed on to a vice-president for a response. The coordinator then passes the answer back to the employee.

Second, staff are treated well. "We are paid well, we are well taken care of, and we get good benefits," said one long-time employee. On top of regular salary and benefits, a "Thrift Plan" matches employee contributions to personal savings plans. The amount the company contributes increases with the length of service. Employees can split their savings among seven funds. Five of them are mutual investment funds, with different levels of risk. One is a money market fund and the final one can be used by employees who bought homes from a major local housing developer to reduce the outstanding principal on their mortgages.

Staff are also compensated for some of the restrictions of living where they do with extra travel days on top of regular vacation time, intended to get them to and from a major centre for their holidays. (The Edmonton-based employees do not get this time).

Syncrude flies in professors from the University of Alberta for an on-site MBA program, with classes taught in the late afternoon. There are also many other on-site educational and training programs.

The children of employees are eligible for awards to cover tuition, fees and some living expenses while they are pursuing post-secondary education. The company also runs a Special Educational Awards Program for local residents that gives grants to aboriginals and to women pursuing non-traditional programs relevant to the oil sands industry at universities, technical schools or colleges.

The third prong in Syncrude's approach to satisfying its employees is an effort to make it possible to combine work and family despite the challenges of distance and shift work. Shuttle busses ferry employees between the communities in which they live and the plant site. A couple who both work at Syncrude have arranged their hours so that the husband catches an early shuttle while his wife gets the baby up, fed and to the sitter. The husband finishes his work day at 2:30 p.m. so that he can catch an early shuttle home to collect the baby and prepare supper. "They joked at first," said his wife, "but he hasn't had a problem." The company has a scheduling system on its electronic mail that everybody can check when they are trying to arrange meetings. Her husband simply blocks out the 2:30-4:30 p.m. time slot every day, so no one tries to book him into meetings after he has to leave.

The same woman commented that people were starting to work part-time to combine work and family. "There is no stigma for engineers," she said, although the concept is not yet fully accepted. "I do get a lot of snide remarks about coming in late. They forget that I get paid less too!" She also noted that she knows women in other areas whose requests to work part-time had been refused.

There are no policies on job-sharing, and compressed work weeks are negotiated by departments rather than individuals. The company allows extended maternity and parental leaves but it has yet to sort through the details of the impact of such leaves. For example, one woman who took a six-month maternity leave was initially denied a merit increase because of a company guideline that says people who are away for six months of a calendar year are not eligible for merit increases.

The main route into management is through the operations side of the company, so, although it is difficult to progress from clerical work directly to management, the company is encouraging women to try non-traditional jobs. It ran a six-week Bridges program in 1991/92 to train and place women in trades and technical jobs. Fifty women applied, 22 were accepted and 13 lasted through the program. All but one of them were placed in non-traditional jobs.

The second time, however, there was not enough interest. The program has been scaled down and extended to male office workers. According to Ms. Atkins, "a lot of the women decided it wasn't what they wanted to do, especially because it was hard to combine shift work with having young kids."

Instead, the company now focuses on informal job shadowing opportunities for anyone interested in working in a non-traditional area. "If someone says, for example, that she's interested in being a process operator, we'll send her over for two weeks to see what it is like." Non-traditional job opportunities and apprenticeship positions are posted regularly and women are encouraged to apply. Now that noticeable numbers of women are in non-traditional jobs, other women are starting to consider such jobs as options.

A skilled trades worker who had done the same type of work in two other companies said, "It's a bit more relaxed here. I don't have to prove myself as much". She felt that was partly because there were more women in such jobs at Syncrude than at the previous places she had worked, and also because Syncrude supports their presence. "The women are going to be hired, and the men have to accept it," she said.

It is not surprising in an organization where only 15% of the employees are women that traditional male attitudes still dominate, and even successful women worry about how they are perceived. Senior managers are treading a fine line in trying to include women and ensure they have equal opportunities without being seen as promoting them on criteria other than merit. One woman's comments highlight the conflicting views. "A lot of the women getting into supervisory jobs have the ability, but they want to *earn* the right to be there." On the other hand, "there are still a lot of old boy types. They go on fishing trips together. . . . We need to ensure that our interviewers are objective."

It takes time to build the momentum needed to overcome such concerns. As Syncrude said in its submission for this book, "We still have a long way to go, but we are making progress."

Syncrude Canada Ltd.
PO Bag 4009 MD Y202, Ft. McMurray, AB, T9H 3L1
Telephone: (403) 790-5911

	Total	No. of Women	% Women
Full-time employees	4,229	652	15%
Part-time employees	15	13	87%
Board members	16	1	6%

Job category (figures based on full-time employees, unless noted otherwise):

Upper level managers	26	1[a]	4%
Middle or other managers	76	3	4%
Professionals	723	184	25%
Semi-professionals & technicians	109	87	80%
Supervisors	315	15	5%
Foremen/women	437	9	2%
Clerical workers	185	180	97%
Sales workers	0	0	0%
Service workers	0	0	0%
Skilled crafts & trades workers	2,248	161	7%
Semi-skilled manual workers	19	13	68%
Other manual workers	0	0	0%

Percentage of full-time employees considered upper level managers:	0.61%
Top-up of U.I.C. during maternity leave:	none
On-site daycare centre?	no
Child/elder care referral service?	no
Employment equity rep. reports to CEO/President?	no
Target numbers for women in management?	yes
Pay equity policy?	no
Employment equity policy?	yes
Mentoring program?	no

Noteworthy benefits:
- gain-sharing plan
- employee savings plan with matching contributions by employer
- academic scholarships for children of employees

Part-time employee benefits:
- same as full-time employees

Notes: (a) General Manager, Materials and Services

Union Gas Limited

Union Gas Limited, a wholly-owned subsidiary of Vancouver's Westcoast Energy Inc., is a natural gas storage, transmission and distribution utility serving approximately 680,000 residential, commercial and industrial customers in southwestern Ontario. It also provides storage and transportation services for other companies in Ontario, Quebec and the United States. It is headquartered in Chatham, Ontario, with regional offices in Windsor, London, Waterloo and Hamilton.

Having a head office in a small centre like Chatham, Ontario, (population 40,000) can be a challenge when it comes to recruiting. Some people are attracted by the advantages of living in a family-oriented community with easy access to outdoor recreational facilities, but others, particularly two-career couples, may see the location as a drawback. The odds of both spouses being able to find good jobs are small, and even if they do, the nature of the work is such that ambitious employees are likely to have to move several times during a career with Union Gas. "We've lost several women to other companies," said one manager, "mainly because of where we are located."

The company tries to overcome this difficulty by helping to arrange interviews for spouses with potential employers in the new community and by working with relocation companies to help staff and their families adapt. When it is not feasible to move the family, or for temporary assignments, the company provides generous travel allowances so that the family members can stay in contact with each other. One woman who spent six months working on a project in Vancouver appreciated that the company flew her home every weekend and flew her husband out to Vancouver for an occasional visit. When both spouses are employees of the company, it will also try to accommodate both careers.

Like many companies these days, Union Gas places a high value on university degrees. It provides educational leaves of up to two years and has been known to relocate employees so that they can attend university.

The company's recruiting brochure shows almost as many pictures of people at play as at work, which gives what seems to be an accurate image of the company as a good place for people wanting to lead balanced work and personal lives. As in any company, there is enough work to keep employees busy for as much time as they want to devote to their work, but excessive hours do not seem to be the norm for men or women.

The company's alternative work arrangements, which include modified work weeks, continuous part-time work and job-sharing, "are for real" according to one employee, although the ability to use them varies with the operational requirements of the department. Employees at the Trafalgar compressor station, for example, designed their own compressed work week schedule to accommodate the station's 24-hour a day operation while giving them a schedule they preferred.

The option of continuous part-time work was introduced for non-management employees in the mid-eighties, and recently extended to management, supervisory and technical staff.

The company has written guidelines for each of the alternative work arrangements. The guidelines set out the process required for approval and factors employees and supervisors should take into account when designing and considering a proposal. The guide to flextime includes a time chart that is used to see at a glance whether the proposal will cause problems with the workload or staff coverage, and all workers in the unit must sign off to ensure that none feel that the proposal will cause a problem for them.

The company also provides good support for employees with children. Staff get three paid half-days per year of Family Sickness Leave, as well as five paid personal days off. A group of employees who were concerned about child care researched a proposal for the establishment of a day care centre in cooperation with St. Clair College's early childhood education program. Union Gas let an employee work full-time on the day care centre project during the planning stages and helped with the initial funding. The bulk of the capital costs were provided by the Ontario Government and the land was contributed by the college. The centre opened in September 1990 and is now self-supporting.

Maternity leaves of up to one year are available, with full company-paid benefits for the whole year and a guarantee of returning to the same job. (In many organizations women taking maternity leaves are only guaranteed a "comparable" job upon return). Many managers are reluctant to take the full year, although eight or nine-month leaves are not uncommon and less senior staff often do take the full leave.

One management employee, who had been on more than one maternity leave, said that during her leaves she had stayed in contact with the office, although the extent of that contact varied. During one leave, which she took from a particularly demanding job, "I practically stayed on the job," she said. "They came to see me every two weeks. I signed papers, dealt with staffing issues, . . ." She was not paid for that time, but said that it was her choice to do it that way. "My boss expects me to develop a plan for how my job will get done while I'm off," she said. "I'm still accountable for what happens." She acknowledged that there are other models. "I know another woman in management here who took the full year off. We brought in an outside consultant to fill her job on a temporary basis."

For those who are having trouble coping with work or personal issues, the company provides a comprehensive employee assistance plan through an outside supplier. The plan is accessible to all employees, regardless of where they are located, through a toll-free number.

Many of the company's work and family initiatives grew out of a 1990 employee task force which found that the number-one workplace issue at the time was balancing work and home life. The task force also identified Canada's increasingly diverse workforce as an issue for Union Gas to address, and the company has established a Diversity Team which includes representatives of the union, management and the technical/analyst/non-union clerical sector. The team's mandate is to identify and make recommendations to a Diversity Council on ways to eliminate barriers to diversity and to suggest ways to help a diverse workforce thrive. The council consists of three senior executives and an equal number of members of the Diversity Team, all of whom must agree to any proposals before they are implemented.

The team and senior management recognize that there is not yet a critical mass of women in senior or even mid-management to be role models and mentors. The two most senior women, as of early 1994, were managers — one of Human Resources Planning and Recruitment and the other a regional manager.

To try to overcome this lack of female leadership, the company occasionally organizes events at which female managers can chat with senior management. The objective of these events is to give the women the exposure that many men may get naturally through informal networking such as at sporting events and casual lunches or drinks after work. One woman found that, perhaps due to being in a small community, people tended to misinterpret "the close personal relationship that is needed for mentoring".

The company has a conservative culture and many of the male employees, even the younger ones, have stay-at-home wives. As a result, said one employee, "they don't understand the issues". There has been a backlash from male staff to initiatives aimed at supporting women. The company has always tried to be scrupulously fair and even-handed in the application of its rules, so staff have some difficulty accepting the notion that equal opportunity may mean treating some staff members differently from others. "The men sincerely believe that women and minorities are getting unfair advantages even though there is no justification for believing that," said one woman, who also noted that it is crucial that the executives be consistent in what they say about the role of women in the firm, whether they are making public statements or chatting informally at social events.

The Diversity Team and Council are working hard to meet the concerns of women and even now the women interviewed felt that "there are tremendous opportunities for individuals here; gender is not an issue." However, "fitting the blue pin-stripe image" is an issue and will be until the company undergoes a major cultural change. "There is a comfort-zone here," explained one employee. "We try not to single people out; we try to treat everybody fairly and consistently. . . . But you do have to be conservative to do well."

Union Gas Ltd.
50 Keil Drive North, Chatham, ON, N7M 5M1
Telephone: (519) 352-3100

	Total	No. of Women	% Women
Full-time employees	2,468	785	32%
Part-time employees	116	112	97%
Board members	9	1	11%

Job category (figures based on full-time employees, unless noted otherwise):

Upper level managers	43	2	5%
Middle or other managers	133	13	10%
Professionals	0	0	0%
Semi-professioanls & technicians	324	56	17%
Supervisors	532	123	23%
Foremen/women	0	0	0%
Clerical workers	638	558	87%
Sales workers	45	5	11%
Service workers	753	28	4%
Skilled crafts & trades workers	0	0	0%
Semi-skilled manual workers	0	0	0%
Other manual workers	0	0	0%

Percentage of full-time employees considered upper level managers:	1.74%
Top-up of U.I.C. during maternity leave:	none
On-site daycare centre?	yes
Child/elder care referral service?	no
Employment equity rep. reports to CEO/President?	no
Target numbers for women in management?	yes
Pay equity policy?	yes
Employment equity policy?	yes
Mentoring program?	no

Noteworthy benefits:
  • full, employer-paid benefits for one year of maternity-related leave
Part-time employee benefits:
  • continuous part-time (CPT) employees who work 30+ hours/month are
    eligible for a reduced package of benefits after 2 years service (or
    immediately, if employee was already an eligible full-time employee who
    transferred to CPT)

FINANCIAL SERVICES: BANKING

American Express

American Express has two companies in Canada: American Express Canada, Inc. and Amex Bank of Canada. American Express Canada, Inc. provides travellers cheques, travel management services for leisure and business travel, merchandise services and insurance and protection services. Amex Bank of Canada provides banking services, charge cards and related cardmember services.

American Express (AMEX) has a reputation for being hard-nosed and competitive, so it is not surprising that its "Best Place to Work" strategy was introduced for pure business reasons. "In 1990 we researched the future workforce and concluded that if we wanted to stay competitive we would have to become one of the best places to work," explained Pheobe Epstein, Vice-President of Human Resources.

AMEX realized that to become one of the best it would have to change a corporate culture that had always rewarded slavish devotion to the company and a focus on individual achievement rather than team work. "We are trying to empower employees to ask for what they need and supervisors to say okay without worrying about setting a precedent," Ms. Epstein continued. "We found that there are very few requests you can't accommodate."

A "work at home" pilot project in a Toronto business travel office grew out of this strategy. Since most business travel is handled by telephone, AMEX decided to let several employees who wanted to work from home give it a try. Participants must have day care for their children and their calls are monitored in the same way they would be in the office. They come into the office once a week.

"It has had some interesting results," said Ms. Epstein. "Somebody who had real productivity problems doesn't any more. . . . The people who are doing it love it. There has been no decline in productivity anywhere. In fact, the only negative we have discovered so far is that the people who have chosen to stay in the office miss the company of those at home!"

Other aspects of the "Best Place to Work" strategy included introducing a child and elder care referral service and a paid sabbatical program. After 10 years of service employees may take a six-month paid sabbatical to do approved community work (or a full year after 20 years of service). Unpaid sabbaticals are also available for employees wanting to do other things with their time.

"It has incredible mental health benefits," said Ms. Epstein, who has seen people take sabbatical leaves from AMEX's international headquarters in New York. "It is no longer perceived as a career killer to take a long break."

AMEX also lets employees buy up to one week of extra vacation time each year, and fund it through pay deductions.

Policies are only as effective as the people implementing them, so managers and executives are being given leadership training, systems have been implemented to give them feedback from peers and subordinates and there is a lot of talk about teamwork, balance and flexibility. "Our manager changed radically as a result of the feedback," said one non-management employee, whose experience had been shared by others.

However attitudes that are as firmly entrenched as those at AMEX cannot be changed overnight. "Conceptually, I agree," said one manager, "but we are not there yet. As an organization we are still very unbalanced." She went on to confess, "I get disappointed when my people don't put in a lot of hours. I do, and I take work home every night." She has three children, and copes by "paying a lot of money" for household help.

Said another manager, "I'm known by my people as a bit of a slave-driver, but I'm trying to change." One manager said she had got feedback from the people who reported to her that they were not happy having to work long hours. "I learned. Now I'm extremely sensitive to that. However," she continued, "my managers cannot possibly do their jobs from 8:30 to 4:30. . . . I am sensitive to family needs but our practices don't yet support that."

The company is trying to change its practices when it comes to hours. Everyone working more than 20 hours a week is eligible for full benefits and in 1993 operations were streamlined by encouraging full-time employees to shift to part-time. About 30 people had done so by the end of 1993 but they still felt the pressure to produce and to put in long hours. One woman who had been working a three-day work week for a year and a half still found herself working 12 hours on each of those three days.

On the positive side, non-management staff appreciated that managers were generally flexible about hours and would allow them time off during the day when they needed it to deal with appointments or sick children, as long as they saw to it that the work still got done. The company allows three personal days, which employees see as a positive signal, yet many felt uncomfortable claiming these days or using their own sick days to care for sick children once the personal days had been used up. "I do take time off for sick kids," said one, "but from my vacation days. . . . I don't take sick days because I don't want people complaining."

Balance is an issue that many of the employees are still struggling with. A manager and mother of three children said, "I used to work all the time. Eventually I understood that it was self-imposed. You have to learn to delegate." She still puts in long hours, although she has delegated the travel aspect of her job to her subordinates. "I talk fast, I walk fast . . . but I'm home at five to put dinner on the table, and I start to work again at nine," after the children are in bed.

What inspires this willingness to work so hard for the company? "AMEX rewards results," said one of AMEX's five female vice-presidents. "It doesn't matter who you are. If you produce and do a good job, you will do well."

All the women interviewed agreed that "promotion in this company really is based on talent", but some felt that women still had to push harder to progress as quickly as men. One woman, who works in a predominantly female area of the company, said, "men who come into our area move on and out quickly. As a woman in our area you have to excel and be very aggressive about your own ambitions."

It also helps if you learn to play golf, at least "well enough not to be an embarrassment on the course," said one woman who attributed her own success to a combination of producing, pushing, mentoring and timing. She felt that women have a tough time breaking into some of the non-work-related bonding that has traditionally helped men make the contacts they needed to get ahead. There are ways around it, however, especially now that there are so many senior women at AMEX to serve as role models and mentors.

"I take being an example to other women very seriously," said one female vice-president, who struggles to fill that role without misleading people. "This is not for everybody. There are choices. I've made some choices that other people may not make. It is not an easy life." Even so, it is not one she or many of the other women at American Express would trade.

American Express
101 McNabb Street, Markham, ON, L3R 4H8
Telephone: (905) 474-8333

	Total	No. of Women	% Women
Full-time employees	1,885	1,304	69%
Part-time employees	121	110	91%
Board members	10	2	20%

Job category (figures based on full-time employees, unless noted otherwise):

Upper level managers	9	5	56%
Middle or other managers	192[a]	108	56%
Professionals	385	191	50%
Semi-professionals & technicians	0	0	0%
Supervisors	96	57	59%
Foremen/women	0	0	0%
Clerical workers	1,203	943	78%
Sales workers	0	0	0%
Service workers	0	0	0%
Skilled crafts & trades workers	0	0	0%
Semi-skilled manual workers	0	0	0%
Other manual workers	0	0	0%

Percentage of full-time employees considered upper level managers:	0.48%
Top-up of U.I.C. during maternity leave:	none
On-site daycare centre?	no
Child/elder care referral service?	yes
Employment equity rep. reports to CEO/President?	yes
Target numbers for women in management?	no
Pay equity policy?	yes
Employment equity policy?	no
Mentoring program?	no

Noteworthy benefits:
- flexible benefits package; can use left-over credits towards fitness club memberships or stock purchase plan; can also purchase 1-5 days of extra vacation time
- sabbatical leave program (company-funded, for approved causes)

Part-time employee benefits:
- same as full-time, if work 20+ hours/week

Notes: (a) 48 of the total and 19 of the women (39%) are at the vice-president or director level

Bank of Montreal

The Bank of Montreal is Canada's third largest bank, with 1,251 branches across the country and $116.9 billion in assets at the end of 1993. It provides full retail, commercial and corporate banking services.

The Bank of Montreal clearly demonstrates how senior management commitment and determination can transform an organization. In 1990 the bank's new president, Anthony Comper, convened a task force on the advancement of women in the bank. As he pointed out to employees in a preface to the 1991 Task Force Report, it did not make competitive sense to have a system in which 91% of the non-management jobs but only 9% of the executive jobs were held by women. Clearly a lot of talent was being overlooked.

The task force conferred widely within the bank and with outside experts. As a result it was able to present a report full of solid data that has become a reference point even for other companies concerned about the role of women within their organizations. It was particularly useful in exposing the facts behind five myths, which are common to many organizations:

1. *Women will just have babies and quit.* The facts showed that women had longer service records than men at all levels of the bank except senior management, where their shorter tenure was largely attributable to the fact that most of the senior women had been hired from outside the bank rather than groomed from within. Bank statistics also showed that 98% of the female employees returned to work following maternity leave.

2. *They're too young, or too old.* There was no significant difference in the average age between male and female employees. In mid-management, the average age was identical, and even in senior management, men were on average only five years older than the women. (The reverse was true in non-management, where women were, on average, five years older than the men.)

3. *They just need more education, and then they'll get ahead.* At the non-management and junior management levels — the main feeder routes to senior jobs — far more women than men had degrees. Lack of education was *not* what was holding them back.

4. *They don't have the right stuff; they're not good enough for more senior jobs.* Significantly more women than men in every job level were rated above average or superior on their performance appraisals.

5. *Time will take care of any imbalance in the numbers.* At the rate at which women were being promoted at the time of the study, by the year 2000 only 22% of the senior managers and 18% of the executives would have been women.

In response to the report the bank promoted a finance specialist, Johanne Totta, to the position of Vice-President, Workplace Equity. She had worked with the task force and was well aware of the issues, but because of her strong financial background she had credibility with other bankers. She reports directly to the president and was given wide scope to make changes. Changes made to date include:

- linking all managers' annual performance reviews to their success in meeting goals they have set for the hiring, retention and advancement of women;
- tracking results quarterly, both statistically and with employee opinion surveys;
- teaching behaviour-focused interview techniques to minimize subjectivity in hiring decisions;
- introducing and actively promoting five types of flexible work arrangements for all levels of employees: flextime (non-traditional starting and ending times), flexible work week (arrangements like compressing the same number of hours per week into fewer days), permanent part-time, job-sharing and flexplace (working from home or another location for some or all of the work week);
- creating national and divisional advisory councils on the "equitable workplace", to oversee the implementation of workplace equity initiatives.

The decision to link managers' performance assessments to their success in meeting equity goals was only implemented in 1993 so it is too early to have data on its effect, but the bank's other efforts are already paying off.

"The bank has changed significantly in the past three years and so have I," said one woman who had started at the bank at age 17 and, after a lot of pushing, worked her way into a branch manager position. "The guidance and leadership from Tony Comper and [Chairman] Matt Barrett made all the difference. Before I felt that I had to be like the men to get ahead. I no longer feel that." Another mid-level manager, who had started 25 years earlier as a teller, agreed. "Until two or three years ago it was difficult for women to progress. It was a boy's club until the new president took over."

In the first two years since the task force reported, women had increased their representation at the executive level from nine to 13%, and in 1993 they got 55% of the promotions to that level, up from 29% in 1991. At the senior management level women got 38% of the promotions in 1993, up from 20% in 1991. This brought their senior management representation to 17% from 13% in 1991. In mid-management, women's representation increased from 34% to 39%, and their share of the promotions increased from 43% to 57%.

One result of the high profile given to the advancement of women within the bank was the emergence of three new myths, which were addressed in the October 1993 follow-up report of the task force.

1. *It's all just quotas now; getting the numbers up is our first priority.* The report points out that managers are responsible for setting their own hiring and advancement targets (not quotas), which reflect what they think they can achieve realistically. Since the mangers are also accountable for the performance of their staff, they are only rewarded if the people they hire and promote are effective.

2. *Men are an endangered species around here.* It is true that more women than ever before are having their abilities recognized with further training and promotion, but at middle and senior levels there are still more men than women being hired and promoted. Talented men are not being neglected.

3. *Advancing women will hurt productivity.* Between May 1992, when flexible working arrangements were introduced, and July 31, 1993, over 2,000 employees (nearly 10% of the staff) had taken advantage of such arrangements. Eighty-four and a half per cent of them opted for flextime, 6.7% for flexible work weeks, 6.3% for flexplace, 1.6% for permanent part-time, and 0.9% for job-sharing. Interestingly, men account for 40% of the flexible arrangements now in place. This widespread use of flexible options has led to a concern in some quarters that productivity will be hurt. The bank's performance in 1993 suggests otherwise: it had its most successful year ever.

People managing such arrangements have found that they actually increase productivity. Staff can arrange their work life to mesh better with their personal lives, so they can focus better on their work; they do not feel themselves pulled in different directions at once. Much less time is lost to people running personal errands on bank time. Employee opinion surveys suggest that people who would otherwise have left the bank decided to stay because of the new options.

One woman who runs a branch that is open 8 am to 8 pm has three people sharing one job. "At the beginning it took more planning," she said, "but that's a one-time effort. Because we have three people to cover the bad shifts, the other employees are also happier."

Of course, not all managers have accepted the new ways. As in any organization, the extent of flexibility and support varies from supervisor to supervisor. But the statistics and employees' comments suggest that the new attitudes have taken hold in most parts of the organization.

"The bank has a 'Flavour of the Month' history," explained one long-time employee, "so there was initial scepticism about the employment equity programs. But because they have been here for two years now and we are hearing pretty consistent messages, it is starting to sink in that it is for real. . . . We've tried to focus on encouraging the receptive types rather than punishing the hard-line opponents."

Senior management is confident that, particularly with its continued promotion of the equity initiatives and solid performance results to back it up, opposition will soon disappear.

Bank of Montreal
129 St. Jacques Street West, 3rd Floor, Montreal, PQ, H2Y 1L6
Telephone: (514) 877-1351

	Total	No. of Women	% Women
Full-time employees	19,780	13,879	70%
Part-time employees	6,709	6,158	92%
Board members	30	4	13%

Job category (figures based on full-time employees, unless noted otherwise):

Upper level managers	197	21	11%
Middle or other managers	8,071	4,554	56%
Professionals	3,256	2,001	61%
Semi-professionals & technicians	36	17	47%
Supervisors	1,227	1,122	91%
Foremen/women	0	0	0%
Clerical workers	6,836	6,132	90%
Sales workers	8	3	38%
Service workers	99	27	27%
Skilled crafts & trades workers	34	0	0%
Semi-skilled manual workers	16	2	13%
Other manual workers	0	0	0%

Percentage of full-time employees considered upper level managers:	1.00%
Top-up of U.I.C. during maternity leave:	none
On-site daycare centre?	no
Child/elder care referral service?	yes
Employment equity rep. reports to CEO/President?	yes
Target numbers for women in management?	yes
Pay equity policy?	yes
Employment equity policy?	yes
Mentoring program?	yes

Noteworthy benefits:
- share ownership program (only available to senior managers)
- educational assistance
- special rates on bank services
- as many "People Care" days as the employee deems necessary can be used to deal with family emergencies

Part-time employee benefits:
- full benefits if work at least half the standard 37.5-hour week
- pro-rated benefits if work at least 7.5 hours/week

CIBC

The CIBC is Canada's second largest bank, with 1,625 branches across the country and $141.3 billion of assets at the end of the 1993 fiscal year. It provides full retail, commercial and corporate banking services.

Revolutionaries are not normally found in a bank, but a group of senior women at CIBC who got together four years ago were perceived that way by some of their colleagues. Evolutionary change was too slow for them; they had a deadline to meet. One of them was pregnant and determined that the bank should provide income support to women on maternity leaves.

They lobbed a few grenades in the form of regular notices on electronic mail to put pressure on senior management throughout the bank. "The executive was unhappy with this, but it got action!" said one of them. Within months the battle was won: the bank introduced a top-up of the unemployment insurance benefits for women on maternity leave.

"I was surprised that the institution acted that fast," said the woman who had been pregnant at the time. "It worked because all these women were behind me and also pushing."

The bank's traditionalists were shaken by the group's activities (at the time comments like, "we've got to get them under control", were heard) but the chairman recognized that it made more sense to channel this energy productively than to try to squelch it. In September of 1991 he issued a strongly worded letter on the role of women in the bank and created the "Chairman's Committee on Women's Issues".

The original women's network still holds monthly meetings and lobbies for change. It is open to the bank's most senior 250 women, although a proposal to expand it throughout the bank is being looked at. "This was always intended to be a central hub of an entire chain," explained one of the founders.

The impact of the women's network and the Chairman's Committee on Women's Issues has been felt at all levels. Even non-management women noted that, "there has been much more openness and flexibility over the past two or three years".

One woman, who had to quit in the past in order to switch to a part-time position from a full-time one while she went to school, and quit again to return to full-time, said, "When I started at the bank I was the youngest teller and everyone in my branch kept telling me 'you shouldn't be in banking'. But now when you see somebody with potential, you *want* them to work for the bank!"

It seems hard to imagine that less than twenty years ago female university graduates were not even allowed into the bank's management training program. Now 14% of the bank's upper level managers are women. This figure puts the CIBC ahead of all the other Canadian banks and is an increase from only 3% in 1987. Likewise, the middle management numbers had increased from 35% women in 1987 to 46% by the end of 1992.

"The glass ceiling still exists but it has moved upward," said a district manager, adding that she did not feel there was a boy's club in the retail side of the bank, where four of the nine district managers in her region were women.

"A 'boy's club' still exists," said another manager, "but it is no longer a power club; it is more like a circling of the wagons". That is unfortunate, since there is no evidence that the bank's efforts to identify and promote talented women have been at the expense of equally talented men. What has changed is that men are no longer promoted automatically over the heads of women, as had been the tradition in this industry.

In fact, it is now much easier for all motivated employees to manage their careers. A clear, easy-to-read "career development" kit helps employees analyze their own strengths, weaknesses and goals and shows them how to investigate and apply for jobs that might suit them. A complementary "staffing process" brochure for managers helps them focus on appropriate hiring criteria.

All vacant permanent positions up to and including the senior vice-president level are posted on an on-line "staffing network", accessible to employees from any touch-tone telephone, 24 hours a day. Some managers still have a preferred candidate in mind when they post a job but many realize they are actually getting more qualified candidates thanks to the posting system.

Another traditional barrier to the advancement of women in the banks was the old system of frequent geographical moves. "There is now less need to move around geographically to get ahead," said one branch manager. For those wanting to move, the "staffing network" gives them ready access to jobs across the country.

Job-share partners can also be found using the "staffing network". Job-sharing is one of several flexible work options introduced recently at CIBC. The bank's "Work and Lifestyle" program was launched with a bang in September of 1993. Managers were given a glossy kit describing the new policies on flexible work hours, telecommuting, part-time work and job-sharing. In the kits were workbooks to help managers assess whether or not particular jobs could be adapted to a flexible working arrangement, and to help employees work through the pros and cons of proposing such an arrangement. Employees who conclude, after assessing themselves and their jobs, that it makes sense to propose a non-traditional working arrangement are given guidance on how to negotiate the deal.

The beauty of these kits is that they serve both to reinforce the message that senior management is committed to the Work and Lifestyle program, and to turn it into a reality by helping people assess the options realistically.

The strategy is working. One assistant manager said that when she told her boss that she was pregnant *he* suggested that she consider the Work and Lifestyle options upon her return. "I said I'd love to job-share, and now we are working on the proposal."

A part-time branch administration officer was having day care problems. "I told the manager about the problem," she said, "and the manager asked if I'd be willing to work at home for the equivalent of one day and spend one day in the branch each week. It works." She is still available to deal with emergencies. "At first the manager was afraid that everybody would want to do it," she added, "but as it has gone on people are learning that I actually *do work* at home. I get far more done at home because there are no interruptions. I can focus."

In the past, noted one employee, managers were censured for agreeing to such proposals. "When I was an administration officer people were coming in with all sorts of requests. I was afraid to be too soft; it caused dissention. . . . People would phone Personnel to complain, and your seniors would come down on you. That environment is no longer the same."

Part-time work arrangements are not yet fully accepted but they are becoming more common, even at the managerial level. A branch operations manager who supervises a staff of 22 is working three days a week. "It's a great opportunity," she said, although, "It's a struggle on the days I'm not in. There is a lot of telephone contact with the branches on those days." She needs to be flexible and sometimes she comes in on her days off. She is paid for her time when that happens.

It is not easy to bring about such radical changes in attitude, and the extent to which the bank has succeeded varies. There tends to be less flexibility in smaller branches, and traditional attitudes are still strongly entrenched in many rural areas. However staff felt that the bank's leadership courses are having an impact. Several also noted that the "Open Forum", an annual opinion survey covering a variety of issues including employee perceptions of their own managers, is a valuable tool. Everybody sees the survey results and unit managers are shown their own unit's evaluations of their personal performance. That feedback is tied into the managers' performance reviews and future performance targets.

In the interviews, staff debated whether the CIBC is a woman-friendly organization that still has a few bad parts or not yet a women-friendly organization, with several good parts. Either way, all agreed that the bank has come a long way and that it is dealing seriously with the parts that need improvement.

CIBC
Commerce Court Postal Station, Toronto, ON, M5L 1A2
Telephone: (416) 980-2211

	Total	No. of Women	% Women
Full-time employees	29,601	21,515	73%
Part-time employees	9,541	8,659	91%
Board members	38	5	13%

Job category (figures based on full-time employees, unless noted otherwise):

Upper level managers	217	30	14%
Middle or other managers	5,832	2,660	46%
Professionals	4,074	2,279	56%
Semi-professionals & technicians	349	181	52%
Supervisors	2,127	1,819	86%
Foremen/women	0	0	0%
Clerical workers	16,576	14,368	87%
Sales workers	206	117	57%
Service workers	129	42	33%
Skilled crafts & trades workers	41	6	15%
Semi-skilled manual workers	12	1	8%
Other manual workers	38	12	32%

Percentage of full-time employees considered upper level managers:	0.73%
Top-up of U.I.C. during maternity leave:	good
On-site daycare centre?	no
Child/elder care referral service?	yes
Employment equity rep. reports to CEO/President?	no
Target numbers for women in management?	yes
Pay equity policy?	yes
Employment equity policy?	yes
Mentoring program?	no

Noteworthy benefits:
- special rates on financial services
- interest-free loans for purchase of computer equipment and software
- educational assistance
- share purchase plan

Part-time employee benefits:
- salary-related benefits are pro-rated

Co-operative Trust Company of Canada

Co-operative Trust was founded more than 40 years ago to meet the needs of Saskatchewan credit unions wanting long-term mortgage financing, estate administration and the ability to invest in long-term guaranteed investment certificates. Since then it has expanded to all provinces except Quebec, and developed expertise in a wide range of financial services. Owned by credit unions and co-operative associations, it is the only national trust company headquartered in Saskatchewan. As of December 31, 1993, Co-operative Trust had $6.7 billion of assets under administration and 10 branches.

Myrna Bentley started in a junior clerical position at Co-operative Trust in 1974 and is now in the key position of Vice-President, Products and Services. She is just one of many women to have moved up the ladder from clerical roles, some of whom had no formal education or experience beyond high school when they joined the company.

"We promote from within, as long as the people have put in the effort to upgrade their skills," explained Maryann Deutscher, Manager, Human Resources. She too had started in a clerical position 14 years ago. She now reports directly to the President; evidence of the importance this organization places on employee development.

The company goes out of its way to make skills and educational upgrading possible for all employees. Tuition and books are paid for up front by Co-operative Trust, rather than being reimbursed after the course has been passed, as is the case in most other organizations. "As a single parent, it would have been hard for me to come up with the money for school otherwise," said one woman who had started in stenographic work and moved into management, thanks in part to academic upgrading.

The company also lets employees juggle their work schedules to accommodate day classes, and rewards academic success immediately with a system of bonuses ranging from $100 to $500. One woman who won an award from the Trust Companies Institute for her outstanding course results not only got the bonus but was flown to Ottawa by Co-operative Trust for an awards ceremony, all expenses paid.

Other types of self-development are also encouraged. One employee is active in Toastmasters, others in organizations like the Canadian Institute of Management.

The commitment to promoting from within is not shaken by maternity leaves. Several women have been promoted just before or during maternity leaves. One woman, who was offered a promotion five years ago just before her baby was born, proposed taking a shorter maternity leave but returning two afternoons a week for the first four months. She also gradually increased the amount of work she was doing from home and eventually returned full-time.

Job sharing, part-time work and flexible hours are common and have been for several years. A woman who has been with Co-operative Trust for six years switched to part-time work after giving birth to her first child. While working part-time she was promoted from a secretarial to a management job, and allowed to share the new position.

The company's perspective is that job-sharing benefits everyone. The employer has two trained people instead of one so there is always backup should one be unavailable.

Part-time work can also benefit both parties. "I'd worked full-time for five and a half years when I went on maternity leave and decided to quit," said one officer. "I soon found that I couldn't afford to stay off". Six months later the company approached her to work on a short-term project and she jumped at the chance. One project followed another and soon she found herself in a two-day-a-week job, which then crept up to three. "My husband works shifts," she said, "and they agreed to let me pick my days to coincide with his days off." Once her children were in school she increased her hours again to work four days a week and later to five, but during school hours only. Twelve years after having started part-time work she returned to full-time.

"At that time," she said, speaking of the early days, "it wasn't a full-time job. But the more I worked, the more I'd be asked to do, so the work level kept expanding. Also, it was a give-and-take situation. When they needed extra help, like during a busy period, they'd get it from me."

An officer who is job-sharing said she appreciated the flexibility left to the job-share partners to structure the arrangement as they saw fit. She and her partner had originally worked five days on, five days off, but found it difficult to make suitable day care arrangements. Now one person works Monday and Tuesday, the other Thursday and Friday, and they alternate Wednesdays.

Staff also appreciate the flexibility they are given in setting and changing their hours to meet personal needs, and the five family care days which can be taken from the employee's bank of sick days.

Given the flexibility, the encouragement of education and the determination to promote from within, why are there still so few women in middle management? The answer lies in low turnover. The men in the middle management positions have been with the company for years. All the women interviewed were confident that as those positions become vacant many of them will be filled with the talented women on staff who are being groomed to move into those roles.

The company is spread in a thin band across the country, but employees everywhere had the sense of being part of a Co-operative Trust family. Internal communication is excellent, so the sense of opportunity is there for everybody. The only thing that holds them back is the wait for available positions.

Co-operative Trust
333-3rd Avenue North, Saskatoon, SK, S7K 2M2
Telephone: (306) 956-1800

	Total	No. of Women	% Women
Full-time employees	195	136	70%
Part-time employees	18	18	100%
Board members	11	0	0%

Job category (figures based on full-time employees, unless noted otherwise):

	Total	No. of Women	% Women
Upper level managers	5	1	20%
Middle or other managers	26	5	19%
Professionals	0	0	0%
Semi-professionals & technicians	9	6	67%
Supervisors	35	21	60%
Foremen/women	0	0	0%
Clerical workers	120	103	86%
Sales workers	0	0	0%
Service workers	0	0	0%
Skilled crafts & trades workers	0	0	0%
Semi-skilled manual workers	0	0	0%
Other manual workers	0	0	0%

Percentage of full-time employees considered upper level managers:	2.56%
Top-up of U.I.C. during maternity leave:	none
On-site daycare centre?	no
Child/elder care referral service?	no
Employment equity rep. reports to CEO/President?	yes
Target numbers for women in management?	no
Pay equity policy?	yes
Employment equity policy?	no
Mentoring program?	no

Noteworthy benefits:
- can use up to five sick days to care for sick family members
- special rates on financial services
- interest-free loan for personal computer purchase
- $5,000 retirement insurance certificate for employees aged 55+ who have 10 or more years of service
- home insurance package available
- educational assistance; cash awards for academic achievement

Part-time employee benefits:
- salary-related benefits are pro-rated; must work 35+ hours/2 weeks

VanCity

With $3.8 billion in assets, 28 branches and over 200,000 members in the Lower Mainland of British Columbia, VanCity is the largest credit union in Canada. It offers a standard range of banking services, and is owned by its customers.

There is an interesting blend of the idealistic and the pragmatic at VanCity (Vancouver City Savings Credit Union). It has developed unique programs for its employees, like the "Living Well" program, which rewards employees for following a healthy lifestyle. Employees give themselves points for things like eating a healthy breakfast, hugging loved ones, composting kitchen waste, and going jogging instead of watching television. The program also rewards credit-union-related activities like submitting ideas to the company suggestion program, having perfect attendance and publishing an article in the staff newsletter. As employees reach various point levels, they earn prizes such as t-shirts, watches, travel certificates and theatre tickets. There are also cash awards.

When VanCity saw what an enthusiastic response the low-cost program got from its employees, its pragmatic side kicked in and it started selling the "Living Well" program to other companies.

In a similar idealistic-pragmatic pairing, its Women's Advisory Council, which was formed in early 1992, has the dual goal of promoting the interests of women within the organization and addressing the needs of female customers.

The Women's Advisory Council is not needed as much at VanCity as at many organizations, although the credit union has not yet reached its goal of having an even split of men and women in management, and the proportion of women in management is still low for an organization in which 75% of the employees are female. Nevertheless, there is little overt sexism. The focus has long been on employee development, regardless of the sex of the employee. "The tone is very egalitarian," said one manager. "There is no locker room mentality here." Longer-term employees felt that this had been particularly true within the past five or ten years, and that presentations to the senior management on "breaking the glass ceiling" have helped improve the awareness of unintentional barriers to women's advancement.

One woman who started as a secretary and is now a mid-level manager noted that even the attitudes of the women themselves have changed. "Women are more aggressive now," she said, "even when they have a family. When I started I didn't want to go further."

The company tries to promote from within, and has recently been particularly successful at doing so for management jobs. For example, in 1992 there were 51 job opportunities at the management level, and 48 (or 94%) of them were filled internally. Of the 427 non-management job openings, 238 (or 56%) of them were filled internally. The company stresses education and training and is still small enough that even head office staff know most of the employees, so career management is easy. "They have offered me positions I hadn't even thought about," said a branch manager who had worked her way through an assortment of positions in different branches.

The company also offers flexibility to its staff. One woman has a part-time arrangement where she does some of her work from home and some from the office. The actual number of hours she works varies with the company's needs, although she puts in a minimum of 17.5 hours a week to maintain her benefits and seniority. When she started working part-time, after the birth of her first child, she worked two days a week in the office but now says that "because of technology I now sometimes don't come in at all. I have a VanCity computer, modem and fax equipment at home."

The credit union has been experimenting with a "passive" job-sharing registry since 1993. People who want to job-share tell human resources staff, who then wait until someone with complementary skills and interests calls in. Given the relatively small size of the organization, it felt that staff who wanted to job-share might not want their colleagues to know unless and until a partner were found. The drawback to this approach is that it is hard for some people to know whether they want to job-share unless they have seen or heard about a specific opportunity. As a result, few people had registered during the first year of the pilot project.

VanCity also allows leaves of up to three years, which are used for activities like child-rearing, education, travel or volunteer work. Since technology changes quickly in this industry, employees on long-term leaves must work for a minimum of one month during each year of the leave, but the month can be split into periods of one or two weeks at a time.

Several approaches are used to help employees deal with child care. A Child Care Coordinator helps staff find suitable care for their children and sends out regular newsletters dealing with issues of concern to parents. For instance, when schools were closed down by a strike, she suggested ways for parents to cope and suggested alternative activities for their children. She also worked with local day care providers to develop 50 new child care spaces, mostly in licensed, home-based day care centres. VanCity gave the centres a one-time grant of $500 per new space; in exchange, the children of its employees got first access to those spaces. In addition, a new head office is being built that will have on-site day care for VanCity employees and for other occupants of the building complex.

The people who work at VanCity enjoy its non-bureaucratic atmosphere. As one manager pointed out, "It is not a big deal to resolve problems. You just pick up the phone." They also like the company's openness to unusual suggestions. Said one, "If it ain't broke, fix it anyway!" This attitude has led to VanCity being the first company to offer many innovations that have now become standard in the financial services industry (like open mortgages and daily interest savings accounts) and others that have not become standard (like Canada's first "socially-responsible" mutual fund, and the first "plain English" loan agreement).

That same openness to suggestions makes staff confident that if they can think of ways to make VanCity an even better place to work, the company will be all ears.

VanCity
515 West 10th Avenue, Vancouver, BC, V6B 5R8
Telephone: (604) 877-7641

	Total	No. of Women	% Women
Full-time employees	737	553	75%
Part-time employees	190	168	88%
Board members	9	4	44%

Job category (figures based on full-time employees, unless noted otherwise):

Upper level managers	19	4	21%
Middle or other managers	86	57	66%
Professionals	102	58	57%
Semi-professionals & technicians	0	0	0%
Supervisors	33	28	85%
Foremen/women	0	0	0%
Clerical workers	493	414	84%
Sales workers	0	0	0%
Service workers	0	0	0%
Skilled crafts & trades workers	3	0	0%
Semi-skilled manual workers	0	0	0%
Other manual workers	1	0	0%

Percentage of full-time employees considered upper level managers:	2.58%
Top-up of U.I.C. during maternity leave:	none
On-site daycare centre?	no[a]
Child/elder care referral service?	yes
Employment equity rep. reports to CEO/President?	yes
Target numbers for women in management?	yes
Pay equity policy?	no
Employment equity policy?	yes
Mentoring program?	no

Noteworthy benefits:
- special rates on financial services
- generous extended leave options

Part-time employee benefits:
- pro-rated to hours worked; must work 17.5+ hours/week

Notes: (a) under construction

INSURANCE AND INVESTMENT

Manulife Financial

Manulife Financial provides insurance and investment products, pension plans, and annuities through a worldwide network of agents, brokers and financial consultants. The company was founded in 1887 and now has over 200 offices worldwide and $38.5 billion in assets, which makes it Canada's largest insurance company. Manulife's corporate head office is in Toronto. Its Canadian operations, which account for 38% of the employees, are based in Waterloo, Ontario.

Manulife is a rarity among Canadian corporations in that its drive to become a good place for women to work began early, in the mid-1970s. The President and Vice-President of Human Resources of the day felt that, since roughly two-thirds of the company's workforce was female, it made good business sense to make the environment a hospitable one for women. They were also pushed along the path by a group called "Women for Advancement at Manulife" (WAM), which was formed by female managers and technical staff as a support and internal lobbying group.

"We don't need it any more," said one recent employee, explaining why WAM no longer exists. Others tempered her statement, but even they agreed that the culture at Manulife is one in which men and women are truly treated equally.

Part of the reason Manulife has achieved that equality without a noticeable male backlash is that its efforts have always been presented to the employees as ensuring equal opportunity and a good working environment for *all* employees. As a result, the number of women at senior levels has not increased as sharply as at some companies and there are still far fewer women at senior levels than in Manulife's workforce as a whole. Nevertheless, the numbers are increasing steadily without any suggestion that women have been promoted for reasons other than merit.

The women in the senior ranks are proud of the supportive, encouraging atmosphere Manulife has provided for women and are conscious of being role models. A senior woman who was one of the first female actuarial students hired spoke of her early days serving on hiring committees for actuarial students, "We'd hire the best, regardless of gender". As time went by this resulted in more and more women being hired. "The company became quite proud of it," she said.

Thanks to those early efforts Manulife was one of the first companies to offer many of the policies which have only recently been adopted by Canada's other best employers for women:

- salary and position level comparisons for men and women are monitored quarterly;
- jobs are posted internally and are open to all;
- employee opinion on equity issues is sought regularly through opinion surveys and exit interviews;
- flexible work options are the norm, and have been formally sanctioned as part of the company's "Lifestyle 2000" program;
- a computerized child and elder care referral and information service is available, and is supplemented by special events such as on-site fairs about summer camps and elder care;
- pre- and post-natal counselling sessions and seminars advise expectant and new parents;
- UIC payments are supplemented for 25 weeks;
- special events such as Kid's Day during the March school break allow employees to bring their children to see where their parents work and to participate in games and activities.

The net effect of these policies, according to one employee, is to signal that "the company really recognizes that we play multiple roles. . . . There isn't a need to separate the personal from business." Assistant V.P., Human Resources, Fern Stimpson, agrees that there is a need for balance. "The vast majority of our employees are now — or might well at some future time be — directly involved in family care. While those employees may have different needs, they will all be looking for a better fit between their personal and professional lives. Manulife would prefer not to lose talented people because their family schedules aren't synchronized with the nine to five business day." It works. Manulife consistently has a lower staff turnover rate than its competitors.

Management also believes that productivity has increased since the company introduced the flexible working options, despite the added challenge of managing them. "The company is goal-based," said one manager. "There is a lot of individual flexibility and autonomy in achieving those goals. That flexibility buys a tremendous amount of loyalty." Another noted that her area was one that did not lend itself to part-time work or job-sharing, but "the flexibility in hours really helps us hire and retain good people."

Non-management women perceived the same flexibility. "As long as the work gets done," said one, "the specific hours spent in the office don't matter." Another appreciated that "there is an assumption of trust, of responsibility, of adulthood".

The level at which it is acceptable to take advantage of the flexible working options is moving steadily upwards. "In the past," said a female vice-president, "you wouldn't get hired as a director or above if you worked a four-day week. That is changing." On the other hand, this organization is no different from most other Canadian organizations in the nineties, in that workloads are increasing phenomenally. Coping with the workload is an increasing challenge.

One way in which Manulife helps is by having everybody in the company linked by computer and many also linked from home by modem. The technology can really help with the balancing act, but it poses its own challenges. "When I first got the computer at home," said one manager, "every time I walked by it I felt a pressure to log on. Eventually I learned to stop checking for messages unless I had a specific reason to do so. But if there is a day when I don't feel great, but well enough to do some work, I'll work from home."

Others appreciate that it enables them to be productive even if they have to stay home to watch over a sick child, and to stay in touch during maternity leaves.

Staff are all convinced that they work a lot more because of the home-based linkage. Even so, its net effect is to reduce stress. "Looking at PROFS [the company's electronic mail system] over breakfast calms me down," said one manager. "It lets me plan my day."

The company's fitness centre at its international headquarters in Toronto is also widely used to combat stress. One manager who has two young children and has been working a four-day week since the first one was born tries to avoid lunch meetings so that she can get to the fitness centre regularly. "It gives me time to myself," she said, and it helps her find the energy to cope with work and family.

A doctor at the company, who was drawn to Manulife 20 years ago because it would allow her to work part-time, said, "My whole experience here has been very positive". She is involved in medical underwriting and also runs the company's health centre. When she and her colleagues analyzed the employee base they noted that 64% of the employees are female, and 50% of them are in their child-bearing years. As a result they have run special courses for staff about pregnancy, menopause, hormone replacement therapy and other issues of concern to women. The company also has an on-line program called, "Taking Care", which provides information about the elderly and child care. "The employees have had good reactions to that," said the doctor.

Taking maternity leave is not seen as a problem or a sign of lessened commitment. One young woman, who was pregnant at the time of the interview, said, "If you want to have kids, Manulife is probably *the* place to be." There are many examples of senior women who have taken maternity leaves with no noticeable impact on their career progression. One management woman said, "I was $6^1/_2$ months pregnant when I got promoted". Another had been promoted during both of her maternity leaves.

Manulife is doing almost all the right things, but there are two trouble spots in this nearly perfect picture: the Canadian operations headquarters in Waterloo, which accounts for 38% of the employees, and the sales force.

In late 1984 when Manulife bought Dominion Life it was agreed that Manulife's Canadian operations would be based out of Dominion's Waterloo headquarters. Unfortunately, Dominion had a much more traditional corporate culture and it still dominates at that office. Management recognizes the problem and that is the only area of the company in which they have felt it necessary to set numerical goals for the hiring and promotion of women.

One of the goals was to have a female vice-president by 1997. That goal has already been met: a female vice-president of human resources was hired in 1993, and a female chief financial officer assumed responsibility for the Canadian operation in mid-1994.

The company also aims to double the percentage of women in senior management in the Canadian operations from 7.5% to 15% between 1992 and 1997.

One senior woman who had considered but turned down a top-level job there said, "I think the senior management there are supportive of women, but that attitude does not go all the way through". In fact, it has become something of a magnet for men who do not like the overall corporate culture. Said one manager, "The men I've known who've gone from here to there are the drinking, boy's club type of guys".

Another trouble spot is sales. Sales is a traditional male area, and while Manulife leads the industry for numbers of women in traditionally male areas like underwriting and actuarial work, it lags in the sales force. In 1993 the sales force remained almost entirely male, with no female branch managers in the Canadian operation, and only one in the American. What particularly disturbed the employees interviewed was that, as one put it, "It is 1993 and there are no aspiring stars in the Canadian field force who are women". Their perception was that "there is no commitment in the field to recruit or promote women".

Apart from these weak spots, which senior management is trying to overcome, the attitude is a positive one. "I've worked for one sexist manager," said a non-management woman who has been at Manulife for 14 years. "He's no longer here. He didn't fit into the culture.

Manulife Financial
200 Bloor Street East, Toronto, ON, M4W 1E5
Telephone: (416) 926-0100

	Total	No. of Women	% Women
Full-time employees	3,854	2,469	64%
Part-time employees	350	307	88%
Board members	16	1	6%

Job category (figures based on full-time employees, unless noted otherwise):

Upper level managers	13[a]	3	23%
Middle or other managers	910[b]	347	38%
Professionals			
Semi-professionals & technicians	1,012[c]	710	70%
Supervisors			
Foremen/women	0	0	0%
Clerical workers	1,291	1,151	89%
Sales workers	0	0	0%
Service workers	0	0	0%
Skilled crafts & trades workers	0	0	0%
Semi-skilled manual workers	0	0	0%
Other manual workers	628[d]	258	41%

Percentage of full-time employees considered upper level managers:	0.34%
Top-up of U.I.C. during maternity leave:	good
On-site daycare centre?	no
Child/elder care referral service?	yes
Employment equity rep. reports to CEO/President?	no
Target numbers for women in management?	no
Pay equity policy?	yes
Employment equity policy?	yes
Mentoring program?	no

Noteworthy benefits:
 • 3 Family Care Days
 • special rates on financial services
Part-time employee benefits:
 • 20-30 hours/week: same as full-time benefits
 • less than 20 hours/week: pro-rated
Notes: (a) VP-level and above
 (b) directors, professionals and managers
 (c) includes supervisors
 (d) includes food service workers

Maritime Life

Maritime Life is a Halifax-based company with other offices in Montreal, Toronto, Mississauga, and Vancouver. It sells a full range of life, disability and health insurance policies, and investment products like RRSPs. As of December 31, 1993, it had $2.6 billion in assets.

Many Halifax-based employers look to Maritime Life as a model of how to treat employees. The company believes that treating its employees well is essential if it is to meet its other business goals of satisfying customers while achieving superior profitability and growth.

Employee and customer satisfaction are measured regularly. Staff are surveyed every year and those surveys have led the company to implement many of the policies now cited by employees as reasons why they like to work at Maritime Life.

For example, the company was one of the first companies in Canada to implement flexible hours, which it did as a direct result of feedback in an employee survey. "It is a god-send to working parents," said one employee, who uses the flexibility to attend school functions as well as to take her children to medical appointments or meet other needs. "Everybody uses it at this company," she said. Schedules can vary day by day, as long as staff are generally available during core hours. "Even at the clerical levels," said another employee, "there is nobody staring over our shoulders."

When Maritime Life was planning its new head office, which opened in 1989, employees were asked what facilities they would like it to include. As a result of their feedback, the head office has a fitness centre, a comfortable staff lounge and cafeteria, and, as of 1992, a day care centre which the company provides rent-free.

The day care centre and the flexible hours are part of a sincere corporate philosophy of encouraging employees to lead balanced work and personal lives. The official work week is 35 hours long, and although management and professional staff work longer hours than that, neither they nor support staff felt that their hours were excessive.

Managers also changed their hours as they entered different stages of their career and personal lives. One senior manager, who typically works about a nine-hour day, said, "Before I had kids I worked much longer hours, but that was part of my push to get into more senior jobs". She now has three children and comments, "I always bring work home, but I seldom do it".

Staff also appreciate the company's willingness to consider options such as reduced work weeks. A manager who was one of the first women to work a four day week found that her day off was generally respected, although she did sometimes have to remind people that she was not available that day. "If I really *had* to come in on my day off, I would," she said, "but I would take another day off to make up for it." In seven years she had rarely, if ever, had to come in on her day off.

Many clerical staff members are also working reduced weeks. One woman switched to a three-day week after having had her third child. "There is no problem with it," she said.

There also seems to be no stigma to taking a maternity leave. One manager's experience with her three maternity leaves may reflect the growing comfort level of both the company and its employees over the years. The first time she was pregnant her colleagues feared that she would not return. She did, after only seven weeks. The second time she took three months off. "My position was held open for me, and I had the full support of my peers and managers," she said. The third time, she pushed the limits even further. Two weeks before her due date she saw a posting for a job that would have meant a promotion to a senior level in a division that was new to her. She applied and told the interviewers that she planned to take $3\frac{1}{2}$ months off. The day before her baby was born she was told that she had won the competition.

The women interviewed felt that any ambitious woman who wants to move up can, although it happens more easily for men. Women miss out on a lot of the informal networking that takes place at hockey games or in the men's room. One woman commented that her male boss would not travel with her for fear of what people might think, and that she could not have lunch with a man for the same reason (although she felt that she could have lunch with two men).

Women are still under-represented in management. One way the company is trying to increase their representation is by actively encouraging talented women to apply for positions they might not have considered. "Maritime Life prefers to hire from within," explained one of them, who is now one of the most senior women in the company. "They would rather spend the time and invest in their own employees even if it will take an extra year or two for them to be really comfortable in their new jobs. The alternative is hiring from elsewhere, and running the risk that the person hired will only stay here for a while."

No women are vice-presidents yet, but there are only four vice-presidents so those jobs are not open often. Most senior jobs are filled by actuaries and it is only recently that many women are entering actuarial studies. The female actuaries on staff feel confident that it is only a matter of time until women reach the senior levels at Maritime Life.

The company's strong anti-harassment policy includes two worthwhile elements often missing in other companies' procedures. It has hired outside professionals to run a toll-free anti-harassment information line. Employees can call the number to discuss their situation, and are guaranteed that no information will be released to Maritime Life without their consent. Another option, available through the Human Resources Department, is a mediation service. There is a panel of mediators from which the employee may choose, and the mediation session is held off-site. No information about it is released to the company without the written consent of the parties involved.

The information package handed out to employees about harassment also suggests that people who have been accused of it consider using these options, particularly if they do not understand why the complaint was made.

Of course, people also have the option of laying a formal complaint. Complainants are guaranteed that they will be told the outcome of the investigation; an important detail that is often overlooked.

The result of these procedures: none of the employees interviewed saw sexual harassment as an issue at Maritime Life.

Maritime Life has created a comfortable, productive working environment. Employees feel they are valued and treated with respect. In turn, they have trouble thinking of anything negative to say about the company, even when probed.

Maritime Life Assurance Company
2701 Dutch Village Rd, P.O. Box 1030, Halifax, NS, B3J 2X5
Telephone: (902) 453-4300

	Total	No. of Women	% Women
Full-time employees	580	430	74%
Part-time employees	12	12	100%
Board members	15	1	7%

Job category (figures based on full-time employees, unless noted otherwise):

Upper level managers	22[a]	4	18%
Middle or other managers	65	20	31%
Professionals	1	1	100%
Semi-professionals & technicians	0	0	0%
Supervisors	31	26	84%
Foremen/women	0	0	0%
Clerical workers	452	377	83%
Sales workers	9	1	11%
Service workers	0	0	0%
Skilled crafts & trades workers	0	0	0%
Semi-skilled manual workers	0	0	0%
Other manual workers	0	0	0%

Percentage of full-time employees considered upper level managers:	3.79%
Top-up of U.I.C. during maternity leave:	average
On-site daycare centre?	yes
Child/elder care referral service?	yes
Employment equity rep. reports to CEO/President?	no
Target numbers for women in management?	no
Pay equity policy?	yes
Employment equity policy?	no
Mentoring program?	no

Noteworthy benefits:
- special rates on financial services

Part-time employee benefits:
- full benefits if work 25+ hours/week
- half the normal benefits if work between 17.5 and 25 hours/week
- no benefits if work less than 17.5 hours per week
- benefits paid to temporary (contract) employees after 1 year of service

Notes: (a) directors, vice-presidents and president

The Mutual Group

The core of the Waterloo-based Mutual Group is Mutual Life of Canada, which provides life and health insurance, annuities, retirement savings products, real estate financing and corporate lending. It is owned by its policy holders. Mutual Life is the country's second largest life insurer in terms of Canadian assets and individual life insurance policies in force. The Mutual Group has offices across the country and in the U.S.A.

Visiting "Mother Mutual", as the firm is nicknamed, seems a bit like stepping into a busy, happy home. The employees chatting in the indoor tropical garden court on their way to grab lunch in the subsidized cafeteria, or to work out in the fitness centre, or to visit their children in the day care centre, seem relaxed and comfortable. They are secure in the belief that they will be treated fairly and given opportunities to grow without having to sacrifice their personal lives.

The company has gone out of its way to provide excellent working conditions, both in terms of the physical surroundings and the structure of daily life. Why? One reason is to attract good people away from nearby Toronto, where salaries are higher and career alternatives greater. As a manager pointed out, "One of the reasons people choose this company and this community is because of the support for family here."

The information kit given to new employees is reminiscent of a camp or college welcoming kit. Full of photos of employees at a company picnic and children at the day care centre, it sends out a clear message that balancing work and personal lives is fundamental to the corporate culture.

Flexible hours are standard, and "If a VP or others at a senior level see you working long hours," said one employee, "they will tell you to go take time with your family." A system of "plus and minus time" compensates employees for overtime worked by letting them apply it towards personal errands.

Part-time work and job-sharing are common. "The question is, what works? What do you need?", explained one employee, noting that she needed flexibility in her schedule; not rigid part-time or full-time. "In the summer," she said, "I had the kids off school and elderly parents to deal with. I offered to forego pay to get some flexibility for the summer, but my boss said no; just do what you need to do."

There are sound business reasons for the flexibility and encouragement of part-time work. First of all, allowing people to work part-time can help trim costs. Some companies have tried to cut costs by eliminating all part-time jobs and compressing them into full-time ones, but Mutual feels that its approach lets it use individual skills as efficiently as possible while retaining high-quality, highly motivated employees.

Second, the variety of work arrangements allows the company to use cross-training to motivate employees. Cross-training serves many purposes. It:

- ensures that there is always back-up should an employee be absent;
- fosters team-work;
- improves communication; and
- provides learning experiences.

It has helped many employees move from clerical to management positions.

Cross-training also recognizes that corporations in the 1990s cannot provide the same career ladders that were available in the past. Instead they can challenge staff through lateral movement. Explained one manager, "We are trying to manage people's abilities so that they don't become brain-dead, given that few can ever get the top jobs".

Managers acknowledge that it can be awkward to work around so many different schedules, but feel it is worthwhile. "I have 18 staff reporting to me," said one manager. "About half of them work some sort of part-time arrangement. . . . Most are parents, but we are also starting to see people who simply want more time to themselves. . . . There is no question that it is harder to manage, but I'd far rather have that than unhappy employees." Added another manager, "I have a job-share arrangement in my group. It has made the job-sharers feel better about what they are doing, so they are more productive".

This is not to suggest that no one works long hours. The lure of the computer is particularly strong. Said one manager, "The senior management in my group are invariably on DAX [the corporate electronic mail system] all evening. It took me a few months to convince them that I wouldn't participate in their evening conversations." Still, she worries about how they perceive her lack of participation. Another said, "I also worked for guys who did that. At first I was sending DAX's at night too. Eventually I let my password expire". She waited nervously to see how they would react to her disappearance from the night DAXers. To her surprise, "When I stopped, there was not a peep out of them. . . . Maybe they really didn't expect me to reply at midnight".

Although the women interviewed did not think their refusal to participate in night-time conversations would harm their careers, it may be too soon to tell. This may become a modern-day equivalent of the sort of networking that traditionally happened when "the boys" went out for drinks after work.

When management women were asked whether they perceived a "glass ceiling" at Mutual they replied: "Glass ceiling? What does that mean?" The company has four female vice-presidents, in Group Marketing, Pension Operations, Corporate Services and Public Affairs. They give the impression that women are getting ahead fast. Still, they only make up 18% of senior management, which is not particularly high given how many women work at Mutual.

The company has a large pool of female talent from which to draw. With 76% of its full-time and 97% of its part-time staff being female, it has far more women among its employees than do most insurance companies. On average, women represented 67.5% of the full-time employees of the seven insurance companies responding to the survey for this book.

The company's focus has been to make the company a comfortable place to work, not to rush women into senior management. This may account for the absence of the male backlash that is seen in so many other companies. Said one female manager, "I've worked here for 18 years. I've never seen a man move up for reasons other than merit and I don't think men feel women are moving up for the wrong reasons".

The Mutual Group is one of the few Canadian companies large enough to offer a lot of choice and challenge in a geographic location that avoids big-city stress.

The Mutual Group
227 King Street South, Waterloo, ON, N2J 4C5
Telephone: (519) 888-2390

	Total	No. of Women	% Women
Full-time employees	2,877[a]	2,190	76%
Part-time employees	212[a]	206	97%
Board members	21	3	14%

Job category (figures based on full-time employees, unless noted otherwise):

Upper level managers	22	4	18%
Middle or other managers	275[b]	75	27%
Professionals			
Semi-professionals & technicians	631[c]	400	63%
Supervisors			
Foremen/women	0	0	0%
Clerical workers	2,161	1,917	89%
Sales workers	0	0	0%
Service workers	0	0	0%
Skilled crafts & trades workers	0	0	0%
Semi-skilled manual workers	0	0	0%
Other manual workers	0	0	0%

Percentage of full-time employees considered upper level managers:	0.76%
Top-up of U.I.C. during maternity leave:	none
On-site daycare centre?	yes
Child/elder care referral service?	no
Employment equity rep. reports to CEO/President?	no
Target numbers for women in management?	no
Pay equity policy?	yes
Employment equity policy?	yes
Mentoring program?	no

Noteworthy benefits:
 • special rates on mortgage-related services
 • flexible benefits program
Part-time employee benefits:
 • eligible for full flexible benefits package; coverage levels pro-rated to hours worked
Notes: (a) includes head office and field staff
 (b) includes professionals
 (c) includes supervisors

Wood Gundy Inc.

Wood Gundy, one of Canada's largest investment firms, is owned 75% by the C.I.B.C. and 25% by its employees. It has 36 offices across Canada as well as specialized offices in New York, London, Tokyo, Los Angeles and Boston. Its clients include businesses, governments and individuals.

In the spring of 1992 Wood Gundy's two top executives, then-Chairman John Hunkin and then-President Richard Venn, summoned the firm's senior women into a boardroom and asked them what the company could do to make itself a better place for women. Sensing that the interest was genuine, the women sprang into action.

With the help of an outside firm, they surveyed Wood Gundy's employees worldwide and identified several areas for improvement. By early September the management committee had accepted a series of recommendations, including:

- a target stating that, by 1993, 30% of the professional staff hired would be women, and, by 1995, 50% would be women;
- having women participate in all recruitment and hiring processes;
- increasing the visibility of Wood Gundy women both within and outside the firm; and
- adopting a zero tolerance policy to personal harassment.

Since then, Mr. Venn (now Chairman) has made it clear, repeatedly, that he and the rest of the senior managers believe that these issues are important and must be acted upon.

Results of the efforts have varied, but overall there has been a tremendous improvement in the status of women at Wood Gundy. The 1993 hiring target was not met but the numbers are improving. The pool of women available who have the appropriate education or experience is limited, but the firm is trying to find creative ways to increase it.

The Private Client Division, for example, whose professional staff was typically only about 10% female, launched a program in 1993 to recruit people from other fields into the brokerage business. It set itself an ambitious goal of 35% female hires, and instructed the hiring managers across Canada to ensure that at least one-third of the candidates short-listed were female. Thirty-five per cent of the offers were made to women, although three of the women declined, so in the end 25% of the people hired were women. The next year the firm placed local advertisements and worked with external recruiters to reach more women. The result: 28% of the division's new hires in 1994 were women.

Another major source of new staff has been Master of Business Administration (MBA) degree programs. Only about 20 to 30% of the graduates from most Canadian MBA programs are female, and only a fraction of them major in finance, so Wood Gundy has sent female professionals to talk to female first-year MBA students to encourage them to specialize in finance. Those talks, together with having more women on campus recruiting teams, are paying off: 50% of the graduates hired in 1993 were women, up from 20% the year before.

The number of women in key decision-making roles within the firm has increased significantly since the Women's Committee was struck in 1992:

- the Management Committee went from having no women on it in 1992 to having three women out of the 23 members by early 1994;
- the Operating Committee increased from 3.2% female (2 women out of 62 people) to 9.9% (8 out of 81) during the same time period;
- directors increased from 3.8% (4 of 99) to 10.2% (17 of 166);
- vice-presidents increased from 11.4% (35 of 305) to 14.8% (55 of 372).

The senior women are mentors and role models for the other women at the firm. The firm's first investment banker to get pregnant did so a mere six years ago. Her male colleagues were pleased, but surprised, that she came back. She has less flexibility in her days than she used to, but she still works more than ten hours a day. That is about the same as the men in her area of the firm, although she notes, "I've often left when the guys are still chatting". She was promoted recently, which she takes as a sign that the organization has accepted the idea of women combining motherhood and careers. Several of the new female senior staff have had children since joining the firm.

The hours in the brokerage business are long (12 hours a day is not uncommon), but there is less after-hours socializing than there used to be and the firm is showing increasing openness to flexible working arrangements. During the 1980s, few employees in investment banking had children; now most of them do. "People are valuing family time more now; men are playing with their kids now," said one employee.

Some of the first women to try flexible working arrangements found that the firm was not ready to accept such arrangements, but one of the pioneers had a positive experience doing her sales job from home for five months following the birth of her first child. The job was done entirely by telephone and the firm outfitted her with all the necessary equipment, including a second telephone line linked in with the company's voice mail system, so most of her clients did not even realize she was working from home. At the end of the summer she decided to return to the office because she missed the social aspect of the office environment. "If I were having another baby I'd definitely do it again," she said.

More recently a manager proposed a four-day work week to an employee after attending a seminar that got the manager thinking about what a "little blip" the early child-rearing years are in most people's lives. "I realized that I should suggest a four-day week to her; that I'd probably lose her otherwise. Senior management supported my decision." Another manager commented: "The Women's Committee has said to us that we can acknowledge the reality of families; that it is a company issue, not a women's issue."

The focus of the women's initiatives to date has been on management women. Support staff still feel overworked and undervalued. Many are routinely expected to work overtime, and get the feeling that because they are paid for overtime or given compensatory time off, it is not seen as a problem to expect them to stay late on short notice. Said one: "The guys come down at 5:30 and you can have your coat on and they'll demand that the work they just handed you get done. They'll work to their schedule regardless of ours. . . . You are warned when you are hired that there will be last-minute things, but I didn't expect it to be all the time". What they find particularly galling is to see the same men who throw last-minute work at them take long lunches or walk out after handing them the work, saying "I've got a dinner date, but I need this done by 7:30 a.m. tomorrow".

That sort of attitude seems particularly prevalent among the traders. "Trading rooms," said one woman, are "big open areas filled with testosterone." Said another: "When you work in investment banking, you learn to yell when you have to," although she felt that the atmosphere in the trading areas has improved over the past two years. "They have learned that there is a difference between generalized yelling and swearing versus put-downs. There is a lot less of the latter now." She attributes this improvement to the leadership and anti-harassment seminars which most staff have attended. There was some grumbling about the seminars, but at least they made people realize that there are laws about harassment and gave them a better idea of what is and is not acceptable behaviour.

Although it is owned by a major bank, Wood Gundy remains entrepreneurial. The bank has allowed the firm to pick and choose those aspects of bank life in which it wishes to participate. Thus, Wood Gundy staff have access to jobs posted in the bank (and vice versa), and the firm can piggy-back on some of the bank's successful women's initiatives.

One borrowed initiative is a gender awareness course that staff felt had a big impact on the people who had taken it. "Two senior men who took the course said it was a real revelation to them," said one long-time employee. "It affected their personal as well as their work relationships. They suddenly realized what women can offer."

In the past two years the organization has gone from being what one employee described as "patriarchal" to having a senior management that is young, open to ideas, and used to career-oriented spouses. Even many of the mid-level managers, who probably feel the most threatened by the increased emphasis on recruiting and promoting women, are starting to appreciate the new atmosphere. Said one woman, "Men are now proud to leave a meeting saying, 'I've got to go take my son to hockey." One is even working a four-day week. And while women are still reluctant to leave meetings to take a child to hockey, one commented, "It is much easier now than it used to be".

Wood Gundy Inc.
161 Bay Street, P.O. Box 500, Toronto, ON, M5J 2S8
Telephone: (416) 594-7000

	Total	No. of Women	% Women
Full-time employees	1,592	710	45%
Part-time employees	0	0	0%
Board members	20	2	10%

Job category (figures based on full-time employees, unless noted otherwise):

Upper level managers	18	3	17%
Middle or other managers	93	16	17%
Professionals	129	39	30%
Semi-professionals & technicians	0	0	0%
Supervisors	35	19	54%
Foremen/women	0	0	0%
Clerical workers	696	531	76%
Sales workers	621	102	16%
Service workers	0	0	0%
Skilled crafts & trades workers	0	0	0%
Semi-skilled manual workers	0	0	0%
Other manual workers	0	0	0%

Percentage of full-time employees considered upper level managers:	1.13%
Top-up of U.I.C. during maternity leave:	none
On-site daycare centre?	no
Child/elder care referral service?	no
Employment equity rep. reports to CEO/President?	yes
Target numbers for women in management?	yes
Pay equity policy?	no
Employment equity policy?	no
Mentoring program?	no

Noteworthy benefits:
- educational assistance: pre-pays course fees

Part-time employee benefits:
- all benefits pro-rated; must work 24+ hours/week

GOVERNMENT

Canada Mortgage and Housing Corporation

The Canada Mortgage and Housing Corporation (CMHC) was set up in 1946 under the National Housing Act to improve housing and living conditions for Canadians. It researches housing markets; runs educational programs; manages, develops and markets government-owned lands; and provides mortgage loan insurance. CMHC has offices in every province and territory.

George Anderson, the former President of the CMHC, had a lot to do with making it a good place to work. In the mid-to-late eighties he shook up the CMHC's traditional management style. "People responded so well to the changes he made and the challenges he gave us that they took hold in the organization," said a long-time employee.

Long before his time, though, the women of CMHC were already pushing for change. A group of them got together in 1975 to discuss how they could promote women within the organization. A Women's Bureau emerged from their meetings, funded and endorsed by senior management. Women were elected from every office and department to guide the bureau.

"The Women's Bureau brought in a lot of good initiatives," said one long-term employee. It established an effective job posting system, improved access to training, paved the way for flexible hours, and improved maternity and paternity benefits. It also laid the foundations for the many innovative options which are now available to CMHC's employees.

The Women's Bureau evolved into a three person employment equity group which is advised by separate, elected panels for women, visible minorities, people with disabilities and aboriginal employees. The advisory panels have a say in every human resources proposal going to the Management Committee and direct access to the Senior Vice-President, Corporate Resources.

The current President, Gene Flichel, also keeps himself directly informed about issues of concern to staff with the help of an elected President's Advisory Council.

This long history of women's initiatives has created a supportive environment for staff with families. "CMHC really encourages family," said one employee, pointing to the child and elder care referral service, the five days of leave available each year for family-related responsibilities, the three days of special leave for emergencies and the generous maternity leave top-up provisions.

A single parent who had to travel a lot for work particularly appreciated the corporation's policy of paying up to $35 a night for child care. Without it she could not have continued doing her job once she had sole responsibility for her children.

Ambitious employees inevitably have to move at some point. "The corporation is very supportive and understanding about moves," said one woman who has moved twice with CMHC. The first time, her spouse, who worked for another organization, had been transferred to Halifax. "They go out of their way to help you find work," she said, grateful that she was able to continue working for CMHC. The second time she accepted a transfer to Ottawa. "The corporation helped my husband find a job," she said, which convinced them it was worth the risk of uprooting the family.

Flexible working hours are standard. Starting times range from 7:00 to 9:30 a.m., and ending times vary accordingly. As a result, it does not stand out if somebody has to leave early to pick up a sick child. Many employees work long hours, but there is no clock-watching. "They know you'll give back any time that you have to take," said one employee.

After a rocky start, part-time work also seems to be gaining acceptance. One woman who has been with CMHC for 10 years worked part-time for six of them. "After my third child was born I wanted to quit, but they offered me the chance to work three days a week. . . . It took a couple of years for people to realize that we [she and others who switched to part-time] were still committed." Once her youngest was in school she returned to full-time work.

She and others who worked part-time felt that the top management was supportive, but there were still several immediate superiors who were not. "I've heard the president say you have to have another life; you have to have balance," said one woman, who felt that the president's public commitment was making it possible for a growing number of employees to use the flexible options.

Forty-two employees signed up for a work-at-home, pilot project which started in July, 1993. It was up to the participants to decide if their work could be done partially from home and to reach an agreement with their supervisors about how to structure the arrangement. Most chose to work from home two or three days a week. Six months into the project, the feedback from both employees and supervisors was favourable, and it seemed likely the concept would eventually be extended to the rest of the corporation.

Maternity leaves and language training create many short-term job vacancies at CMHC. It has turned these absences into opportunities. Acting assignments are used to keep employees learning and motivated. From the corporation's point of view, this not only produces happier employees, it also ensures that people are cross-trained so they can fill in for each other on short notice, and that those being considered for promotion have a wide range of experience.

One novel approach to cross-training used by CMHC is a job exchange. "I felt that I was becoming too specialized," said one woman who participated in such an exchange. She wanted experience in a new area, but was nervous about leaving a job in which she was comfortable and doing well. She and her supervisor explored the idea of a job exchange. She traded jobs with another employee for a year, with a review at the end of it. "My boss was supportive of the move and it happened very quickly," she said. "At the end of the year the person I had traded jobs with and I were both happy with the switch, so it became permanent. It was great to have the chance to try it first."

Many managers are good about career counselling and mentoring. One secretary who was bored after six years in the same job approached her boss for advice. He helped her move into a junior management position, and she is now working on a human resources management certificate as part of a program taught on-site for employees by Carleton University. The Corporation pays for tuition and books, and classes are scheduled so that they are half on the employer's time and half on the employee's.

The overall atmosphere for women is definitely positive, but there are still entrenched "boy's club" attitudes which can make work frustrating for some. "I've had some experience with the glass ceiling," said one woman. "You work hard long hours, but somehow you're never quite there." The women find themselves excluded from a lot of informal networking that takes place over drinks after work or in the men's change room at corporate hockey league games.

Ironically, all the talk about providing a family-friendly workplace can backfire. "Men assume that a woman has to juggle family and work so they assume that she doesn't want to have more responsibility," said one woman, who has no children. Said another, "Women have to make it known, repeatedly, that they are interested. With men it's more by default". Women felt that they had to be more aggressive and push harder to prove themselves and get ahead.

Despite the frustrations, the female employees felt positive about CMHC. "I wouldn't want to work anywhere else," said one, summing up the views of many.

Canada Mortgage and Housing Corporation
700 Montreal Road, Ottawa, ON, K1A 0P7
Telephone: (613) 748-2176

	Total	No. of Women	% Women
Full-time employees	2,624	1,447	55%
Part-time employees	67	61	91%
Board members	10	1	10%

Job category (figures based on full-time employees, unless noted otherwise):

Upper level managers	42	5	12%
Middle or other managers	518	188	36%
Professionals	867	326	38%
Semi-professionals & technicians	168	49	29%
Supervisors	114	85	75%
Foremen/women	0	0	0%
Clerical workers	853	788	92%
Sales workers	0	0	0%
Service workers	0	0	0%
Skilled crafts & trades workers	1	0	0%
Semi-skilled manual workers	12	1	8%
Other manual workers	49	5	10%

Percentage of full-time employees considered upper level managers:	1.60%
Top-up of U.I.C. during maternity leave:	generous
On-site daycare centre?	no
Child/elder care referral service?	yes
Employment equity rep. reports to CEO/President?	no
Target numbers for women in management?	yes
Pay equity policy?	yes
Employment equity policy?	yes
Mentoring program?	no[a]

Noteworthy benefits:
 • generous educational leave provisions
 • self-funded leave program
Part-time employee benefits:
 • salary-related benefits pro-rated; others same as full-time employees; must work 25+ hours/2 weeks to qualify
Notes: (a) pilot project

City of Montreal

The employees of the City of Montreal provide public services such as road maintenance, garbage collection, support to cultural events, and firefighting to Montreal's one million residents. Most of the employees are unionized, by one of six unions and staff associations.

"I sent a man to hospital once," said a woman whose career path had taken her from being a hairdresser to a legal secretary to a labourer. "It was a reflex. He tried to 'help' me into a truck." She grinned. "He hasn't tried again."

She was part of a first wave of female blue-collar workers hired under a special program started in 1988 to increase the representation of women in blue-collar, technical and trades positions. Interested women were briefed about specific jobs and potential career paths within the City. Workshops prepared them to deal with the problems that often arise when women enter non-traditional jobs. Once they were on the job, regular group meetings gave them the chance to share their experiences, and give each other moral support and advice.

Since the program's introduction, the City has filled 25% of its blue-collar vacancies with women. As a result, the representation of women in blue-collar jobs increased from 49 women, or 1.3% of the positions, in August of 1987 to 292 women, or 7.2% of the positions, by December of 1993.

Blue-collar women are still often given a rough ride when they arrive in a new group, but they feel that the City's diversity training seminars have improved the behaviour of men. They have also developed strategies for coping. "At first I blushed," said the former hairdresser, "but now I respond in the same tone. . . . If someone goes too far, though, I'll say so."

They also note that some of the men now acknowledge that the presence of women has made even their jobs easier because they now have better equipment to do heavy tasks. As a result, everybody's rate of workplace injuries has gone down.

The program for women in blue-collar jobs was part of the City's employment equity program, which was launched in 1987. Women have made major inroads since then in every job category except fire fighters (where there were no women in 1987 and only two by December, 1993) and foremen (where their numbers increased from three, or 1.1%, to seven, or 2.5%, during the same period). In other categories, progress has been dramatic:

- women in senior management increased from one woman out of 66 senior managers in 1987 (1.5%), to 12 out of 78 (15.4%) by December, 1993;
- in other management jobs, they went from 12.1% to 24.3%;
- in professional positions, they increased from 13% to 28.8%;
- among other white-collar positions, they increased from 41.7% to 53.3%;
- their total representation in the workforce of the City of Montreal increased from 16.1% to 24.5%.

In such a large and diverse organization, attitudes inevitably vary from department to department, but the women interviewed felt that attitudes were generally good. "There are no barriers or systemic blockages," said a senior manager who was originally one of only two women in her area.

Some women have been allowed into positions for which they were not yet fully qualified. For example, a bright secretary with several years experience at the City moved into a professional position while she was still working on a related bachelor's degree.

Another woman got a senior management job for a three-year trial period even though she lacked the required experience. This can be a risky strategy. "I was one of the first women in my area," she said, "and the department is still mostly male. I often wonder if I'm a token."

Another senior manager, who has made a strong, public commitment to hiring more women in her department, discovered that it can take special effort to find qualified women. "When I took over this department there had been no management women before me and my subordinates were all men and all resistant," she said. Fifteen days into the job she had 12 summer job openings to fill. "The list I was shown had only two women on it. I told them that wasn't good enough. I wanted a list that was 50-50." They looked harder, and produced a new list. There were good women out there, but, she said, "they simply didn't see them".

When candidates are equally qualified she will choose the women. Once she has decided who to hire she meets one-on-one with men who lost out to equally qualified women to discuss the rationale for her decision.

It will take years to reach the City's goal of having women in every job category in numbers proportionate to their external availability in those job categories. Like many organizations, the City of Montreal is not doing much hiring these days and employees on the "availability list" (a list of employees working on temporary assignments because their jobs have been eliminated) get priority. For historical reasons, that list contains mainly men in areas that have traditionally been male dominated.

Women also feel that a lack of formal career counselling makes it harder for them to get ahead. "The City is good at getting the women in," said one manager, "but it doesn't follow up and help them continue."

Informal networking still plays a big role in promotions and transfers. The senior manager who had demanded the 50-50 list said her male employees were so used to the informal network that one of them actually asked her how he was supposed to let her know about his career aspirations if she didn't play hockey, golf or use the men's room. He was startled when she answered that he should book a meeting with her and they would sit down to discuss his future.

Because informal networking is so important, women who take long maternity leaves have trouble keeping their careers on track. The City allows a leave of up to two years but so far it seems to be mainly unionized staff who take long breaks. The experience of one ten-year manager who took a $1\frac{1}{2}$ year maternity leave may explain why. While she was away, her department was reorganized. Her job no longer exists; she is now on the availability list.

Being on the availability list is not all bad. Employees on it still receive full salary and whatever work can be found for them. They may be exposed to other departments, which can help their long-term career prospects.

Another manager, who took a two-year break following the birth of her second child, did so because, while she was pregnant, her mother was diagnosed with cancer. "Before I had the kids, I was a workaholic," she said. The children and her mother's illness changed her priorities. She asked to come back on a three-day work week. It was approved for a six-month trial but she found it hard to supervise for only three days a week. "I would have loved to job-share," she said, but that is not yet an option at the City.

Part-time work is rare. The professionals' union worries that it would be used by management as a way to cut hours, regardless of the employees' wishes. Nevertheless, alternative working arrangements are being discussed.

Most managers interviewed did not find their hours excessive. They felt the City was a good place for people wanting to lead balanced work and personal lives. An on-site day care centre opened in 1992 and work is under way to open a second one in conjunction with the Université du Québec Montréal. The City continues to look for ways to improve itself as an employer of men and women.

City of Montreal
413, rue St-Jacques, 4e étage, Montréal, PQ, H2Y 1N9
Telephone: (514) 872-3237

	Total	No. of Women	% Women
Full-time employees	11,404	2,791	24%
Part-time employees	0	0	0%
Board members	51[a]	16	31%

Job category (figures based on full-time employees, unless noted otherwise):

Upper level managers	78	12	15%
Middle or other managers	717	174	24%
Professionals	660	190	29%
Semi-professionals & technicians	0	0	0%
Supervisors	0	0	0%
Foremen/women	283	7	2%
Clerical workers	3,966	2,114	53%
Sales workers	0	0	0%
Service workers	1,662[b]	2	0%
Skilled crafts & trades workers	4,038[c]	292	7%
Semi-skilled manual workers			
Other manual workers			

Percentage of full-time employees considered upper level managers:	0.68%
Top-up of U.I.C. during maternity leave:	varies[d]
On-site daycare centre?	yes
Child/elder care referral service?	no
Employment equity rep. reports to CEO/President?	no
Target numbers for women in management?	yes
Pay equity policy?	yes
Employment equity policy?	yes
Mentoring program?	no

Noteworthy benefits:
- five days for personal or family emergencies
- some agreements also provide for two floater days
- discounts on some fitness club memberships

Part-time employee benefits:
- there are no permanent part-time employees; no benefits for casual and temporary employees

Notes: (a) elected council
(b) firefighters
(c) also includes all manual workers
(d) generous top-up for management and professional employees; average for others

City of Toronto

The City of Toronto is responsible for the provision of public services such as garbage collection, public health, local parks and community centres, and firefighting. It is governed by 16 elected councillors and a mayor.

The City of Toronto is one of only two organizations in this book to have proportionately more women in senior management than in the organization's workforce as a whole. In fact, when it comes to professionals, the City looks like it has an over-representation of women, but the professionals category in the City consists largely of nurses and other health professionals, 96% of whom are female. The opposite extreme is seen in the service workers category, which seems to have a higher proportion of men than at many other organizations because it includes fire fighters, roughly 99% of whom are male.

Apart from those extremes, few departments in the City are now almost exclusively male or female. Why has the City done so well at getting a balanced representation of women in management and professional positions? A large part of the credit goes to having started early. A Mayor's Task Force on the Status of Women in Toronto was set up in 1973, and it triggered fast action that has not let up since. In 1977 it became one of the first organizations to adopt an Equal Opportunities Program for its staff, and by 1979 it had hired a full-time staff member to work specifically on equal opportunity issues. By January of 1980 it had elected equal opportunity representatives for every department, and in 1982 the status of equity issues was given a boost with the appointment of Equal Opportunity Senior Managers in each department.

"Part of my job is to challenge and teach," explained one such manager. "I do a lot of counselling of my peers about how they need to change their overall attitudes towards the employees." She worked in a particularly tradition-bound department, so she found herself asking her peers things like why they assumed employees were only good if they worked long hours, when extreme hours might actually indicate an inefficient use of time.

A thorough review of the first decade of equal opportunity initiatives concluded that progress was still too slow. As a result, starting in 1985, every department head had to set goals for the representation of women at various levels within his or her department, and timetables for achieving them. Progress is measured every three years and department heads must justify the lack of progress if their goals are not met. That was the added incentive they needed: the numbers really started to improve once that measure had been implemented.

To help managers meet their goals without sacrificing quality, the City has been active in outreach recruiting (recruiting with the help of community groups in the communities from which the City is lacking representation) and has developed innovative programs to help women move into non-traditional jobs. One such program is BRIDGES, which involves 35 days of training spread out over four or five months. Classroom sessions and shop training teach participants about mechanical principles, occupational health and safety, and how to use basic tools and equipment. Panel discussions with women in trades and technical occupations, and worksite visits help participants explore job possibilities. They are also led through self-assessments to get a better idea of whether they would really enjoy such work. Finally, they spend one month on the job in an area of interest to them.

The BRIDGES program has been so successful that the City now consults to other organizations wishing to establish similar programs, and its own representation of women in entry-level labouring and construction jobs had increased from 1.8% in 1986 to 6.8% by 1990. (Ironically, the program has been suspended within the City pending the outcome of a dispute over whether seniority should be looked at corporation-wide or only within a bargaining unit when a job vacancy occurs. BRIDGES typically takes women from one union local and trains them for jobs in a different one.)

The City also provides university preparation courses to help more women on staff qualify for management jobs, and pays child care expenses for women who would be prevented from attending a training course without the financial support.

The environment is a welcoming one for people who want to balance their work and personal lives. A woman working in the legal department, for example, commented that "a lot of the female solicitors who come to the City do so in order to combine kids and a career". The City tops-up U.I.C. payments for both the 15 weeks of maternity leave and another 10 weeks of parental leave, one of the few organizations to do so. It has provided on-site day care since 1980, and managers with children find that co-workers understand that they need to leave at specific times to pick children up at the day care centre. As a result, they report that late afternoon meetings are now rare.

There are no formal policies on alternative working arrangements, but permanent part-time, job-sharing, telecommuting, flexible hours and compressed work weeks are all happening. Access to them depends a lot on managers and supervisors. One woman found that her department had changed radically in the five years she was there. "After my first maternity leave I asked for a three-day week. It was refused, but then several others also asked and the Commissioner decided to allow it. After my second child was born I hadn't planned to come back, but my manager suggested that I put together a proposal to work from home. Now I do two days at home and one in the office. I had to buy my own computer, and at first there was some jealousy, but I pointed out that I am only paid for the three days, and that nothing is stopping them from making their own proposal." She said that, in her department, there are now several people job-sharing, others working flex-time and some working compressed work weeks.

The change in attitude in her department reflects the efforts the City has made in training and educating managers about the needs of a diverse workforce. It also reflects recent retirements of managers with traditional attitudes. In many departments staff commented that "the old guard is disappearing". The public health department is an interesting case in point. "When I came," said one employee, "the Medical Officer of Health was king. The inspectors were paramilitary. The department was authoritarian. . . . Now 83% of the department is female, more than half are public health nurses, and we are in the forefront of modern management practice (although we are still far from perfect)." Added another, "Women pushed for education programs; men saw the department's role as enforcement".

There are still some problem areas for women, particularly among clerical workers, fire fighters and outside workers.

Clerical work has historically been undervalued at the City, with the result that these employees feel unappreciated and overworked. Several who started in the seventies and early eighties have made it into management. Here as elsewhere, though, that happens less often now, as greater emphasis is put on formal education rather than length of experience with the organization. Women are flocking to training programs (women represented 29% of the workforce in 1990, but half the participants in all training and development courses), but they are less likely than men to take management training courses. They are also less likely to take external courses or any that require taking a leave of absence.

Women in the traditionally "macho" areas of fire fighting and outdoor work note that attitudes towards women are not improving very quickly. "The [anti-harassment and gender awareness] courses they have sent people on did help," said one employee, "but they are sending the supervisors, not the guys who are doing the harassing."

There are some concerns about male backlash against the equal opportunity initiatives, but as long as the women moving up are good at their jobs they can overcome it, as did one woman who started as a litter picker in 1988. "I'm a good worker, dependable," she said. "I got offered the chance to become a foreman. The guys think I got it because I'm a black woman. I think I got it because I know what I'm doing, I speak good English and I write well. . . . At first there was another woman with me, but she quit because she was offended by the way the guys talked. I didn't let it get to me. I'll tell them off if they are being rude. . . . At first when I became a foreman the guys didn't want to talk to me, but eventually they decided I was OK. We get along well now."

One of the most promising aspects of the City's approach to equal opportunity issues is its thorough research. Its detailed analysis of trends in employment, training, salaries and other related issues means that it can pinpoint problems and try to address them. It has the challenge of working with four very different unions and staff associations in doing so, though, so major change cannot happen overnight. Nevertheless, its steady approach has already made a big difference, and seems likely to continue to do so.

City of Toronto
City Hall, Personnel Service Division, 2nd Floor, West Tower, Toronto, ON, M5H 2N2   Telephone: (416) 392-7193

	Total	No. of Women	% Women
Full-time employees	7,118	2,137	30%
Part-time employees	66	63	95%
Board members	16[a]	4	25%

Job category (figures based on full-time employees, unless noted otherwise):

Upper level managers	115	37	32%
Middle or other managers	341	125	37%
Professionals	693	432	62%
Semi-professionals & technicians	662	257	39%
Supervisors	224[b]	45	20%
Foremen/women			
Clerical workers	564	388	69%
Sales workers	0	0	0%
Service workers	2,027[c]	649	32%
Skilled crafts & trades workers	429	17	4%
Semi-skilled manual workers	422	49	12%
Other manual workers	1,641[d]	138	8%

Percentage of full-time employees considered upper
level managers: 1.62%
Top-up of U.I.C. during maternity leave: good
On-site daycare centre? yes
Child/elder care referral service? no
Employment equity rep. reports to CEO/President? no
Target numbers for women in management? yes
Pay equity policy? yes
Employment equity policy? yes
Mentoring program? no

Noteworthy benefits:
• can use 6 sick days for care of ill dependents
• self-funded leave program
Part-time employee benefits:
• pro-rated based on number of days worked
Notes: (a) elected council
(b) includes foremen/women
(c) consists of skilled workers in office, trade and service functions (e.g. secretary, bookkeeper, firefighter, real estate appraiser)
(d) consists of all entry level workers (including those in agriculture, labour, construction, transportation, communications, office and service work)

Loto-Québec

Loto-Québec was established by an act of the Quebec National Assembly in December, 1969, with a mandate to set up and operate lotteries in the province. It has recently been given additional responsibility for establishing and operating casinos and a network of video lotteries. The Crown corporation is headquartered in Montreal, with ten regional offices throughout Quebec. Almost all the employees are unionized, by one of five different union groups or associations.

Loto-Québec was under no legal compulsion to implement an employment equity policy, but it did so in 1988 under the leadership of David Clark, who, as president from 1985 to 1991, was troubled by the underrepresentation of women in many parts of the organization.

The employment equity policy set out four objectives:

- increasing the number of women in management and professional positions;
- increasing opportunities for support staff;
- developing a good quality of life at work; and
- ensuring pay equity.

The organization set a goal of having 30% female managers within three years. It did not force managers to take specific actions to reach that goal, but the policy suggested ways to do so.

Apparently suggestions were not enough, so at the end of the three years Loto-Québec decided to take stronger action. The most common route to management was through the sales force, an area where women were seriously lacking, so the corporation developed a one-year internship program for sales representatives, which combined academic training with on-the-job apprenticeships. In light of the employment equity goal of increasing opportunities for support staff, applicants had to have at least six years experience with Loto-Québec. At the time, only 17% of the sales representatives were women, but there were a lot of longserving women in support roles at the organization who were eager for the opportunity to learn.

The program was so successful that by the third year the internships were made available to men too, as the corporation had met its goal of having female representation in the sales force proportionate to the external availability of women in sales.

Based on that successful model, the corporation has just launched another internship program: an 18-month program for electronics technicians, who are responsible for activities such as installing and servicing telecommunications and computer equipment.

The vast majority of staff are unionized, and the unions agreed to waive seniority for hiring and promotion decisions in under-represented areas. Instead, if the candidates were equally qualified, preference would be given to hiring women.

These initiatives have led to a significant improvement in the representation of women in Loto-Québec's workforce:

- the percentage of female middle and other managers increased from 17% in 1988 to 22% by late 1993;
- women's representation among professional staff increased from 26% to 35% during the same period;
- among sales workers, female representation increased from 12% to 26%.

These numbers were achieved without a net increase in the total workforce.

Unfortunately, in its eagerness for action, the corporation lacked a certain finesse in implementation. An early attempt at encouraging women to network and learn by holding a women-only training session caused outrage among the men. To the allegation that "your career is over unless you wear a skirt", one long-time employee responded, "I point out to them what happened earlier; that it used to be that men moved up *much* faster than women with the same degree." That may well be true, but it suggests that reverse discrimination is happening now, which is not the corporate policy and would understandably raise hackles if it were.

The backlash from the men at Loto-Québec continues, and the men and women seem to be two solitudes. On an individual level, many women have managed to break down the walls dividing them but women still comment that "in meetings with men, women are excluded from the chit-chat" and that a lot of informal networking goes on without them. They have used creative strategies to try to change the way the game is played. One manager commented that she and another female manager discuss films instead of sports in casual boardroom conversations, and find that men are coming over to join in. Another said, "I can't join them in the men's room, but I can catch them in the elevator". She brought a proposal to the attention of senior management using the elevator approach.

Management women commented that "at 5:00 p.m. the guys will meet in somebody's office" and, while "not a lot of work gets done between five and eight, some important politics do". Added another, "If you miss out on that, you can miss some boats".

The women recognize the organization's political nature, but are reluctant to join in. One felt that the impact of after-hours socializing was decreasing. "It is a question of styles: when it was all men in management, first they went through a phase where they all worked late. Then everybody went to Nautilus together after work. Then education became the fashion. Now that there are more women there is less of this trendiness; women won't follow it."

The company is trying to stress other virtues, like work and family balance, and men are beginning to appreciate the growing flexibility. One man recently took a two-month parental leave, and, as one manager pointed out, "There are starting to be more men who have to leave to pick their children up at day care".

The corporation is encouraging work and personal balance in other ways too. Professional employees have access to three floater days, to use as they choose, and in the summertime everyone works a 35-hour, $4\frac{1}{2}$ day week. Women can take up to two years maternity leave, and can phase in their return to work by working part-time for a portion of those two years.

The long leaves, which management women are still reluctant to take but are widespread among support staff, are seen as a wonderful opportunity for staff development by both managers and the employees they supervise. Said one woman, "As a manager, I, too, used to be reluctant to hire women of child-bearing age. I'm not any more, because we have a good internal job posting system and I can get good people to fill in". Said a non-management employee, "You can no longer manage your career upward, but you can laterally. . . . The two-year leaves give great opportunities to broaden and motivate yourself by trying other jobs".

The typical hours of work are not excessive by private industry standards. Some managers stick to an eight-hour work day, although ten hours is probably more typical. Support staff are generally able to contain their hours to a standard work day.

Employees with young children appreciate the convenience of both the on-site day care centre, which opened in 1990, and a medical clinic in the head office building which will see sick children on short notice. The day care centre has informally agreed that if the medical clinic says a child's illness is not contagious, the child may return to the centre. "Because of the doctor in this building," explained one woman, "if my child gets sick, I end up taking half an hour off work instead of a full day."

Loto-Québec still has a way to go in its employment equity efforts, but it has done more than many organizations and it continues to push on. The results of its efforts are examined annually by senior management. Awareness sessions are being held for all managers to try to bridge the barriers between male and female staff, and the corporation is making good headway in promoting a work and lifestyle balance.

Loto-Québec
500 Sherbrooke St. West, Montreal, PQ, H3A 3G6
Telephone: (514) 282-8000

	Total	No. of Women	% Women
Full-time employees	630	306	49%
Part-time employees	20	14	70%
Board members	8	2	25%

Job category (figures based on full-time employees, unless noted otherwise):

Upper level managers	5	2	40%
Middle or other managers	86	19	22%
Professionals	175	61	35%
Semi-professionals & technicians	84	49	58%
Supervisors	0	0	0%
Foremen/women	0	0	0%
Clerical workers	234	163	70%
Sales workers	46	12	26%
Service workers	0	0	0%
Skilled crafts & trades workers	0	0	0%
Semi-skilled manual workers	0	0	0%
Other manual workers	0	0	0%

Percentage of full-time employees considered upper level managers:	0.79%
Top-up of U.I.C. during maternity leave:	generous
On-site daycare centre?	yes
Child/elder care referral service?	no
Employment equity rep. reports to CEO/President?	no
Target numbers for women in management?	yes
Pay equity policy?	no
Employment equity policy?	no
Mentoring program?	no

Noteworthy benefits:
- subdized fitness club memberships for some categories of employees
- four weeks vacation after the first year
- some categories of employees have 3 floater days for personal needs
- allow up to two years' maternity leave

Part-time employee benefits:
- pro-rated to hours worked

Municipality of Metropolitan Toronto

The Municipality of Metropolitan Toronto (Metro) was created in 1953 to provide more effective and efficient delivery of government services in the greater Toronto region. It is the sixth largest government in Canada, serving the 2.3 million residents of the cities of Toronto, North York, Scarborough, Etobicoke, York and the Borough of East York. It is responsible for services such as the police force, ambulances, welfare and child care. Its activities are overseen by an elected council of 34 members: 28 representatives of individual wards plus the six mayors of the local municipalities.

"The culture of Metro is set by Council," said Carol Ruddell-Foster, a senior manager who was herself a councillor for many years. That culture is one that strives to have a workforce that reflects the population it serves. Another senior manager, with 15 years experience at Metro, agreed. "Having a directly elected council has made a big difference. The 28 full-time councillors take more interest and ownership in these issues than used to be the case. As a result, even resistant senior managers are being pulled along by Council."

Metro has a full-time employee dedicated to advancing the role of women within the organization. As a result of her initiatives and those of Council, Metro has many policies and facilities that encourage a balance between work and personal lives. Flexible work hours, compressed work weeks and voluntary part-time arrangements are common in office environments and gaining acceptance in operational areas. Pay and benefits are excellent. Staff particularly appreciate the on-site fitness and day care centres. Children of Metro employees also have access to day care spots in Metro day care facilities throughout the region.

Maternity leaves of one year have become the norm, and corporate policies support many other types of leave, including six days which may be taken from an employee's sick days to care for ill dependents, and a self-funded leave of absence program.

Leaves allow Metro to use cross-training and secondments to keep staff motivated at a time when there are limited opportunities for promotion because of shrinking funding for government services. One woman who moved from a clerical position into management attributed her success to a combination of having had good mentors and having been given lots of opportunities to learn about different areas through secondments.

Many of the women in Metro management today started in clerical jobs, but it has become difficult to make that transition without advanced education. To overcome that barrier, Metro, the City of Toronto and York University run an on-site university preparation program for female employees. The course is offered on shared employer/employee time at lunch and in the late afternoons, so that even those with demanding family responsibilities can attend.

Over half of the graduates so far have gone on to take university or college courses, and the preparation course has been extended to male employees. Graduates of the course and their supervisors agreed that it helped the participants' on-the-job performance and improved their self-confidence.

In another creative approach to employee development, the Homes for the Aged division and Canadian Union of Public Employees (CUPE) Local 79 developed an academic upgrading course for nursing attendants, in cooperation with Centennial College and the Ontario Women's Directorate. The section was having trouble recruiting qualified Registered Nursing Assistants (RNAs), so the program was designed to help nursing attendants get the academic background they would need to enter an RNA program.

Response to the upgrading program was overwhelming. Applicants wrote two sets of qualifying exams to ensure that anyone admitted to the two-year program would have a reasonable chance of success. Those who did not qualify were advised about ways they could upgrade their skills. Metro contributes half the tuition costs and half the time needed to attend classes.

Metro also offers a program based on the City of Toronto's BRIDGES program to help women move into trades and technical jobs. (See City of Toronto listing for details). A community services worker who joined the BRIDGES program spent a month working with a team of arborists. "I loved that month," she said. The work was physically demanding, and "at first they test the hell out of you, but . . . I had an excellent crew to work with; we still keep in touch. Now I'm doing training for certification as an arborist." She and her husband have set up a part-time business in the field, and she is exploring job opportunities within Metro that would draw on her new skills.

Education is also made easy with the help of a "self-study learning centre" which offers dozens of computer, video and audio-based career enrichment courses which can be used during the work day or at home.

Even with all these supportive policies, few of Metro's senior executives are women. Some senior men's attitudes are, as one woman put it, "stuck in a time warp". Overall, however, the culture is not one that is hostile to the idea of women in senior positions. On the contrary, some talented women have moved rapidly through management ranks.

Those who have done so understood that movement within the organization is based on informal networks and word-of-mouth. There is no clear path to follow. "There are problems with the promotion process," admitted a human resources manager. "It is long, labour-intensive and not well understood." There is not, as yet, a formal system for spotting and developing "high-potential" employees.

An engineer, who has worked at Metro for 13 years in male-dominated areas, felt that mentoring was crucial. "I was promoted to manager when I was very pregnant with my first. The promotion was effective two weeks before I was off for a four-month maternity leave. I'm sure my boss had to fight hard for that."

In a system that relies heavily on mentors, the departure of a mentor can have unsettling career implications for those who have depended on the mentor. Many employees at Metro who do not have strong mentors are particularly uncertain about their status because there are no routine performance appraisals. Several employees felt that such appraisals could help them become aware of weaknesses which might be impeding their progress, and could help managers have a better idea of the aspirations of their employees.

Low turnover and shrinking budgets also make progress slow for women aspiring to senior management. The pressure from Council, though, seems unlikely to vanish. With time, the number of women in senior management will likely increase.

Municipality of Metropolitan Toronto
55 John Street, Station 1055, Metro Hall, Toronto, ON, M5V 3C6
Telephone: (416) 397-7143

	Total	No. of Women	% Women
Full-time employees	11,080[a]	5,352	48%
Part-time employees	2,774	2,192	79%
Board members	34[b]	12	35%

Job category (figures based on full-time employees, unless noted otherwise):

Upper level managers	21	2	10%
Middle or other managers	210	92	44%
Professionals	1,368	1,008	74%
Semi-professionals & technicians	2,525	1,748	69%
Supervisors	948	410	43%
Foremen/women	128	3	2%
Clerical workers	2,146	1,619	75%
Sales workers	0	0	0%
Service workers	3,171	2,208	70%
Skilled crafts & trades workers	239	4	2%
Semi-skilled manual workers	976	39	4%
Other manual workers	2,008	355	18%

Percentage of full-time employees considered upper level managers:	0.19%
Top-up of U.I.C. during maternity leave:	average
On-site daycare centre?	yes
Child/elder care referral service?	yes
Employment equity rep. reports to CEO/President?	no
Target numbers for women in management?	yes
Pay equity policy?	yes
Employment equity policy?	yes
Mentoring program?	no

Noteworthy benefits:
- top-up of Workers' Compensation Board payments to 100% of net pay with no deduction from sick bank
- self-funded leave program

Part-time employee benefits:
- pro-rated; must have at least one year of service
- Homes for the Aged part-time employees have their own contract

Notes: (a) includes temporary and casual staff (21% of full-time staff are temporary); benefits for temporary staff are similar to those of permanent employees

(b) elected council

Ontario Provincial Police

The Ontario Provincial Police (OPP) provides police services to those parts of Ontario that do not have their own forces, and patrols provincial highways. It also helps municipal police forces, the coroners' service and provincial ministries by providing special investigation and enforcement services. Approximately 21% of the staff are civilians.

It has been 20 years since the first female officers were hired by the OPP. Thirty-six women were included in that original group, of whom 15 remain. The number of female non-civilian (or "uniform") staff increased over the next few years to about 100 and stayed there, hovering at about one to two per cent of the uniform staff. The women were confident that over time they would assimilate naturally within the police force and that no special measures were needed.

That confidence was shattered by a 1991 article in the police association newsletter scoffing at new provincial legislation that mandated that the force aim toward 50% female representation. The man who wrote the article is no longer on staff, and the article triggered the creation of an OPP Women's Network. The network has worked closely and successfully with the police association to overcome some of the misconceptions about the role of women within the force.

Since 1992, 50% of the new hires have been women. Women now account for 8.3% of the OPP's non-civilian staff and a raft of measures are in place or in the works to ensure that the number keeps increasing. The target is 14% by the end of 1995.

There's an oddly schizophrenic attitude about the hiring of women, even among the women themselves. There has not been a major effort to explain the methods being used for recruitment, so even women worry that, in the rush to meet the numeric goals, unqualified people will be hired.

"They are trying to push us to the forefront," said one woman who is now an acting sergeant. "We would rather get there on our own abilities." Yet when she and others were asked if they believed women were getting hired or promoted for reasons other than merit, they answered with an unequivocal "no".

Rather than lowering its standards, the OPP has revamped its approach to recruitment. "Traditionally we went out and spoke to law and security classes in colleges and universities," explained Inspector Irena Lawrenson, the OPP's Employment Equity Coordinator. "When we were talking to classes that were 80 to 90% white male, that's what we were getting in our recruits." Now the OPP is using new approaches to try to broaden the recruitment base while keeping standards high. For example:

- An outreach coordinator is identifying employment agencies, advocacy groups, associations and clubs that have strong links within the communities where the police force lacks adequate representation. At the same time, all districts have set up employment equity committees which have been charged with making presentations about the force to these groups. Every second presentation is to be made specifically to a women's group.
- Women and others who may be curious about police work but nervous about making a permanent commitment to it are being encouraged to join the auxiliary forces, which are now being seen as a sort of internship program. Traditionally, 20% of the auxiliary members end up becoming officers, and 20% of the members are female. Simply persuading a larger proportion of the female auxiliary members to switch to permanent staff would have a big impact on the numbers.
- The force is considering making presentations to university and college students in programs that have high female representation, and are in subject areas where the skills and interests of the students may overlap with police work. For example, nurses and social workers are similar to police officers in that they deal with victims and other people needing help. Students in these classes could be encouraged to consider applying their skills within the police force.

The women who have become officers find that being a woman can actually help them deal with tricky situations. "My relative lack of physical strength has *never* been a drawback," said a woman who has been with the OPP for 19 years. "The fact that I am a woman has helped diffuse situations, like one case of family violence where the man came roaring out to the car and you could see he was all ready to slug the police officer, until I got out and he saw that it was a woman. His arm just dropped."

Another woman tells a similar story. "I'm 5'5" and I weigh 120 pounds. I've arrested a guy who was 6'2". I managed to take him in just by talking to him. A man in that situation probably would have got into a fight. . . . On the other hand, if I think there's going to be a problem, I'll back off and wait for help. So would a guy," she said.

Male staff also worry about unqualified women getting hired, but individually they seem to respect and get on well with their female colleagues, and recognize that their presence has benefitted the force.

Women are proving to be particularly good at handling sensitive issues like sexual assault. As a result, they are starting to cluster in certain types of work. This poses a dilemma for the force. While many of the women are good at dealing with issues like sexual assault and feel fulfilled by doing so, Inspector Lawrenson worries that they will get burned out from the emotional stress. She also feels that it is important that men not neglect the personal skills needed to do such work.

Women are also gravitating towards "soft" policing; jobs like community services officers, which are similar to public relations jobs in other organizations. Community work has traditionally not been highly regarded within the force but the OPP is in the midst of a major redesign that will bring a community orientation to all types of police work. If the new approach takes hold, the skills women bring to the force will become more highly valued, and women's promotion prospects should be enhanced.

Now that the OPP is managing to find good female recruits in numbers proportionate to the population, it has turned its attention to ensuring that there are no systemic barriers to promotion. "There is a system for promotion but it doesn't work very well," said one officer. "Because it is such a male-dominated workforce you second-guess yourself. You tend to under-estimate your abilities. Yearly performance reviews don't happen yearly, and when they do they are too subjective and vague."

New forms and procedures that will require an annual review for all rank-and-file officers and will incorporate comments from at least three external sources are expected to be implemented in the fall of 1994. Inspector Lawrenson explained the rationale for using external reviewers:

"Men expect women to work the same way they do, so that's what they reward. By going external, to the organizations we deal with on a day-to-day basis, we'll get a more balanced sense of how an officer is doing. The external reviewers can be people like Crown attorneys, the Children's Aid Society, community policing committees, local truckers — as long as it is someone who knows the officer's work."

One of the barriers with which the OPP is still grappling is work and family balance. It is only recently that significant numbers of female officers are having children. "I'm a little bit apprehensive about what will happen if I get pregnant," said one. "The talk is that you get set back in your career."

The three field chief superintendents have just made a video in which they discuss the issue of work and lifestyle balance. One of them points out that maternity leaves are a human resource planning issue, not a women's issue. He points out that a man off for an injury is no different than a woman off for a maternity leave, from a staffing perspective, except that the maternity leave allows time to plan how the workload will be dealt with.

The new OPP headquarters, due to open in 1995, will contain a day care centre. However, employees are dispersed throughout the province, and most police jobs require shift work for which it can be difficult to arrange child or elder care. Shifts are usually scheduled long in advance, which helps employees make regular arrangements. However emergencies inevitably arise in police work. Employees must make contingency plans for how their children will be looked after if they cannot get home at the usual time.

Family situations are also taken into account in human resource planning. Although the force has the right to demand that an officer move to a new district on short notice, it rarely does so if the move will cause family problems. "The force is willing to hear about problems and will react to them," said one officer.

Flexible working options, like job sharing and part-time work are only available officially to civilian staff at the moment, but part-time work for uniform staff is being tested.

A woman who, during her 18 years with the OPP, has had many contacts with other police forces is glad she chose to work for the OPP. "The OPP treats women better than any other police department I know of," she said.

Ontario Provincial Police
50 Andrew Street South, Orillia, ON, L3V 7T5
Telephone: (705) 329-6600

	Total	No. of Women	% Women
Full-time employees	5,936[a]	1,072	18%
Part-time employees	0[b]	0	0%
Board members	0	0	0%

Job category (figures based on full-time employees, unless noted otherwise):

	Total	No. of Women	% Women
Upper level managers	137[c]	9	7%
Middle or other managers	999[d]	24	2%
Professionals	0	0	0%
Semi-professionals & technicians	3,346[e]	361	11%
Supervisors	0	0	0%
Foremen/women	0	0	0%
Clerical workers	734	625	85%
Sales workers	0	0	0%
Service workers	488[f]	192	39%
Skilled crafts & trades workers	0	0	0%
Semi-skilled manual workers	0	0	0%
Other manual workers	275[g]	56	20%

Percentage of full-time employees considered upper level managers:	2.31%
Top-up of U.I.C. during maternity leave:	generous
On-site daycare centre?	no
Child/elder care referral service?	no
Employment equity rep. reports to CEO/President?	yes
Target numbers for women in management?	yes
Pay equity policy?	yes
Employment equity policy?	yes
Mentoring program?	no

Noteworthy benefits:
 • self-funded leave program
 • one-year leave available for foreign or intergovernmental employment
Part-time employee benefits:
 • pro-rated

Notes: (a) numbers very different for civilian and uniform staff. E.g. 8% of
            uniform vs. 55% of civilian jobs are held by women
       (b) part-time employee numbers not available
       (c) includes civilian senior management (33% female) and senior
            commissioned officers (4% female)
       (d) sergeants and staff sergeants
       (e) constables
       (f) communications and security staff
       (g) caretakers and maintenance staff

HEALTH SERVICES

Credit Valley Hospital

The Credit Valley Hospital is 366-bed, acute care facility that serves the Mississauga area of Ontario. It opened on November 5, 1985. More than 3,600 babies are born at the hospital each year, and its emergency department sees 60,000 patients a year.

It's odd to think of a Canadian hospital as an entrepreneurial organization, but Credit Valley is one. When it was set up nine years ago, the founders hired a nucleus of energetic, assertive, ambitious people to get it going. Most of them have stayed, and have hired in their own image. As Jocelyn Garrett, Associate Vice President, Marketing/Public Relations, put it, "everybody here *knows* they are the cream of the crop" so they have the self-confidence to work cooperatively.

Cooperation and teamwork are fostered in many ways. President Dean Sane holds regular employee forums, at which he discusses issues ranging from budget constraints to accreditation. All staff are encouraged to attend and to ask questions. To try to keep the atmosphere informal, the president has been known to set up a platform for a "fireside chat", complete with housecoat and slippers. When he had to discuss the implications of the Ontario government's cost-cutting "social contract" legislation, he sat on empty cardboard boxes. He is eager for feedback (an attitude found at all levels), and when it was pointed out to him that many shift workers could not attend a daytime chat, he added an evening session. The forum is also videotaped, and the tapes are made available to all units to watch when they have a few spare moments.

Hiring is done by committee. The more senior the person being hired, the more people will have input into the hiring decision.

Employees are recognized by a peer-nominated-and-selected "employee of the quarter" award. In a sector where employee turnover tends to be high, Credit Valley has a much lower turnover rate than most — a fact that is making the "long service awards" dinner become larger and larger. ("Long service" is defined as five years or more at this nine-year old institution). Despite the cost, anyone who has worked at the hospital for more than five years is invited to come every year thereafter. The Hospital gets outside sponsorship so that it can continue this team-building tradition.

Many decisions are made and implemented by cross-functional, multi-level committees. For instance, a change in the type of food offered might have input from nutritionists, nurses, the finance department and the cleaning staff. Staff at all levels are encouraged to volunteer for committees and set up new ones if they see a need. One nurse, for instance, initiated a "problem solvers committee". Other committees include quality of work life, personal security, health and safety, employee wellness, child care, various employee awards committees and a social and recreational club, which organizes staff events and also arranges staff discounts from local merchants.

Flexible work arrangements are common at Credit Valley, and have an unusual twist: employees who want to work full-time when there is no full-time job available are often able to "time-share". For example one woman works 80% at one job and 20% at another. The flexibility of these arrangements means that the hospital can allocate staff resources in an efficient, effective manner; the employees can take on new challenges without making a sudden jump into a completely new type of work; departments can improve their communication and cooperation with one another since the same employee may work in different departments; and employees' personal needs can be met.

Those who do not want to work full-time also find the hospital accommodating. An employee who does a standard 50-50 job-share commented that she brings more energy and efficiency to her work than she would if she were working full-time, and that the hospital benefits directly because, if one person gets sick or goes on vacation, there is a back-up person who is fully versed in the job.

However, even working "part-time" at as hard-driving an institution as Credit Valley means long hours. As one manager put it, "I do work more than the official number of hours, but I did when I was full-time too". She is happy to have the opportunity to mesh her personal life with work, and feels that her decision to do so has always been respected and supported.

There is no sense that people working part-time or job-sharing are frowned upon or are limiting their careers in any way. Nor does pregnancy seem to harm careers. One woman was hired into a vice-president position even though she was visibly pregnant at the time of the interview.

A mid-management employee took a six-month maternity leave followed by a one-year educational leave to finish a Masters of Business Administration degree. She was pleasantly surprised that the hospital was willing to let her come back into a director-level position part-time. She wanted to be able to use the skills she had learned from her new degree, but did not want to work full-time while her child was still so young.

Before her leave, she had already taken advantage of the hospital's strong commitment to education. She was given a half-day off each week so that she could attend courses which were only available during the day. She made up the time on evenings and weekends.

Some employees, particularly shift workers, have occasionally found it difficult to get time off to care for a sick child (they typically have to use their vacation time or unpaid leaves), but management is extremely flexible when it comes to arranging staff time so that employees can go to school.

The Hospital also puts on its own education days and encourages its employees to attend educational events elsewhere in the city. These can range from the hospital's annual "Women's Health Day", which is a full day of seminars offered to all female staff that covers issues such as breast cancer, menopause, stress management, and balancing work and family, to participating in outside seminars about new medical developments.

Educational videos are also produced, and made available to part-time and casual workers to watch during breaks or at departmental meetings.

Even staff without a lot of formal education find that their abilities are recognized and that they are challenged to develop them in new areas. Two women at different levels commented that they were amazed and pleased to be allowed to teach, even though they lacked the paper qualifications. "They let me do the teaching job based on my experience," said one, "even though I didn't have the formal education." The other, who was one of the first people hired by the hospital, said that she felt the selection committee chose her because she had the sort of personality that fit with the hospital's approach.

That approach is one which has produced a tightly knit group. One employee commented, "This is not just a workplace; it is a community." Another, who works with the hospital's 500 volunteers, was away on jury duty for three weeks. "When I came back," she said, "it was like coming home."

Credit Valley Hospital
2200 Eglington Avenue West, Mississauga, ON, L5M 2N1
Telephone: (905) 820-2639

	Total	No. of Women	% Women
Full-time employees	876	763	87%
Part-time employees	764	717	94%
Board members	23	6	26%

Job category (figures based on full-time employees, unless noted otherwise):

Upper level managers	10	5	50%
Middle or other managers	23	19	83%
Professionals	475	434	91%
Semi-professionals & technicians	25	17	68%
Supervisors	69	59	86%
Foremen/women	0	0	0%
Clerical workers	145	140	97%
Sales workers	0	0	0%
Service workers	110	89	81%
Skilled crafts & trades workers	19	0	0%
Semi-skilled manual workers	0	0	0%
Other manual workers	0	0	0%

Percentage of full-time employees considered upper level managers:	1.14%
Top-up of U.I.C. during maternity leave:	good
On-site daycare centre?	no
Child/elder care referral service?	yes
Employment equity rep. reports to CEO/President?	no
Target numbers for women in management?	no
Pay equity policy?	yes
Employment equity policy?	yes
Mentoring program?	no

Noteworthy benefits:
- staff discounts at local shops, restaurants, etc.
- group home and automobile insurance available

Part-time employee benefits:
- earn 13% of base salary in lieu of benefits; are eligible for Hospitals of Ontario Pension Plan and group home and auto insurance; can use the computerized child care referral service

Mount Sinai Hospital

Mount Sinai was established as a 33-bed hospital in 1923 by a group of women active in Toronto's Jewish community. Their goal was to build a hospital that would serve that community and provide a strong teaching centre for young Jewish doctors. Since that time, it has expanded to a 546-bed, multi-disciplinary hospital. It has a strong research focus, and, in 1992, was the first Canadian hospital to receive a four-year accreditation award from the Canadian Council on Health Facilities Accreditation. It admits over 20,000 patients a year, and deals with some 31,000 emergency cases and 540,000 outpatient visits annually.

A woman who started at Mount Sinai when she was a single mother with three children and little work experience told the following story: "My son was picked to play the lead in a Christmas play that was going to be held at 1:30 in the afternoon. I told him I couldn't go. The day of the play our chief operating officer ran into me in the hallway and asked why I wasn't my normal self. When I told him, he said, 'What are you doing here?' and found someone to race me through a blizzard to my son's school. My son was on stage when I got there. He looked up, saw me, and announced, 'There's my mom!'."

What distinguishes Mount Sinai from most employers is its genuine focus on individuals. "There is so much support from everyone around you," said one employee. "I'm here for the long haul because of the people."

Whether it is encouraging a ward clerk to take a six-month leave to travel while she decided whether or not she wanted a career in nursing, or sending an injured housekeeper for English and computer lessons so that she could become a secretary, this hospital manages to combine the close, family atmosphere of a small hospital with the excitement and challenge of a teaching hospital.

"I chose Mount Sinai because it is *the* place in terms of values," said Doris Grinspun, its internationally known Program Director, Nursing. The managers and supervisors recognize that the hospital will get the best out of its staff if it discovers and meets their needs and aspirations.

How does a large, complex organization manage to do that? With a culture where mentoring is second-nature and inter-departmental co-operation is superb. That way the hospital knows what its people want to do and are capable of doing, and is able to guide them to the educational and job opportunities that will meet their needs and the hospital's.

"Within three months of my coming here," explained a staff nurse, "the Director of Nursing spent an hour and a half with me, asking what my career goals and strengths were. She then gave me special assignments to build on them."

Progress can be swift for employees who show that they have ability and interest. Beverly Lanigan-Gilmour, the Director of Human Resources, started as a recruiting officer at a time when the hospital was doing massive hiring. Shortly after her arrival, the director got sick and was off for three months. "It was a sink-or-swim situation," said Ms. Lanigan-Gilmour. She swam. She was promoted to Manager within a year, to Assistant Director two years later and to Director four years after having started at Mount Sinai.

More recently, a young woman who started as an administrative director was promoted to Assistant Vice-President and then to Vice-President of Administration within four years of joining. Her background was as a nurse; unusual in this position, which is still held by men at most hospitals. "When I came here I was working for a well-respected, male vice-president," she said. "He was an important mentor for me, but even when he left, the organization was prepared to take some risks with me."

It helped that she had just completed graduate work in hospital administration. Education is highly prized at Mount Sinai, and the hospital will go out of its way to make it possible for staff members to pursue further education.

"When I came to Canada, Mount Sinai accepted me with open arms and gave me lots of opportunities even though I had no Canadian experience," said a woman speaking with a heavy accent despite her 17 years in the country. The doctor who ran the laboratory in which she was working gave her time off to take the courses she needed to get her Canadian certification. "I'd come in really early to get extra work done," she said, adding that it was her choice to do so, not his request. Once she had her certification, the work she was doing for him was no longer appropriate so he offered to help her get a job elsewhere. "I told him I wanted to stay at this hospital, so he helped me get my current job, even though I had no experience in the area," she said.

Staff from clerks on up have their courses paid for and are allowed to schedule their hours to work around class times. As their educational levels increase their supervisors help direct them into new jobs to take advantage of their increasing knowledge.

Of course, no organization is perfect, and even at Mount Sinai some supervisors are less accommodating than others. But even employees who had run into problems with individual supervisors felt that, as one nurse put it, "If you are interested and wish to pursue things, the opportunity is there".

Mount Sinai also recognizes that to get the best from its staff it must ensure that their personal needs are met so that there is no needless stress interfering with work.

A head nurse who had problems with her nanny was given the opportunity to get things straightened out at home and greater flexibility in her hours to avoid a recurrence of the problem.

The Director of Public Relations, Jodi MacPherson, had a baby and soon afterwards a set of twins, shortly after joining the hospital. She was amazed by the reactions she got when she announced the pregnancies. Both times "the chief operating officer was genuinely pleased, not upset," she marvelled. Her doctor ordered her to go on complete bed rest 24 weeks into the second pregnancy. "They were more concerned with my health," she said, than with any impact the disruption would have on the hospital. She quickly got bored in bed, and "they saved me" by providing a fax machine and the other equipment she needed so she could work from her bed. "It kept me sane," she said, and at the same time the hospital was still able to benefit from her expertise and have the time to train others to cover for her during her eventual maternity leave.

Since the birth of the twins she has worked a four-day week, with a lot of flexibility in when and where she gets the work done. "I put in a lot of hours," she said, "but I can spend time with my kids and still do my job well."

The hospital trusts its employees and values their opinions. Commenting on this, one employee noted that even when she was at the clerical level she was consulted about the physical layout of her work space. When the hospital was investigating new computer systems she travelled with the President, the Vice-President, Finance, and other senior hospital officials to study the systems in place at other hospitals. "I was never left out of the decision making process," she said.

The ward clerk who had gone travelling for six months did decide to become a nurse, and was able to schedule her hours around her class times. The injured housekeeper is enjoying her work as a secretary, and also works in the gift shop to support her son, who she is raising alone. "They knew I was coming from housekeeping," she said, "but they didn't treat me with any less respect. I'm supposed to start at eight, but I'm always there at seven. I also often work through lunch, but if I need a day off, there is no problem. They recognize and appreciate my work."

Mount Sinai Hospital
600 University Avenue, Toronto, ON, M5G 1X5
Telephone: (416) 596-4200

	Total	No. of Women	% Women
Full-time employees	1,672	1,291	77%
Part-time employees	772[a]	681	88%
Board members	54	11	20%

Job category (figures based on full-time employees, unless noted otherwise):

Upper level managers	10	7	70%
Middle or other managers	96	70	73%
Professionals	896	760	85%
Semi-prof & technicians	120	70	58%
Supervisors	37	25	68%
Foremen/women	0	0	0%
Clerical workers	266	240	90%
Sales workers	0	0	0%
Service workers	0	0	0%
Skilled crafts & trades workers	18	0	0%
Semi-skilled manual workers	17	2	12%
Other manual workers	212	117	55%

Percentage of full-time employees considered upper level managers:	0.60%
Top-up of U.I.C. during maternity leave:	good
On-site daycare centre?	yes
Child/elder care referral service?	no
Employment equity rep. reports to CEO/President?	no
Target numbers for women in management?	no
Pay equity policy?	yes
Employment equity policy?	no
Mentoring program?	no

Noteworthy benefits:
- pre-paid leave program
- on-site fitness classes

Part-time employee benefits:
- get 12-14% of regular hourly rate in lieu of benefits (and 4-12% for vacation pay)

Notes: (a) includes casual staff

St. Elizabeth Visiting Nurses Association of Ontario

Founded in 1908, the St. Elizabeth Visiting Nurses Association is one of the major providers of home nursing care in Ontario. Staff include registered nurses, registered nursing assistants (called registered practical nurses in some jurisdictions), homemakers and health care aides. The bulk of the organization's work consists of home visits by nursing staff. It also has a "shift nursing" service, which provides continuous care by the same in-home nurse or nursing assistant for several hours in a row. It is a non-profit organization, whose funding comes mainly from the provincial government, but also from donations and fees paid by some clients.

There's an almost missionary zeal to the women who work at St. Elizabeth Visiting Nurses Association. One employee explained it this way: "As a student at Seneca College I went out with a St. Elizabeth nurse for a morning and that's all it took. One morning with this magnificent nurse who showed me that you could touch a child in a way that would take away the fear when she was having an injection, deal with dying patients with the most sensitivity I have ever seen, and really enjoy what you were doing. St. Elizabeth has a rule that you have to work for two years after you leave school before they'll hire you. Those were the longest two years of my life."

The wait was worth it. Fourteen years later she is still there and still convinced that "St. Elizabeth is the best way to be the greatest professional you can be".

The four women who have led St. Elizabeth through its 86-year history have given it the stability and closeness of a family; the drive and energy of a winning team. The result is a group of women so committed that even long working hours and relatively low pay have not dampened their enthusiasm and team spirit.

Many of the employees chose St. Elizabeth over its competitors because of a warmth and caring that was evident even in their job interviews.

"I'd been in the country for four years," said one woman, who is a member of a visible minority group. "This was the first place where I had a real interview. They actually wanted to know you." A registered practical nurse (RPN) turned down a full-time job elsewhere to work at St. Elizabeth part-time "because of the way I felt after the interview". A nurse who is now a manager contrasted her two-hour interview at St. Elizabeth to a 15-minute one at a competitor and reached the same conclusion.

The genuine interest even in potential employees is a conscious part of St. Elizabeth's human resources strategy. Only candidates who seem to share the organization's values are hired.

Once in the door, new nurses and nursing assistants are integrated quickly with the help of a six-week preceptorship program. New hires are paired with an experienced visiting nurse who has volunteered and been specially trained to be a preceptor. During the six weeks the new staff move from joining the preceptor on her rounds and observing how she works, to caring for the patients together, to the preceptor observing while the new nurse does the care. Then, for a few days, the new nurse will care for some of the preceptor's patients on her own, and the preceptor will get feedback from the patients and from the new nurse as to how she did. The preceptors typically stay friends and mentors to those who were paired with them.

Mentoring seems to be an ingrained part of the organization's culture. Sometimes the talents of an employee will be spotted by others and she will be encouraged to apply for progressively senior positions. Other times, the employee herself will ask for more responsibility.

"When I told my manager that I was interested in management," said one woman who had been a visiting nurse for years, "I was asked to help her do things and given a range of experience that would help me make the move." She was soon asked to fill in for a district manager who was on a maternity leave, and, at the time of the interview for this book, was poised for a permanent move into management.

Whenever possible employees are promoted from within. Since most nurses in Canada are women, this explains why seven of the eight senior management positions and all of the middle management positions are held by women. (The only man in senior management is the Vice-President, Finance/Administration.) Employees are encouraged to come up with new ideas and to try to implement them. This helps management spot those with management potential and keeps staff motivated and challenged.

A district manager who was feeling the need for a new challenge was offered a chance to spend a year working in public relations. St. Elizabeth paid for her to take university courses in public relations and marketing. Another one was seconded twice to work on special projects developing new services, and has since moved into a newly created marketing and fund-raising position that grew out of the second project.

The organization prefers to take people who know the front lines well and train them for management specialties, rather than bring in outsiders who have little real understanding of the operation. That approach, combined with active staff committees, ensures fast, open communication between management and staff, and has given St. Elizabeth tremendous market responsiveness. This has been key to its rapid growth, which continued throughout the recession, and to its ability to avoid deficits at a time of shrinking government funding.

St. Elizabeth has also been able to stay lean and efficient by making good use of part-time work. "The Association is very supportive in allowing you to work around bringing up a family," said a supervisor who has been with St. Elizabeth for 18 years. She had started part-time and got her first experience in management while filling in for a woman on a maternity leave. Others switch to part-time while working full-time on university degrees.

St. Elizabeth was one of the first organizations to let nurses job-share, which it has done since 1983. The job-share partners each work 50% of a standard job, and they split vacations and benefits evenly. It is up to them how they schedule their time: they can alternate days, weeks or even months. The organization also has what it calls four-fifths positions, where a nurse works four days instead of five but has her own caseload and gets benefits (some pro-rated to 80%) instead of the pay in lieu of benefits given to part-timers.

The flexible working arrangements are not only used by mothers. Further education is encouraged, and a bursary system helps defray some of the expenses. Every effort is made to adapt work schedules to fit school timetables. Several of the women on one team were taking Tuesdays off to get their community health certificates. One manager took every Friday off for $2\frac{1}{2}$ years while she did a master's degree. "My colleagues picked up the slack for me," she said, while noting that their support inspired even greater commitment from her. "St. Elizabeth is a lifestyle. You are recognized for hard work, and there is a respect and loyalty that goes both ways."

St. Elizabeth provides for personal and professional development in other ways too. It encourages its employees to go on work-related courses and seminars and has sent some nurses on specialty training. It recently developed a mental health program that helps clients who have or are recovering from psychiatric illnesses make the transition back into the community. Staff who were interested in working on the mental health team, including a part-time employee, were sent on a $2\frac{1}{2}$ month training program at the Clarke Institute of Psychiatry.

Employees are also encouraged to get involved in outside community organizations. This helps staff develop personally and helps the organization attain a higher profile and a good network of contacts in the communities it serves.

Being a part of the community — both the wider community in which it finds its clients, and the narrower community of St. Elizabeth Visiting Nurses — is the major attraction of this organization to its employees. They became nurses to work with people and to help people, and they feel that St. Elizabeth gives them a wonderful opportunity to do both.

St. Elizabeth Visiting Nurses Association of Ontario
10 Gateway Blvd., Suite 650, Don Mills, ON, M3C 3A1
Telephone: (416) 429-0112

	Total	No. of Women	% Women
Full-time employees	285	279	98%
Part-time employees	516	500	97%
Board members	15	8	53%

Job category (figures based on full-time employees, unless noted otherwise):

Upper level managers	8	7	88%
Middle or other managers	15	15	100%
Professionals	215	214	100%
Semi-professionals & technicians	0	0	0%
Supervisors	0	0	0%
Foremen/women	0	0	0%
Clerical workers	47	43	91%
Sales workers	0	0	0%
Service workers	0	0	0%
Skilled crafts & trades workers	0	0	0%
Semi-skilled manual workers	0	0	0%
Other manual workers	0	0	0%

Percentage of full-time employees considered upper level managers:	2.81%
Top-up of U.I.C. during maternity leave:	none
On-site daycare centre?	no
Child/elder care referral service?	no
Employment equity rep. reports to CEO/President?	yes
Target numbers for women in management?	no
Pay equity policy?	yes
Employment equity policy?	no
Mentoring program?	yes

Noteworthy benefits:
Part-time employee benefits:
- paid 10.5% to 12.5% of salary in lieu of benefits
- may join pension plan after 1,500 hours' service

HOSPITALITY SERVICES

Canadian Pacific Hotels & Resorts

Canadian Pacific Hotels & Resorts (CPH&R) owns 26 hotels and resorts across Canada. They include well-known hotels such as The Empress, in Victoria; the Banff Springs Hotel, in Banff; The Royal York Hotel, in Toronto; Le Chateau Frontenac, in Quebec City; the Hotel Beausejour, in Moncton; The Prince Edward, in Charlotte-town; the Chateau Halifax, in Halifax; and the Hotel Newfoundland, in St. John's. Approximately half its employees are unionized.

Employees from Vancouver to Toronto insisted in interviews that "CP Hotels & Resorts is *the* best chain in Canada." That pride stems partly from the chain's ability to keep a small company feeling despite its size. Employees move around the country a lot so they get to know each other. It gives them a sense of working in a closely knit team rather than in isolated hotels.

Management and supervisory jobs are posted across the country unless an internal candidate is being groomed for the position, and moving from one hotel to the next gives employees a breadth of experience that the chain feels is important as people rise through the ranks. As a result, said one employee who has worked at several of the hotels, "I've found a really good support network through the company". That's just as well, because it is almost impossible to combine that sort of movement with having a family. "I don't own property and I'm not married," she said.

Employees also meet each other on training courses. "This company is interested in developing employees on a continuous basis," said one manager, "and they realize that when things are in a low-morale period it is important not to pull back." Even when sales are down, courses and team-building events like Christmas parties go ahead as usual.

Training focuses on the importance of people skills, which also weigh heavily in hiring and promotion decisions. As a result, the chain has many supportive supervisors who are flexible in meeting employees' needs. One manager, for example, worked a four-day week temporarily and did much of her work from home to keep her terminally ill mother out of hospital. It is not just senior managers who benefit from such flexibility. An apprentice chef who had only been on staff for a few months was given seven weeks off to participate in a culinary tour of Italy.

The company is experimenting with alternative working arrangements, but the 24-hour-a-day nature of the business means that shift work and odd hours are inevitable for many workers. "I know when I start!" said the apprentice chef, but ending times are unpredictable. Parents find it a difficult balancing act, and even single people find their social lives curtailed. "I'm married to a very large, grey building," said one of them.

Nevertheless, when two human resources managers in Vancouver proposed job-sharing, the company was willing to give it a try. They each work three days a week. The day of overlap ensures that nothing falls between the cracks. The company feels that the extra cost of that day and of giving them each full benefits is worthwhile because it benefits from the expertise of two professionals instead of one, and there is always coverage should one of them be absent. The job-sharers think they are more productive working three days a week than they would be working full-time. They work closely with an assistant, who had filled in for them during their maternity leaves, so, as one of them explained it, "The department heads view our department as having three people they can talk to". The job-sharers participate in a management incentive (bonus) program on a pro-rated basis.

The job-sharing trial has raised hopes for many others who are eager to strike a better balance between their work and personal lives. A few are now working reduced work weeks, but they still find that they are carrying a full workload. One woman who is officially working three days a week acknowledged that she is really condensing the same job into less time, for less pay. She wastes no time in the office and works from home with the help of a fax machine and a modem. She also comes in for meetings on her days off. Another employee, who would like to be able to do more work from home, felt that the idea had not yet been accepted. "They are afraid to start something," she said.

The difficulties of hours and travel may be one reason why the large numbers of female graduates from hospitality management programs are not reflected in the numbers of women in management in the industry. CPH&R is making good progress in changing that pattern. The percentage of its women in middle management is roughly the same as the percentage of its female full-time employees. Two of its hotels are now run by women. The Royal York Hotel hired its first female head of catering in 1990. She had the challenge of replacing a man who had been in that department for fifty years and who insisted on staying there for another six months to assure himself that she knew what she was doing!

She noted that now half the Royal York's executive committee is female; a dramatic shift during her four years with the hotel.

CPH&R has also made progress in getting women into other traditionally male areas of the hotel industry. A beverage supervisor, for example, commented that while hers is a physically demanding job, involving lifting beer and liquor cases and moving portable bars, "It doesn't take as strong a person as you would think to do it. It is not true that to do a physical job you have to be strong."

The first female bellperson at one of the hotels said that she enjoyed the physical aspect of the job, which involves carrying luggage. Once she had proved to her co-workers that she could do it, most of them accepted her presence. As to the clients, "I've had good reactions, especially from female guests".

Senior management of the chain recognizes that it needs to support the women who are breaking down the barriers. Women still face traditional attitudes and need strategies for dealing with them. Said one, "You just have to put your foot down. They'll push you as far as they can. It's up to you to push back". Another woman took a softer approach: "Sometimes you have to give them a gentle reminder".

Discussions like that take place at CPH&R's quarterly Women in Management meetings. "Women in Management" is a networking group set up to support women in management in the chain and to provide role models for women graduating from hospitality schools. Company support enables the group to bring in high-profile speakers. In October, 1993, it linked into a live, satellite-run conference on working women put on by the American Management Association. Its members particularly appreciate the networking opportunities the group provides. "Men network with things like sports," said one manager, "Now I feel that I can call these women and ask them a question." Women in Management was launched in Ontario, but it has offered to help other regions wanting to set up similar groups.

The hospitality industry does not pay well compared to many other industries, but it has some nice fringe benefits, like free or deeply discounted room, food and beverage rates for staff and their families. CPH&R also rewards employees who bring group bookings to the chain by giving them a percentage of the revenues generated by their referrals. There are cash awards, ranging from $25 to $25,000, for employees who suggest ways to improve hotel operations. Long-service awards start with pins at three years and move into gifts at five years and beyond.

In an industry that tends to have high turnover, CPH&R gives out more long-service awards than most. It believes that keeping its employees happy and motivated is the key to success.

CP Hotels & Resorts
1 University Avenue, #1400, Toronto, ON, M5J 2P1
Telephone: (416) 367-7111

	Total	No. of Women	% Women
Full-time employees	7,464	3,082	41%
Part-time employees	2,230	1,085	49%
Board members	8	0	0%

Job category (figures based on full-time employees, unless noted otherwise):

	Total	No. of Women	% Women
Upper level managers	12	2	17%
Middle or other managers	637	267	42%
Professionals	0	0	0%
Semi-professionals & technicians	0	0	0%
Supervisors	636	249	39%
Foremen/women	0	0	0%
Clerical workers	335	290	87%
Sales workers	0	0	0%
Service workers	5,517	2,371	43%
Skilled crafts & trades workers	0	0	0%
Semi-skilled manual workers	0	0	0%
Other manual workers	0	0	0%

Percentage of full-time employees considered upper
   level managers: 0.16%
Top-up of U.I.C. during maternity leave: none
On-site daycare centre?   no
Child/elder care referral service?   no
Employment equity rep. reports to CEO/President?   no
Target numbers for women in management?   no[a]
Pay equity policy?   yes
Employment equity policy?   yes
Mentoring program?   no

Noteworthy benefits:
- free and discounted room, food and beverage rates across the chain
- rewards for group referrals
- awards for suggestions

Part-time employee benefits:
- some benefits pro-rated; pension plan available if have two years of service and have worked a minimum number of hours

Notes:
(a) target intake of 50% women into Career Development Program, but not numbers of women in managhement overall

Pan Pacific Hotel

The Pan Pacific Hotel is a five-star hotel located on Vancouver's waterfront. It has 506 rooms and is owned by the Tokyu Canada Corporation. Employees are not unionized.

"My friends think I'm crazy for the amount of time I put in here," sad a woman who started as a secretary at the Pan Pacific Hotel when it opened in January, 1986, and within a few years had worked her way into management.

She had been turned down for the management job the first time she applied, but the Director of Human Resources sat down with her to discuss why she had not got the job and what she needed to do to have a better chance the next time. She followed the director's advice and enrolled in a professional certification program. The company paid for her courses even though she was not working in the area of her studies.

The hotel industry, because of inevitable drawbacks like long, sometimes unpredictable, hours and weekend and night work tends to have a high rate of turnover. The Pan Pacific has turned this to its advantage by making it clear to employees that there is a lot of opportunity for growth and personal development. It is common to change jobs every six months and for staff to move through the ranks quickly.

One woman started at the hotel as a waitress after graduating from university. "I was really depressed," she said about starting as a waitress after four years of university, but she had always been interested in the hotel industry and that was the only job open at the time. The hotel management assured her that there would be many opportunities and, true to their word, she moved quickly through different areas. Five years, five promotions and one maternity leave later, she was enjoying an interesting management position.

Returning from maternity leave posed its own challenges. She decided she did not want to work full-time while the baby was young, and proposed job sharing. The hotel was uncomfortable with the idea but did let her try working four days a week during the summer, taking the fifth from her vacation time. By the end of the summer she was more convinced than ever that she wanted to work part-time. "It was the first time the hotel had done it and it was a big deal for them," she said, explaining why, after lengthy debates, she finally had to force the issue.

"I told them I was going to have to leave. I was not going to choose the hotel over my son. It was a very hard thing to do because I love the job. . . . I'm very, very happy where I am and I didn't want to give it up." After a lot of discussion, a three-day work week was approved.

Other employees watched the experiment eagerly. At the time of the interviews, another manager was trying to negotiate a four- day week but still facing a hesitant upper management. "The one area that is still a problem is maternity," said a long-time employee. "We do what we need to but not much beyond that."

Despite this frustration, with which senior management seems to be starting to grapple, the women at the Pan Pacific are fiercely loyal. Much of that loyalty is attributable to a strong team atmosphere, where employees at all levels have opportunities to get involved in the decision-making process and are given a high degree of autonomy.

An employee relations committee has representatives on it from all departments. Everyone can bring ideas or concerns forward through their committee representative and everyone sees the minutes of the committee meetings. Other committees are formed as needed to address specific tasks or issues. "The committees are really listened to," said one employee, "and you get feedback even if they can't do what you asked for."

An accountant, who had worked at other hotels before joining the Pan Pacific, said, "This has been the most enjoyable and rewarding job by far. . . . They treat you like you are an important part of the team". She and others particularly appreciated the company's educational subsidies and free, on-site courses, like one on public speaking. "You can take training just because of your own interest, even if your department won't benefit," said a manager. Since people switch jobs so often, the Hotel recognizes that it can benefit if it encourages staff to follow their interests and get training in other areas.

The Hotel recently offered English-language training during the slow season. The course attracted many employees, especially from areas like housekeeping. Housekeeping staff tend to be recent immigrants with minimal knowledge of English, with the result that they do not feel as much a part of the team. English-language training may help them become better integrated into the life of the hotel.

All employees also participate in a formal performance review twice a year. As part of the review process they indicate where in the hotel they would like to go next, and their supervisors discuss with them what they need to do to get there. A secretary who wanted to broaden her experience took a computer course at night. When she told her boss about her studies, her job was reorganized so that she could work on the team responsible for implementing a new computer system.

There are still some "old boy" attitudes, but the hotel has been creative and open in its staffing process. It is one of the few hotels to have a female operations manager (the second most senior position). Her appointment was doubly unusual because she did not have an operations background; she had originally been the hotel's director of human resources.

It has also had a female doorperson, a position that is generally one of the best paid in the industry, thanks to tips, and is an almost exclusively male domain. Hotel kitchens also still tend to be male-dominated, but, at the time of the interview, the Pan Pacific had a female sous-chef, two female senior chefs and several other women at more junior levels.

The women in male-dominated areas still felt that "You have to be a little bit more aggressive; you have to demand the respect". However they did not perceive any barriers to their advancement.

The company hires people who are assertive, professional and hardworking. A young woman who started as a hostess was quickly brought into a new project in which she was given broad cross-training and worked as a trouble-shooter in a newly opened restaurant. Her expertise was then put to use developing a training manual. "It was very hectic," she said, "I had no social life." But she clearly felt it was well worth the trade-offs.

Pan Pacific Hotel
#300-999 Canada Place, Vancouver, BC, V6C 3B5
Telephone: (604) 662-8111

	Total	No. of Women	% Women
Full-time employees	412	227	55%
Part-time employees	60	29	48%
Board members	6	2	33%

Job category (figures based on full-time employees, unless noted otherwise):

Upper level managers	6	2	33%
Middle or other managers	56	18	32%
Professionals	0	0	0%
Semi-professionals & technicians	0	0	0%
Supervisors	35	17	49%
Foremen/women	0	0	0%
Clerical workers	18	11	61%
Sales workers	8	6	75%
Service workers	289	144	50%
Skilled crafts & trades workers	0	0	0%
Semi-skilled manual workers	0	0	0%
Other manual workers	0	0	0%

Percentage of full-time employees considered upper level managers:	1.46%
Top-up of U.I.C. during maternity leave:	none
On-site daycare centre?	no
Child/elder care referral service?	yes
Employment equity rep. reports to CEO/President?	yes
Target numbers for women in management?	no
Pay equity policy?	no
Employment equity policy?	no
Mentoring program?	no

Noteworthy benefits:
- cultural exchange programs with Japan and Singapore. Of the 7 employees who had gone by early 1994, 5 were women

Part-time employee benefits:
- same benefits if work an average of 25+ hours/week

MANUFACTURING

Avon Canada Inc.

Avon is one of the world's largest cosmetics manufacturers and distributors. Its Canadian operation, which includes marketing, production and shipping facilities, was started in 1914 and is based in the Montreal suburb of Pointe-Claire. The products are sold by nearly 58,000 women to whom the comments below do not apply as they are not employees of Avon; they are independent dealers.

Avon's biggest strength as an employer is its ability to motivate its staff. Communication is excellent, and is aided by English- and French-language employee panels which meet directly with management four times a year to discuss issues of concern. Employees who are not on the panels also find senior management approachable. "The executives dine with the rest of us in the cafeteria every day," said a secretary who had been with the company for over 30 years.

Even junior employees feel included in decision making and are aware of how the company is doing. Bonuses and a profit-sharing plan are available to all employees, including part-time workers. The amount of the bonus increases with the length of service. "We know about the good and the bad," said one employee. "When we had a particularly good year they brought around champagne and we all celebrated."

To a large extent, the tone at Avon Canada was set by Christina Gold, who was its president until late 1993 when she moved on to oversee the entire North American operation. Her ascent from clerical ranks to the top of the company is legendary, and inspires confidence in others that they too can go as far as they want to go.

"If you are good," said a woman who worked her way up through 10 positions in as many years and bore three children in the process, "they open the doors for you. They ask you about your career aspirations in your performance evaluation, and I've been offered positions I never would have expected."

Others agreed, and also appreciated the flip-side: "If you want to advance at Avon, you can. If you want to slow down for a while, that's OK too," said a 20-year employee who had taken two maternity leaves, one of which was extended because her child had serious health problems. "They always look at the human side of things."

In looking at the human side, the company shows tremendous flexibility when people need time off to deal with personal problems, and offers a wide range of programs to support the emotional and physical well-being of its employees. Many of the company-sponsored courses and seminars are of particular interest to women, such as an annual, in-house clinic where gynaecologists and breast-cancer specialists are available to examine staff and discuss women's health concerns. It also offers self-defence, smoking cessation, weight loss, retirement planning and English and French language courses.

Where the company falls down is in failing to institutionalize some of the flexibility. "I would have liked to have had flex hours or have been able to job-share when my kids were small," said one employee. No flexible working arrangements exist at Avon. Such arrangements would involve subjective decisions about who could take advantage of them and the company is reluctant to provide options that cannot be applied uniformly.

The concern about uneven application of policies may not be unfounded. Even now employees commented, "A lot depends on your supervisor. . . . and there are some very chauvinistic men around here." The manufacturing plant, for example, while headed by a women, seems to be a man's world. "Men have more clout than women on the floor," said one employee who works in the plant. Another agreed. "It is still a boy's club, and advancement there is tough for women. Women do apply for non-traditional jobs, but they make them go through all these tests, to the point where they'll never get picked."

Even in the plant, though, working conditions are positive enough that many employees, male or female, stay for life. In fact, working at Avon is often a family tradition. "I started here as a student," said a 16-year employee. "My dad had been here for 35 years, so I knew a lot of the people through him." Another woman, who was about to enter her 40th year with the company, commented proudly that her daughter was now a manager with the firm and several of her family members had worked at Avon over the years. "Avon is a comfort-type of place," said one employee, explaining why she had stayed.

Avon Canada Inc.
5500 Trans-Canada Highway, Pointe Claire, PQ, H9R 1B6
Telephone: (514) 695-3371

	Total	No. of Women	% Women
Full-time employees	751	560	75%
Part-time employees	296	194	66%
Board members	5	2	40%

Job category (figures based on full-time employees, unless noted otherwise):

Upper level managers	17	8	47%
Middle or other managers	49	23	47%
Professionals	136	93	68%
Semi-professionals & technicians	16	14	88%
Supervisors	31[a]	13	42%
Foremen/women			
Clerical workers	147	131	89%
Sales workers	219	219	100%
Service workers	0	0	0%
Skilled crafts & trades workers	33	0	0%
Semi-skilled manual workers	103[b]	59	57%
Other manual workers			

Percentage of full-time employees considered upper level managers:	2.26%
Top-up of U.I.C. during maternity leave:	none
On-site daycare centre?	no
Child/elder care referral service?	no[c]
Employment equity rep. reports to CEO/President?	yes
Target numbers for women in management?	no
Pay equity policy?	no
Employment equity policy?	no
Mentoring program?	no

Noteworthy benefits:
 • educational assistance
 • discounts on Avon products
 • free travel medical assistance program (for personal and business travel)
Part-time employee benefits:
 • not eligible for dental and long-term disability
 • are eligible for end-of-year performance bonus
Notes: (a) includes foremen/women
   (b) includes other manual workers
   (c) employee assistance program includes general information on child and elder care

Cott Corporation

Cott is the largest bottler of private-label soft drinks in North America. In addition to its product development and manufacturing organization, it also owns Retail Brands International, a marketing consultancy, and The Watt Group, a graphic design firm. Cott's operations are based in the Toronto region, but it also has offices in the Montreal area, the United States and, through subsidiaries, elsewhere in Canada and internationally. It has grown rapidly in recent years, from $31 million in sales in 1989 to $665-million in the 1993-94 fiscal year. Cott has had a female president since mid-1992.

Cott is definitely not a company for wall-flowers. Rapid growth has meant that there are plenty of opportunities for people who are bright, hard-working, independent and not above a bit of self-promotion.

"You have to be confident in your abilities and speak up," said one woman who started as a receptionist, but within months had moved into management in the traditionally male domain of manufacturing. Others agreed. "You have to create your own opportunities," said a product manager, who missed the extensive training and development programs available at her previous employer. Another woman had learned the lesson the hard way: "I've had someone brought in over me when I could have done the job. They just assumed I was too busy; that I would not want it." Since then, "I've gone to my boss and the [head of her division] to say I need more, so that I have a sense of what is going on elsewhere in the company".

The lack of training was a concern for many of the employees. "They give you the opportunities, but not always the tools and training to back you up," said one manager. The company has grown so quickly that, rather than train and develop its own employees, it tends to fill vacancies from the outside. "They are afraid to move people who are doing a good job to a more senior job because of the retraining time," added the same manager. The company has recognized that this tendency has started to chip away at morale, and it recently hired a vice-president of human resources, who has as a top priority developing job descriptions so that it will be feasible to post jobs internally.

In the meantime, getting ahead is easier if you are close to the centre of power. The company is spread out over several sites so "being in the corporate office is an advantage. It gives you more visibility, and you are aware of the opportunities," said one manager. Otherwise, it is crucial that "you find yourself a mentor; you have to develop networks that tell you what opportunities are available".

A lot of the networking takes place late in the day. "There does seem to be a work ethic that takes you past five o'clock," said a support staff member. "After five p.m. is sometimes chat time." Since most employees are young, single and excited by their work, this is not a problem for them. They spend long hours at the office but there is a lot of flexibility in scheduling those hours. If someone has been putting in a lot of time on a big project or travelling, no one will look askance if they come in late or leave early the next day. People are trusted to get the job done and to know when to call it quits. "It is up to you to pick up your stuff and go home if you need a break," said one employee who travels a lot.

There are no set policies on flexible hours, but there are a few extreme examples of them. One woman, who is in an office supervisory role, works from 3:45 a.m to about 3:30 p.m., and has done so for the past nine years. She likes being able to get so much work done in the early hours when there are no interruptions. The supervisory aspects of her job are handled once the rest of the staff arrive.

Another woman, who breeds show horses, worked from 5:00 a.m. to 1:00 p.m. for a while so that she could ride her three horses before dark. It worked out well for the company since she was responsible for producing a report that had to be complete and on the managers' desks by 9:00 a.m.

The plant workers have less flexibility, as they work scheduled shifts, but, unlike the office staff, they are paid for overtime. Even in the plants there is a lot of flexibility if, for example, a family member is ill.

The company thinks of itself as family-oriented, and in times of personal crisis the message is definitely "family first". Cott organizes family-oriented events, like a group outing to the circus and a family picnic, and Heather Reisman, the president, writes in the corporate newsletter about the importance of balancing work and personal lives. Nevertheless, staff wonder how genuine the commitment is. Given the youth of the staff, it has not really been put to the test. Few women have become pregnant, and there are no precedents yet for options like job sharing.

One woman who had negotiated a phased-in return from her maternity leaves at The Watt Group before it was bought by Cott is still officially only working a four-day week, although "I'm on the phone constantly on the fifth day." She believes that the president's commitment is genuine. "They'd like me to work five days, but Heather was very supportive of my staying on four days." Other woman, though, worry that being of child-bearing age will make senior managers hesitate to promote them. When everybody is working so hard and the business is growing so fast it is natural for an employee to worry that she will be passed over for promotion if she is going to be absent for a few months.

Senior management seems genuinely interested in hearing about these and other employee concerns. Doug Anderson, the new Vice-President of Human Resources, commented that "Heather is the first boss I've had who has more books on organizational behaviour on her shelves than I do!" Cott has recently hired a manager of corporate communications to improve internal communications and help ensure that management hears about staff concerns before they explode into major problems.

The company is also exploring other ways to keep employees happy and motivated. A profit-sharing plan was introduced early in 1994. It not only provides for employee purchases of company stock (matched two-thirds by the company), but also grants options to every employee to buy 200 shares at a fixed price once the employee has been with the company for six months, and includes a one-time gift of shares to reward service prior to the profit-sharing plan having been introduced. All employees may participate in the plan.

None of the concerns raised by staff were explicitly gender related. There is no sense that anyone is held back because of being female. Being a woman may pose challenges when dealing with some customers or suppliers, but the company has not let that influence who gets the opportunity to tackle which assignments. A woman, for example, is working on developing Asian business. The company felt confident that she could overcome any cultural biases she might face. Generally, Cott seems open to any talent that thrusts itself forward, no matter how it is packaged.

Cott Corporation
207 Queens Quay West, Suite 800, Toronto, ON, M5J 1A7
Telephone: (416) 203-3898

	Total	No. of Women	% Women
Full-time employees	1,150	350	30%
Part-time employees	0[a]	0	0%
Board members	10	1	10%

Job category (figures based on full-time employees, unless noted otherwise):

Upper level managers	41	4	10%
Middle or other managers	87	20	23%
Professionals	40	22	55%
Semi-professionals & technicians	72	33	46%
Supervisors	45	11	24%
Foremen/women	0	0	0%
Clerical workers	117	108	92%
Sales workers	103	24	23%
Service workers	0	0	0%
Skilled crafts & trades workers	2	0	0%
Semi-skilled manual workers	42	12	29%
Other manual workers	601	117	19%

Percentage of full-time employees considered upper level managers:	3.57%
Top-up of U.I.C. during maternity leave:	none
On-site daycare centre?	no
Child/elder care referral service?	no
Employment equity rep. reports to CEO/President?	yes
Target numbers for women in management?	no
Pay equity policy?	no
Employment equity policy?	no
Mentoring program?	no

Noteworthy benefits:
- share purchase and share option plans

Part-time employee benefits:
- salary-related benefits pro-rated; no minimum number of hours to qualify

Notes: (a) data not available

Freda's Originals

Freda's Originals is a high-quality clothing design house which specializes in corporate attire. Major clients are in the financial services, transportation and government sectors. The Toronto-based manufacturer had annual sales in 1993 of nearly $4,000,000.

To be one of the best, an employer does not have to have a lot of formal policies. Thousands of Canadians work in firms employing fewer than 100 people, and these companies can be wonderful places to work. One such company is Freda's Originals. Freda Iordanous and her husband, Demos, came to Canada from Cyprus in 1971, when Freda was barely out of her teens. Soon after they arrived they started Freda's Originals, which quickly developed a market niche in high-quality uniforms.

Their customers range from the Bank of Montreal, for whom they design an optional line of clothing, to airlines like Canada 3000 and tourist attractions like Ontario Place, for whom they design staff uniforms. One of their most challenging projects to date was to design the outfits worn by 6,000 Expo '86 employees in Vancouver. Freda won that contract in a competition with 650 other designers. She ended up creating 100 designs and supplying 80,000 sets of clothing. The walls of Freda's 20,000-square-foot office and factory are lined with letters of appreciation from customers citing the quality and reliability of the company's work.

Freda also has a small showroom on the premises where she sells original fashions that incorporate fabrics and design details that would not be practical or affordable for uniforms. The showroom helps keep her in touch with the tastes and preferences of the people who end up wearing her clothes.

In 1991 Freda's won the Canada Award for Business Excellence in the small business category. The private sector jury was particularly impressed by the way Freda's created a niche market for its business fashion clothing.

The majority of the employees are female, which is typical in the fashion business. Freda's has a permanent staff of 52 full-time and 13 part-time employees, and a roster of others (accounting for about two per cent of its annual payroll) who work out of their homes when extra help is required. Before anyone is hired to work at home, they spend some time at the factory becoming familiar with the lines and demonstrating their own skills, to ensure their work is of a high enough standard.

When one thinks of the clothing trade, crowded sweatshops with huddled, underpaid immigrant workers may come to mind. The clean, brightly lit, comfortably air-conditioned room where Freda's employees cut, sew and press the clothes stands in stark contrast to that image. The atmosphere is relaxed and friendly. One presser jokes as she lines up little strips of cloth that it is "like baking cookies". And while Freda's certainly does hire immigrants, pay levels are at or slightly above industry norms.

Over and over again the words "It is like a family" come up in interviews. "Freda never says 'Do it'," says one sewing machine operator who has been with the company for 10 years. A colleague, who manages the company's store after having worked out of her own home for many years, adds, "She involves you in the business . . . 'Do you like that? Do you think people are going to like it?'."

This theme of respecting the views of employees came up over and over again. "You need to use your head", said one woman in the finishing department. "They ask our opinions", said another, who works in sales. When it comes to holiday schedules or coping with the workload, "We talk to each other and coordinate" who is doing what and when.

Freda and Demos's pride in the quality of their products is shared by the staff. One presser, who has been with the firm almost since it started 20 years ago, sees her job as not only pressing the garments, but doing a final screen to ensure that they meet the firm's quality standards. "I feel very comfortable here," she said, "They trust me, and I treat it like it was my own company. We are all professional here."

They take care in hiring to ensure that new hires fit with the firm's quality approach and familial atmosphere. "They make sure not to hire troublemakers" commented the presser; a line echoed by Freda. "We have people here from all nationalities," said Freda. What is important is to hire people who will work well with the others and meet the firm's high standards.

One of the sewing machine operators, in comparing Freda's to the firm where she had worked previously, felt that the avoidance of a piecework approach to pay was crucial to maintaining the quality standards and the cooperative atmosphere. However, employees' performance is measured daily, with a computerized tracking system that calculates each employee's efficiency (speed and non-rejections). Those who do particularly well receive bonuses, which are determined weekly. The employees did not seem troubled by the performance measurement system, and, while none mentioned the bonuses in discussing pay, several stressed their appreciation for the fact that "we are always paid on time" and that Freda will go to great lengths to try to avoid laying off staff.

One sewing machine operator had a sickly three-year-old son when she started. As a result, she had to be accessible to the child's care-giver. At her previous employer, she said, they would "just wait till 12 o'clock and give me the message. By then the boy would be burning in fever. . . . Here it is different". If there is a call for her she is paged right away. As a result, she said, "You don't worry so much. I can be relaxed. I know that if my son has a problem, I'll hear about it right away." Also, she said, "If you have a family and you need to take some hours off, they never, never go against it". Because the company shows concern for her, she reciprocates by feeling more committed to the firm and working harder.

These sentiments were echoed by another employee whose husband had been quite ill. "They were very cooperative with me. If I needed help in any way, even moneywise, . . . they were very understanding. . . . If I needed to go home it was no problem."

While it would be difficult to offer elaborate benefits while staying competitive, one employee commented, "She helps us any way she can. For example, with fabrics and patterns. Not every company gives its patterns to the employees. I can cut anything I want". Another added, "She wants us to feel good too, in her clothes". This concern for staff is rewarded by low turnover. Several of the employees have worked there since the firm was founded, and almost all have stayed over five years.

Said one employee, summing up the attitude at Freda's, "If you think that they care for you, you really care for them".

Freda's Originals
86 Bathurst Street, Toronto, ON, M5V 2P5
Telephone: (416) 366-0304

	Total	No. of Women	% Women
Full-time employees	65	58	89%
Part-time employees	13	12	92%
Board members	2	1	50%

Job category (figures based on full-time employees, unless noted otherwise):

Upper level managers	2	1	50%
Middle or other managers	4	3	75%
Professionals	1	0	0%
Semi-professionals & technicians	1	0	0%
Supervisors	2	2	100%
Foremen/women	4	3	75%
Clerical workers	3	3	100%
Sales workers	4	4	100%
Service workers	0	0	0%
Skilled crafts & trades workers	30	28	93%
Semi-skilled manual workers	4	4	100%
Other manual workers	10	10	100%

Percentage of full-time employees considered upper level managers:	3.08%
Top-up of U.I.C. during maternity leave:	none
On-site daycare centre?	no
Child/elder care referral service?	no
Employment equity rep. reports to CEO/President?	yes
Target numbers for women in management?	no
Pay equity policy?	yes
Employment equity policy?	no
Mentoring program?	yes

Noteworthy benefits:
• no benefits (apart from government-required programs, such as CPP)
Part-time employee benefits:
• n/a

Merck Frosst Canada Inc.

Merck Frosst is Canada's largest research-based pharmaceutical company. Its headquarters are in Kirkland, Quebec, and it has offices in Halifax, Quebec City, Ottawa, Toronto, Winnipeg, Edmonton, Calgary and Vancouver. Its research focuses on discovering, developing, manufacturing and selling medicines, over-the-counter drugs and other pharmaceutical products. Merck Frosst also makes and sells a range of products for animal health and agriculture.

Orders at "Annie's Take Out" service are booming these days. Annie Tougas was a member of the Work and Lifestyle Task Force Merck Frosst set up in April, 1993. It was her idea to have the cafeteria prepare pre-cooked dinners that employees could bring home with them and pop in the microwave for a fast reheating for dinner. The task force members, who were drawn from different parts of the company and varied personal backgrounds, had expected the service would appeal mostly to busy working mothers. They were surprised to find that an even bigger user group has been single employees.

Annie is getting tired of being known for what seemed like an obvious idea in retrospect, but it symbolizes the impact the employees themselves have had in making Merck Frosst a good place to work, especially for people who want to balance their work and personal lives.

Even before the task force, staff initiatives were already making a difference. "If you believe in something strongly," said one secretary, "get signatures to show management that you have peer support and the idea will be considered."

It was that sort of thinking that led to the creation of Merck's day care centre, which opened two years ago. Employees had the idea, researched the costs and demand for such a service, and made a convincing proposal to management. Persuaded, Merck subsidized the centre's construction to the tune of a million dollars and still provides about $100,000 a year for ongoing operations and capital costs. The 60 spaces filled almost immediately. Employees are active in running the centre.

One employee, whose son is in the day care centre, said its presence has had a spill-over effect on her entire department. "It changed the mentality. The day care closes at six. We no longer have as many meetings, they are not as late, and they are more productive."

Working parents feel far less stress thanks to initiatives like these. "This company has a lot of stress relievers," said one employee, and not just for parents. About 10% of the employees have used the company's employee assistance plan, many of them taking advantage of its recently launched elder care program. Stress management courses are available. Membership in approved fitness clubs is 85% paid for by the company, up to a maximum of $400 per year.

The aim of minimizing stress is just one aspect of the company's focus on people. It is also seen in who they hire, their support for education and career development, and a general flexible approach. One 34-year employee benefited from all three aspects of the Merck personality. "I had knocked on 50 doors before I got in here," she said. "I hardly spoke English. They gave me a chance." She started in the plant, but over the years she learned English and computer skills, and she now works as an executive secretary. She also raised two children during those years and says, "The attitudes are great!"

Despite the flexible and nurturing environment, there are still not many women in senior management or in most of the non-traditional fields. The company has set and is actively working towards targets for the numbers of women in most job categories, but low turnover makes for slow progress.

In some areas, the company is doing extremely well. The number of women in sales increased from 12% to 34% in the space of a year and a half of targeted recruiting. One woman, who was one of the first in technical sales at Merck, said, "It was a relief to come here. The sales people were not as macho as at my previous employer. Here we weren't tested or embarrassed. . . . I never felt treated any differently here because I was a woman."

An engineer working in building services, another traditionally male domain, noted that "15 to 20 per cent of the engineering grads are women, but nearly half the engineering staff in my department are women."

The company's focus on education and career development helps the women it hires move ahead. The company pays for tuition and books, and strongly encourages employees at all levels to pursue further education even when it may not be directly related to their current job. One woman, for example, started as a part-time translator. She decided to do a bachelor's degree in industrial relations, which the company financed. When she saw a posting for a job in human resources, "They took a chance on me". She has now been with the company for twenty years, and has moved steadily upward in the human resources department.

Many workers who started in clerical positions have, with the company's encouragement, completed university degrees and moved into more senior positions. Most jobs are posted, and "You are encouraged to keep trying, even if you don't get the job the first time," said a woman who started as a secretary and is now a senior financial analyst and nearing the end of her Bachelor of Commerce degree. Effort is rewarded.

The flip-side to the focus on education is that staff are now expected to have, or be working towards, a degree in order to move out of clerical jobs. This frustrates some long-service employees who feel that experience with the company should count for more than it does. "As a person with years of experience you'll end up training university graduates with no experience," said one.

Merck also offers many courses which are geared towards personal development. These include monthly "Power Breakfast" seminars which are held before work and typically draw about 150 employees, English and French language courses, and a three-day, off-site, pre-retirement course which is also open to spouses. The company is developing a learning centre that will have videos and tapes in French and English on a range of topics, such as stress management, financial management and personal health.

The company's flexible attitude helps employees find time for further education or whatever else is important to them. Flexible working hours and compressed work weeks have been formal options since the late 1980s. One woman started as a clerk-typist working three days a week, ten years ago. Four years later, after having had a second baby, she got divorced and could no longer afford to stay part-time. "My boss gave me a full-time job and encouraged me to go back to school. I started taking courses on my own, but he suggested a specific program." She is now half-way through a Bachelor of Science degree and is moving up the career ladder.

There are plans to introduce job sharing in the near future, and a pilot program of home-based, or "flexplace", work is under way in the translation department. Employees are eager to have a flexplace option. Many feel that they could accomplish more from home. Said one manager, "My most productive days are when my kids are sick, because I'm working from home".

The company is also flexible in how it handles maternity leaves. "When I was pregnant [nine years ago] I found that the company was quite open to my situation," said one manager. "I wanted to come back earlier than normal, but part-time. They agreed to let me do that. I took a total of six months instead of four, but about half of that was working part-time."

Pregnancy does not seem to harm career progress. One manager moved through five positions in six years and bore two children in the process.

Merck Frosst also wants to provide a physically pleasant working environment. "A lot of our capital projects are done to improve the quality of life of the employees," said a woman who works on such projects. Everyone from secretaries to researchers also spoke proudly of the "gorgeous" equipment the company provides. "The equipment here is top-of-the-line," said one employee, "and here they give you courses so you can learn how to use it!"

The result of all these initiatives: tremendous pride in working at Merck Frosst. The employees feel that company is committed to them, and they, in turn, are extremely committed to the company.

Merck Frosst Canada Inc.
16711 Route Transcanadienne, Kirkland, PQ, H9H 3L1
Telephone: (514) 428-7920

	Total	No. of Women	% Women
Full-time employees	1,136	464	41%
Part-time employees	132	68	52%
Board members	8	0	0%

Job category (figures based on full-time employees, unless noted otherwise):

Upper level managers	50	6	12%
Middle or other managers	142	37	26%
Professionals	246	99	40%
Semi-professionals & technicians	51	27	53%
Supervisors	17	6	35%
Foremen/women	20	3	15%
Clerical workers	168	149	89%
Sales workers	251	90	36%
Service workers	0	0	0%
Skilled crafts & trades workers	46	1	2%
Semi-skilled manual workers	45	4	9%
Other manual workers	100	42	42%

Percentage of full-time employees considered upper level managers:	4.40%
Top-up of U.I.C. during maternity leave:	none
On-site daycare centre?	yes
Child/elder care referral service?	yes
Employment equity rep. reports to CEO/President?	no
Target numbers for women in management?	yes
Pay equity policy?	yes
Employment equity policy?	yes
Mentoring program?	no

Noteworthy benefits:
• fitness subsidy
Part-time employee benefits:
• none

Calgary Herald

The Calgary Herald is one of two daily newspapers in Calgary, and one of 18 papers in the Southam Newspaper Group. Its average circulation is over 127,000 copies a day.

"We take the Herald for granted because we so often see what it could be at the expense of what it is," said a woman who has worked at many newspapers over the years, explaining why a visitor could easily get mixed messages about the paper from its staff. It has some problem areas for women, particularly in the editorial department, but on balance it seems to be one of the best newspapers in the country at which to work, for women and men.

An employee who was being funded by the Herald to pursue a management certificate at the University of Calgary noted that the Herald does a lot of the good things that she was learning about in her classes; things like giving employees autonomy and responsibility, encouraging self-improvement even when it is not directly related to the job, and letting staff at all levels talk with senior management at "brown bag" luncheon sessions.

Employees feel that the Publisher, Kevin Peterson, is the driving force behind many of the good things the Herald does for its employees. He has implemented several of the recommendations of the 1989 Southam Task Force on Women, including providing on-site day care (and continuing to support it, even during difficult economic times) and implementing a formal policy supporting alternative working arrangements. He intervened personally when he discovered that a sales representative was being sexually harassed by a client: he joined her on the next call to that client, and made it clear that he was prepared to lose the business if the harassment did not stop. It stopped.

He has also inspired other changes indirectly. For example, an off-the-cuff remark about women needing a "rent-a-mentor" led to the founding of a mentoring program by two female employees. Interested employees can volunteer to be mentors or ask to be mentored. They can even suggest who they would like to have as their mentor. Once the pairing is made, it is up to the individuals how they choose to run the arrangement. As of early 1994, 21 women were being mentored. One commented that her mentor helped give her insight into the corporate hierarchy, the decision-making process, how her actions were perceived by others, and how she could further her career.

The mentoring program is one way women at the Herald are hoping to overcome what they see as systemic barriers to the advancement of women into the senior management levels. Relative to other daily newspapers, the Calgary Herald has a good base of women from which to draw: a larger proportion of its total workforce is female than at the other newspapers responding to the survey for this book, and women are well represented among the management and professional ranks as well as in the sales force. Where they seem to hit a roadblock is in moving into senior management.

The Herald has two strong women in senior management: Catherine Ford, the Associate Editor, and Sharon Henwood, the Director of Marketing Resources. However, even they felt that there were unintentional forces making it difficult for women to get ahead at the paper. "In order to succeed in this business I suppose I took a naturally aggressive, domineering personality and sharpened it to a fine point," said Ms. Ford. "Nobody should have to be this aggressive in order to be successful. Natural feminine abilities, even if that in itself is a discriminatory statement, should be allowed to flower in any working environment. We shouldn't have to have a loud voice, be aggressive and play golf."

Other women on staff admire them but are not sure they either can or want to follow in their footsteps. "It would be good to see women go higher in the organization," said one employee, "but the women at the top are so tough; they are intimidating role models. I don't think I'm like that. It would be nice if they could maintain female attitudes rather than taking on male attitudes."

For the moment it seems that they cannot. "The only people these days who are allowed to be feminine are the men," said Ms. Ford. She and others noted that if a man leaves a meeting that is running late for household reasons, he is "showing his sensitive side"; if a woman does the same she is "not committed to her work".

The paper is still struggling to find the best way to overcome the barriers that seem to be keeping women from playing a larger role, particularly in the editorial department. Some of the senior men recognize that giving women more say in the content of the paper could help combat declining circulation, but there is not yet any agreement on how to give them that say.

The paper has experimented twice with reserving a job for a woman. The first was a sports writer position that was created specifically for a staff member who had already written sports articles for the paper. It was not posted. The other was a columnist. That position was posted, but the posting stated that it was for women only. That caused an uproar that extended beyond the newsroom, but it seemed to be the only way a women would ever be chosen. Explained Associate Editor Ford: "Their [men's] definition of news is much different, . . . what they want to read can be much different, so when you say you want a columnist and you have a male power structure picking the columnist, you are not going to pick someone who writes about a lot of soft issues. . . . There was a big, big backlash about that job posting, but at least it was honest. If we are not going to hire a man, why put some poor guy through a hiring panel when he's not going to get it? Why lie? Why pretend?"

The challenge is even greater given the difficult economic times. How do you introduce more women into the ranks while cutting staff? The economic squeeze has also meant that the pressure and time demands on staff are increasing. While some are able to take advantage of the alternative working arrangements, others find that overtime "is becoming an expected norm".

To a certain extent the pressure is relieved by an on-site fitness centre, an employee counselling program, and a lot of flexibility in dealing with crises such as sick family members. The day care centre also helps relieve stress, and not only for those whose children attend it. Explained one manager, "You're in a meeting and somebody's getting a bit hot under the collar and all of a sudden you see little kids walking by. . . . It breaks the tension".

There is some tension at the Calgary Herald these days, but there is also a lot of pride in working for an organization that cares about its employees and is trying to improve. Said one woman, "I came here from a horridly paternalistic, sexist organization. My goals for a new employer were that it be humanistic, people-oriented, and give me a sense that what I did was important". Several years later, the Calgary Herald still does.

Calgary Herald
P.O. Box 2400, Station "M", Calgary, AB, T2P 0W8
Telephone: (403) 235-7100

	Total	No. of Women	% Women
Full-time employees	583	229	39%
Part-time employees	206	117	57%
Board members	14[a]	2	14%

Job category (figures based on full-time employees, unless noted otherwise):

Upper level managers	10	2	20%
Middle or other managers	14	6	43%
Professionals	21	9	43%
Semi-professionals & technicians	134	36	27%
Supervisors	43	19	44%
Foremen/women	17	0	0%
Clerical workers	74	72	97%
Sales workers	85	53	62%
Service workers	14	14	100%
Skilled crafts & trades workers	160	22	14%
Semi-skilled manual workers	19	4	21%
Other manual workers	0	0	0%

Percentage of full-time employees considered upper level managers:	1.72%
Top-up of U.I.C. during maternity leave:	good
On-site daycare centre?	yes
Child/elder care referral service?	no
Employment equity rep. reports to CEO/President?	no
Target numbers for women in management?	no
Pay equity policy?	no
Employment equity policy?	no
Mentoring program?	yes

Noteworthy benefits:
- discounts on placing advertisements and announcements
- free newspapers
- one paid floater or personal day per year
- share purchase plan
- educational assistance; half the funds advanced upon approval of course, balance upon completion

Part-time employee benefits:
- pro-rated to hours worked; must work 20+ hours/week
- educational assistance plan pays 50% of tuition fees for part-time employees (vs. 100% for full-time employees)

Notes: (a) Southam Inc. board

Canadian Broadcasting Corporation (CBC)

The Canadian Broadcasting Corporation (CBC) was established by Parliament in 1936 to serve as Canada's national public broadcaster. Its English and French radio and television services reach about 99% of the Canadian population. It also broadcasts some programs in native languages and runs an international shortwave radio service.

Fran Cutler, the CBC's Manager of Employment Equity, started her career with CBC radio in 1964 as a producer of current affairs programs. She replaced a woman who had also replaced a woman. Ms. Cutler feels that the CBC, particularly on the radio side, has long been open to women in responsible positions. With the encouragement of many mentors, male and female, she worked her way through the production ranks and was appointed the Director of Radio Programming for CBC North in 1985.

Ms. Cutler insists that her experience was not unusual. "By no means was I a pioneer," she said. "During my 28 years in radio programming there were always lots of women in journalistic and managerial positions." That is true, but there was also plenty of room for improvement, which has taken place. For example:

- 214 women were in management and professional positions in December 1976, but they represented only 10.2% of the 2,099 managers and professionals on staff. The total number of managers and professionals in December of 1993 was almost the same (2,157) but 761 (or 35.3%) of them were women;
- the percentage of radio and television producers who were women increased from 16.7% in 1976 to 45% in 1993;
- the proportion of female announcers increased from 11.4% in 1976 to nearly 36% in 1991;
- the proportion of female journalists increased from 18.2% in 1976 to 40.6% in 1991;
- production, design and staging services were already nearly 30% female in 1976, but had increased to 46.5% female by 1993.

The CBC has done several things to improve the proportion of women in such jobs. It reviewed all its policies on hiring, promotion and termination, and is still reviewing other employment-related policies to ensure that none contain unintentional barriers to women. There is now at least one woman on every selection board for hiring and promotional decisions.

All senior managers include hiring and promotion targets for women in memoranda of understanding they sign with the President. Results are measured and reported quarterly.

The CBC has been active in outreach recruiting and has run training and apprenticeship programs to increase the representation of women in engineering and technical jobs, where their numbers are still low. For example, in 1992 the CBC worked with Toronto Women in Film and Television (TWIFT) and the federal government to give training workshops and job shadowing opportunities to women interested in lighting, camera and editing work. The workshops ran between April and October 1992. By the fall of 1992, 78% of the women who had completed the training were working in the industry. In early 1994 they sponsored three more courses; this time in video editing, production and story telling.

In the spring of 1993 the CBC resurrected a program that had been suspended for two years following major staff cutbacks. That program funds apprenticeships for women (and other under-represented groups) who want to work in areas such as reporting, production, research, and technical jobs. The apprenticeships typically last for two months to one year during which the trainees get on-the-job training, coaching and mentoring to help them compete when job vacancies arise.

As a result of efforts such as these, there have been substantial improvements even in those areas where female representation is still low. For example, the percentage of women in technical jobs increased from 2.1% in 1976 to 7.5% by 1993.

Unfortunately, at the same time as opportunities really started to open up for women, the CBC shifted to a contract orientation in hiring. As the figures in the chart show, over a quarter of the full-time employees are on "temporary" contracts. Half the contract workers are women, whereas women make up only 35% of the permanent full-time staff. These year-to-year contracts can last for a decade or more. While working conditions are similar to those of permanent employees, contract workers do not perceive themselves as having the job security of permanent employees, although many are offered work on other shows if the ones they have been working on are cancelled. They are not eligible for a company pension.

Few of the women interviewed had experienced any sexist behaviour but they did feel that there were less tangible factors impeding their progress, especially a lack of mentoring. The organization is so large and complex that it is difficult to figure out the informal rules and plan a career path without help. Many employees felt that success depends on having the right connections, and that men are more likely to be mentored than women. "It is frustrating to see them get mentored along whereas we are set to sea," said one woman. Another, who had benefited from good mentors during her years at CBC, also believed that being "part of the locker room set" helped some men get ahead.

Ironically, because men within the CBC are so aware of the Corporation's desire to be a good place for women to work, they are reluctant to give women even constructive criticism. "It is a problem," said one woman who worked in a non-traditional area, "You are told the job you are doing is okay even if it isn't." Said another, "I've never been told that I've done something wrong, but I know I've made mistakes. Men get hauled up on the carpet for their errors." Without adequate feedback women cannot learn as much and will not progress as far.

Several also felt that men got more support staff and equipment than women in comparable positions. Sometimes this was because men at comparable levels were more likely to have been recruited from outside, so they had more bargaining clout to start with. But many women also seem willing to cope with less support. "I know I'm only compounding the problem because I will come in at seven to get the job done," said one. "There is recognition if you do well," said another, "but it is harder for you to succeed because you are not given the same help or resources". Here too, mentors could help the women understand what support they should insist on before accepting a new job and advise them as to how to get it.

Long hours are common at the CBC, partly because many of the staff really enjoy their work and find it hard to pull back. The corporation's openness to long-term leaves helps prevent burn-out. Educational and special leaves for developmental experiences such as volunteer work or travel can be as long as two years. As far back as 1980, the special leave policy explicitly recognized employees' "dual role as CBC employees and as members of family groups", and allowed leaves to attend to family obligations.

Even so, many of the jobs at CBC are difficult to combine with having a family, and will be no matter what the organization does. As one former news reporter explained, "We all make choices. There is a rush to being a reporter. It is hard to give that up to be with a baby".

The hours of work are long and unpredictable, especially in technical and production jobs, and can involve long stretches of travel. Interestingly, even the male technicians have started reassessing their priorities. A growing number are taking parental leaves, turning down projects in order to have more time with their families, and considering options like job-sharing.

The organization is so large and diverse that the acceptance of flexible work arrangements varies wildly. Choices vary by job, by manager, by department and by city. There were 32 different unions and staff associations in 1993, so even the formal options available to employees varied. (Negotiations were under way in 1994 to cut the number of bargaining units dramatically.) When it comes to the informal, many employees said they had supportive managers who did not care when and where the work got done as long as it got done. Others faced rigidity. "Ultimately," said one employee, "it is your immediate boss who sets the tone."

Overall, the tone at the CBC is positive. Women have a wide array of interesting job options available to them as long as they learn to negotiate the maze.

Canadian Broadcasting Corporation
1500 Bronson Avenue, P.O. Box 8478, Ottawa, ON, K1G 3J5
Telephone: (613) 724-1200

	Total	No. of Women	% Women
Full-time employees	12,649[a]	4,940[b]	39%
Part-time employees	52	48	92%
Board members	15	3	20%

Job category (figures based on full-time employees, unless noted otherwise):[c]

Upper level managers	44	6	14%
Middle or other managers	584	133	23%
Professionals	1,744	580	33%
Semi-professionals & technicians	4,160	1,005	24%
Supervisors	84	32	38%
Foremen/women	119	4	3%
Clerical workers	1,631	1,243	76%
Sales workers	196	119	61%
Service workers	3	2	67%
Skilled crafts & trades workers	342	78	23%
Semi-skilled manual workers	304	23	8%
Other manual workers	27	12	44%

Percentage of full-time employees considered upper level managers:	0.35%
Top-up of U.I.C. during maternity leave:	good
On-site daycare centre?	no
Child/elder care referral service?	yes
Employment equity rep. reports to CEO/President?	no
Target numbers for women in management?	yes
Pay equity policy?	no
Employment equity policy?	yes
Mentoring program?	no

Noteworthy benefits:
Part-time employee benefits:
• pro-rated, if work 60% or more of a standard week
• eligible for pension plan
Notes:
    (a)   includes 9,238 permanent and 3,411 "temporary"
    (b)   includes 3,237 permanent and 1,703 "temporary"
    (c)   breakdowns based on permanent employees only

The Gazette

The Gazette is Montreal's only English-language daily newspaper. It is one of the 18 papers in the Southam Newspaper Group. Circulation is approximately 157,000 copies a day during the week, and 230,000 on Saturdays.

Women have been far more successful at The Gazette than at most newspapers, and they are well represented in much of the organization. Four of the 11 senior managers are women, and it is one of the few newspapers in Canada to have a female editor-in-chief. Women also make up a significant and growing number of the mid-management and professional positions.

Why are women doing better at The Gazette than elsewhere? There are three main reasons:

- there has been strong top-level support for promoting women;
- there is a commitment right from the top to having what one staff member called "a civilized environment";
- sincere efforts are being made to accommodate work and family balance.

Joan Fraser, the Editor-in-Chief, co-chaired the 1989 Southam Task Force on Women. Staff feel that she "has been very influential in creating a supportive environment" at The Gazette. That Task Force made 10 recommendations to Southam newspapers. The recommendations ranged from having the president of the Southam Newspaper Group circulate a strong policy statement supporting the role of women within the organization, to a controversial recommendation that became known as "broads for bucks": that the pay of publishers and senior managers be linked in part to their efforts and success in recruiting, developing and promoting women.

David Perks, who was the publisher of The Gazette at the time, was an outspoken supporter of this recommendation. He tried to implement it at The Gazette, although the proposal never took effect. While some women feel that their rise has been partly attributable to Southam's effort to promote women, they are also confident that they would not have got their jobs without the required skills and ability.

Management is committed to expanding the role of its women but "the rank and file has been much less supportive," according to one female staff member. Some areas remain male bastions, like the distribution side of the circulation department. "I've never had to put up with sexism here *except* from the guys in the circulation department," said one long-time employee.

Other areas, like advertising sales, have traditionally been more open to women, and are particularly so at The Gazette. "A lot of successful female sales reps have paved the way in our department," said a sales representative who had started four years earlier as a secretary. Results are measurable, so it is easy for women who are good at sales to prove themselves.

Part of the reason for the newspaper's commitment to getting women into senior positions may be to combat its falling circulation. Many North American newspapers are suffering from falling readership these days, but The Gazette has the added challenge of being an English language paper in a city whose English-speaking population is on the decline. Input from female staff members may help the paper appeal to a broader audience and reverse the loss in female readership. "As a result," said one member of the editorial staff, "now they are interested in hearing our views. In the past our contributions were more likely to have been ignored."

In addition to the editor-in-chief, several other key editors are women. The culture of the newsroom has changed dramatically during recent years. One former reporter said that in the past, "If you didn't go to the bar with the managing editor and the boys and bat your eyelashes and talk baseball, there was no room for you in the newsroom culture. That has completely disappeared."

Management's commitment to changing the traditional rough-and-tumble environment may be one reason why The Gazette's employee assistance program has never reported sexual harassment to be an issue in its general compilation of statistics on usage. "I am confident," said one employee, "that if there was a sexual harassment issue it would be dealt with fairly."

While there may no longer be overt sexism in the newsroom, it remains a difficult place for women wanting to combine motherhood and a career. "I don't think I could do my job if I had children," said one women who had worked her way up from a reporter to management ranks. Managers, male or female, need to put in long hours, and the normal route into their jobs is via the copy desk. That involves working nights in an area where women feel they are still not well accepted.

Nevertheless, most staff are positive about the attitudes towards combining work and family at The Gazette. It is one of the few newspapers to have a formal policy on alternate work arrangements, which include a reduced work day or week and job-sharing. "Anyone who wants to work a four-day week can," said one staff member, although there are rare occasions when such a request will be turned down for practical reasons. About half the classified staff are now on some form of reduced work week and several editorial staff work three-day weeks.

There is a flexible attitude towards hours at the paper, both on a daily basis and during times of personal crisis. The experience of one woman whose husband was very ill was typical. "The publisher and the director made it very clear that I should take all the time I needed," she said.

The Gazette is one of the few newspapers in Canada to top-up UIC payments during maternity leaves, and "women don't seem to be penalized for having kids," said one employee. It has taken a pragmatic approach to maternity leaves of management women. Rather than trying to replace or live without women during their maternity leaves, it rewards managers for staying in touch and doing some work from home.

Before going on a maternity leave, a manager negotiates an agreement with her manager under which she specifies what work she feels she can continue to do while on leave in exchange for a "return to work bonus". The bonus will top up her UIC benefits to 75 to 100% of her normal salary. The amount of the top-up depends on how much work she agrees to do. To qualify for the full 100%, she must receive her in-basket on a regular basis, take phone calls, be available to attend meetings, and generally deal with most of her normal workload. The company provides any needed equipment, such as fax machines, computers, and printers. If the manager finds that she committed herself to doing too much, she can revise the agreement and accept a lower bonus. If she asks that no contact be maintained during her leave she only gets the normal top-up, which is a flat 38% of the maximum UIC payment.

The Gazette also provides three floater days which can be used for personal reasons at any time of year and five winter break days which can be taken between November and May.

These policies, combined with the positive attitude of senior management and the leadership of strong women, make The Gazette a good place for women wanting to work in the newspaper industry.

The Gazette
250 St. Antoine West, Montreal, PQ, H2Y 3R7
Telephone: (514) 987-2222

	Total	No. of Women	% Women
Full-time employees	743	258	35%
Part-time employees	125	66	53%
Board members	14[a]	2	14%

Job category (figures based on full-time employees, unless noted otherwise):

Upper level managers	11	4	36%
Middle or other managers	31	10	32%
Professionals	136	39	29%
Semi-professionals & technicians	34	10	29%
Supervisors	83	20	24%
Foremen/women	20	0	0%
Clerical workers	143	112	78%
Sales workers	72	50	69%
Service workers	7	0	0%
Skilled crafts & trades workers	127	6	5%
Semi-skilled manual workers	0	0	0%
Other manual workers	79	7	9%

Percentage of full-time employees considered upper level managers:	1.48%
Top-up of U.I.C. during maternity leave:	average
On-site daycare centre?	no
Child/elder care referral service?	no
Employment equity rep. reports to CEO/President?	no
Target numbers for women in management?	no
Pay equity policy?	no
Employment equity policy?	no
Mentoring program?	no

Noteworthy benefits:
- 3 floater days
- 5 "winter break" days off between November and May; available to all but production staff, who have other days off set out in their agreement
- share purchase plan
- subsidized English and French language courses
- educational assistance
- Gazette discount card, for discounts on various goods and services
- free home delivery
- reduced rates on advertisements and announcements

Part-time employee benefits:
- if work 20+ hours/week, most of the same benefits except no paid vacation days, and no floater or winter break days
- may join pension plan after completing 700 hours of work or having earned 35% of the year's maximum pensionable earnings

Notes: (a) Southam Inc. board

OTHER SERVICES

Manpower Temporary Services

Manpower Temporary Services is an international company that supplies temporary workers to businesses. It has over 1,100 offices in 31 countries. In Canada there are more than 60 offices across the country, many of which are franchised. The information below is based on the Toronto-area franchise only, which covers much of southern Ontario. It does not apply to the temporary workers that Manpower places; they are independent contractors.

The federal government no longer uses the name "Manpower", but Manpower Temporary Services does. It has built a strong reputation for being a good employer for women; a reputation which it feels more than makes up for today's narrow connotations of the word manpower.

This is a field which has traditionally attracted women, but Manpower excels at promoting them into senior levels. The employees believe that Manpower has "a lot more female executives than others" in the industry, and that "even versus other Manpower franchises, the Toronto organization has a lot more women in management and upper management". Six of its eight senior executives are women, including the two vice-presidents, one of whom is responsible for operations and the other for finance and administration.

What draws so many promotable people to Manpower? Clearly not the pay. The industry as a whole does not pay well, and even many of Manpower's own employees believe that "the competition does pay significantly more." The low pay is partially compensated for by a bonus scheme, but in tough economic times that amounts to little, if anything.

The people-orientation of the work seems to be a major factor in what draws women to it. Manpower has also given its employees enough autonomy, combined with solid training, to give them a strong sense of ownership in their work.

"Sometimes I think, 'Am I nuts? This is not my business. What am I doing this for?'," said a branch manager. Yet, "I feel like it *is* my own business." Another employee, who works only three days a week officially but acknowledges that "they phone me constantly on Thursday and Friday", sees part of the attraction as being that "we are left on our own; there is nobody breathing down our necks. We make our own decisions about, for example, whether to reimburse a client [the company has a 100% satisfaction guarantee] or to pay a temp" in a questionable circumstance.

Others commented on the opportunity to learn and to grow as being strengths of Manpower. Many of the women who are now management employees started as temporary workers being placed by the company. "Manpower expects a lot from its employees," said an office manager. Added another manager, "The company made me do more than I ever thought I could".

Marv Goodman, the recently retired founder of Manpower's Toronto franchise "was a very good mentor and leader," said one employee, "but he's typical of the leadership of this company". His son, company President, Bob Goodman, has also been instrumental in making Manpower a good place for women. He is open to any suggestions employees have about things that might make the workplace better for them. For example, two branch managers approached him about the possibility of job sharing. He agreed to give it a try, and it worked out well.

One former branch manager said that when she sheepishly told Bob that she was pregnant with her third child since joining the organization, he replied, "I've always looked at maternity leave as an interruption, and believed that you are permanently committed. It is not a setback". This attitude is reflected by the fact that most employees do return after pregnancy (though some choose less demanding positions), and that many of the managers are now having babies. "The service reps are so well trained that they can fill in for us," said one manager. (The service representatives are the entry-level staff who screen and assign temporary workers to fill customer orders.) From the representatives' perspective, it gives them the opportunity to broaden their experience and hasten their progress into management.

Manpower employees also cited the company's excellent internal communication. Manpower has built a reputation on superb customer service. The notion that everybody has a customer, be it internal or external, has permeated the organization. "We have to give good customer service to each other," said one non-management employee. "We are a team," said another.

A weekly sales report goes out to all branches, fostering some internal competition, but other branches and head office staff are quick to congratulate those doing particularly well in a given week. "One good thing about working with other women," said one employee, "is that the communication is a lot better here, especially when you are doing a good job."

They feel that Manpower's systems and standards are second to none.

Staff are not on commission, so there is a strong sense of team-work and they feel that they can take the time to get to know the temporary workers and the clients well. "We spend two to three hours with each temp when we first hire them," said one. As a result, said another, "We develop a personal relationship with them, and a lot of loyalty builds up".

Employees also take pride in what they consider the firm's "integrity". It has an employment equity committee which works with outreach groups to try to train people from disadvantaged groups to be service representatives. It also works with clients to try to encourage them to overcome biases. Said one manager, who has worked in this industry for many years, "There is a lot of racism out there. We have to educate our clients (and ourselves) to overcome it."

As the sun set and the snowflakes fell outside the cramped boardroom where staff were being interviewed for the book, they could not stop talking about the many things they feel the company does right. Said one, "I live and breathe Manpower".

Manpower Temporary Services (Toronto) Ltd.
124 Eglinton Avenue West, 4th Floor, Toronto, ON, M4P 2H2
Telephone: (416) 480-1212

	Total	No. of Women	% Women
Full-time employees	89	82	92%
Part-time employees	10	10	100%
Board members	3	1	33%

Job category (figures based on full-time employees, unless noted otherwise):

Upper level managers	8	6	75%
Middle or other managers	22	20	91%
Professionals	0	0	0%
Semi-professionals & technicians	0	0	0%
Supervisors	2	2	100%
Foremen/women	0	0	0%
Clerical workers	9	8	89%
Sales workers	4	4	100%
Service workers	44	43	98%
Skilled crafts & trades workers	0	0	0%
Semi-skilled manual workers	0	0	0%
Other manual workers	0	0	0%

Percentage of full-time employees considered upper
    level managers: 8.99%
Top-up of U.I.C. during maternity leave: none
On-site daycare centre? no
Child/elder care referral service? no
Employment equity rep. reports to CEO/President? yes
Target numbers for women in management? no
Pay equity policy? no
Employment equity policy? no
Mentoring program? no

Noteworthy benefits:
Part-time employee benefits:
  • none (unless negotiated)

The Rider Group

The Rider Group, which was founded in 1982, specializes in the business travel market. It has 26 business offices across the country and another 80 locations at the offices of major clients, such as the federal government. Annual Canadian sales total more than $450 million. Ninety-eight per cent of those revenues come from the business travel side, but it has also expanded into travel-related software development, corporate communications and vacation travel services.

"Pure basic business instincts" are what convinced the senior management of The Rider Group to recognize, develop and promote female talent, according to one female manager with the company. The Rider Group more than doubled in size overnight when it got the contract to be the exclusive provider of travel services to the federal government in 1991. The Chairman, Mark Rider, and President, Scott Anderson, scrambled to find good managers to handle the new business and ended up promoting bright, assertive women quickly.

They found that there was a lot of female talent within their own company, and more available outside in the form of women with experience in other travel or hospitality firms. These women thrived on challenge and change, and were willing to work hard.

The Rider Group has recently realized there is another benefit to having women at the senior levels: more and more corporate and government clients comment favourably if they see women in positions of authority at the bidding table. The presence of senior women signals that the company is in tune with the times and not restricting its talent pool.

To some extent, the women in management selected themselves. Rider had a reputation for being aggressive and innovative. Most of the women who are in senior management today went after their positions with a vengeance. One woman who had a lot of experience in business travel contacted the company when she heard rumours that it would be expanding to her city. Company representatives met her and promptly hired her to open up the new office. When she felt that she needed a more senior position to get the job done properly, she asked for it, explaining why the promotion was necessary and in the company's best interests. She got it.

Another senior woman was offered a series of promotions by the chairman and the president, but, upon reflection, she acknowledged that they were not just handed to her. "I was vocal," she said.

The employees at every level are Type 'A' personalities: driven, assertive, energetic, and highly career-motivated. They work long hours. They think and talk about work even when they are not there. Even junior employees call in regularly while they are on vacation.

What appeals to them about the company is its energy: the excitement and opportunities of growth. The company is young, and it is staffed with young people. Innovation and creativity are encouraged. "This is not a company where you get a lot of direction," said one manager. "It is geared towards self-starters. If you've got an idea, don't ask — just go do it."

Women at the entry levels felt the same sense of opportunity. "There are always lots of positions available you can go for," said one woman who had started in the mail room but quickly moved through other areas of the company. "Human Resources keeps us well informed [most jobs are posted internally], and you also end up talking to a lot of people."

Apart from formal job postings, the rapid growth makes it possible to expand and restructure jobs to match the strengths of the people filling them. "Whatever you enjoy doing," said one employee who had been with the company for less than a year, "you can move into it and focus on it."

On the other hand, while lateral opportunities are good at the junior levels, those employees did feel a barrier blocking them from management. With the rapid burst of growth in the early nineties the company had hired a lot of managers and perhaps not enough people to support them. As a result, support staff are desperately needed in the support roles, and there are not many openings at junior levels of management. If a new manager is going to be hired, the company looks for someone who will bring outside experience or academic qualifications to the job. Senior management recognizes that this hurts morale and has started working on ways to identify and develop in-house talent.

Despite this frustration, morale is reinforced continually with staff social events like pub crawls and baseball outings, and reward programs. Staff are nominated from each department for a monthly "I Made A Difference Award". Winners are those who "have gone above and beyond the call of duty, shown a positive attitude and contagious working spirit, had an individual and/or team achievement, shown excellence in customer service, or improved upon past performance". Winners have a trophy on their desk for a month and their names are added to a plaque. Occasional travel rewards help compensate for the low pay, which is comparable to that at other firms in the travel industry.

Staff also appreciate the lack of bureaucracy. "I can go ask people at my level or above for help. People don't say, 'That's not my job'," said a secretary who finds that she is constantly being asked to take on new roles.

There are enough women in senior roles to have a big impact. They are looked to by the junior women as role models, and within their own ranks they appreciate that "there is no more female bravado. The women here have become more supportive of one another. We are getting to the point where you can flub something," said one of them.

Others felt that might be going a bit far. They can open up and bounce ideas and concerns off each other, but most still feel that, when it comes to dealings with the men, "you can't show a chink in your armour".

It is not yet clear whether those suits of armour come in maternity size. One manager had just been approached about moving into a new, more senior position when she realized she was pregnant. "I thought, 'Oh god, how am I going to tell the men at work?'. I finally got my nerve up . . . and I gave them the option of not giving me the new position." The reaction was a pleasant surprise. "It didn't make any difference; we are just planning around it. . . . Even Mark Rider said, 'I think that's great!'"

She spread the word to other employees, because there are still lingering fears among management women about how pregnancies will be perceived. Those who have been there for a few years say that the reaction she got was definitely a change from the past, but they felt the attitude change was a genuine one. From a purely business perspective, it does not make sense to lose talented women for the sake of a few months' maternity leave. And, for the moment, that really is all that is at stake. Everyone is scrambling so hard to keep up with the rapid growth that no one would think seriously about requesting a shorter work week or an extended leave, except in dire circumstances. Those who do have children are sure not to let them interfere at all with their work. "I had worked with [a female manager] for two years and I never even knew she had a child," said one support staff member.

Attitudes are improving, but The Rider Group is still far from being a 'family-friendly' workplace. Balancing work and personal lives is not part of the culture. However, women who are ambitious and self-confident, who love a fast pace with lots of change and innovation, will find exciting opportunities at The Rider Group.

The Rider Group
370 King Street West, Suite 700, Toronto, ON, M5V 1J9
Telephone: (416) 593-8866

	Total	No. of Women	% Women
Full-time employees	600	480	80%
Part-time employees	30	15	50%
Board members	0	0	0%

Job category (figures based on full-time employees, unless noted otherwise):

Upper level managers	18	4	22%
Middle or other managers	52	37	71%
Professionals	10	3	30%
Semi-professionals & technicians	25	5	20%
Supervisors	30	25	83%
Foremen/women	0	0	0%
Clerical workers	100	80	80%
Sales workers	16	10	63%
Service workers	30	24	80%
Skilled crafts & trades workers	330[a]	300	91%
Semi-skilled manual workers	0	0	0%
Other manual workers	0	0	0%

Percentage of full-time employees considered upper level managers:	3.00%
Top-up of U.I.C. during maternity leave:	none
On-site daycare centre?	no
Child/elder care referral service?	no
Employment equity rep. reports to CEO/President?	no
Target numbers for women in management?	no
Pay equity policy?	no
Employment equity policy?	yes
Mentoring program?	no

Noteworthy benefits:
Part-time employee benefits:
- must work 15+ hours/week to get health benefits; others pro-rated to number of hours worked

Notes: (a) consists of counsellors, ticketing staff, couriers, and accounting staff

PROFESSIONAL SERVICES

Price Waterhouse

With 25 offices from Halifax to Vancouver, Price Waterhouse is one of Canada's largest professional services firms of chartered accountants and business advisors. It offers a full range of services in audit, taxation, corporate finance, corporate recovery, valuations, litigation support, and management consulting.

More than half the entry-level professional staff members hired by Price Waterhouse since the early eighties have been women, but a disproportionate number of them leave the firm before becoming partners. Price Waterhouse recognized the problem of high female attrition rates as early as 1988 and set up a task force on Family and Lifestyle Programs and Policies to address it.

As a result of that task force's report, the firm improved its maternity benefits and introduced two flexible work programs in 1989: part-time, under which professional staff at the managerial level and above could work as little as 60% of a full-time schedule (plus proportionate overtime); and core hours, which allowed those same levels of staff to limit their office hours to 10:00 a.m. to 4:00 p.m., and do the balance of their work from home.

About 100 women, particularly those with young children, seized the opportunity to work part-time, and a few opted for core hours. But by 1992 the firm was still losing a lot of talented women, and the number of women at the senior levels was still low compared with many other accounting firms. It hired outside consultants to interview 32 highly rated women who had quit the firm, to find out why. It also held focus group discussions with female employees and undertook a nation-wide survey of staff attitudes.

As a result of that input, a three-year plan was approved by the management committee in 1993, and audit partner Brenda Vince was named Partner Responsible for Women's Initiatives. Chairman Bob Brown pointed out in a special newsletter announcing the program that "Women's initiatives are becoming a business imperative for the 1990s [particularly] when you consider that as many women as men are attracted to our profession and more and more women are entering the most senior ranks of our clients".

The three-year plan includes:

- launching a child and elder care referral service (introduced in early 1994);
- implementing a new staff appraisal program that links every employee with a "development counsellor", in the hopes of fostering more mentoring (announced in late 1993);
- providing gender awareness and sensitivity training to partners, and incorporating such training into the management training program (a seminar was pilot-tested with Vancouver office partners in 1993 and is being introduced in the rest of the firm);
- giving managers better guidance about how to work with flexible work options;
- setting up a process for routine, independent interviews of all highly rated women who leave the firm;
- developing better procedures and policies for dealing with sexual harassment;
- conducting annual staff opinion surveys to monitor progress (the first survey was held in the fall of 1993).

The reactions of men in the firm to the announcement of the Women's Initiatives were mixed. "Some were surprised that there was an issue," said a manager from the Vancouver office.

The firm's few female partners are aware of being role models, and some see themselves as advocates for women in the firm. One of them, Kathleen O'Neill, joined the firm in 1975. She was not happy with how things were going when she returned to work following the birth of her first child in 1981, so she left. The firm did not want to lose her, and in 1983 she negotiated a return on a four-day-a-week basis. She had two more children, and in 1988, with the help of a powerful mentor, she was the first person to be promoted to partner while working part-time. She had a fourth child the next year and continued to work four days a week until late 1993, when she felt ready to return to full-time work.

"Having more women, especially female partners, has led to a significant change in attitude," she said. "We are starting to realize that it is important to work *effectively*, not just to focus on hours."

There is a changing tone at partner's meetings; they are no longer as socially oriented. "They think twice now about going to strip clubs [after meetings]," said one partner. "Maybe a lot of men felt uncomfortable with the game too." And, while a few clients still resist dealing with female partners, a growing number want to hear that the firm is recognizing and promoting talented women.

The women trying to work their way up to the partner level still have to be outstanding compared to some of the men who make it. "It is not yet true that an 'average' woman can do as well as an 'average' man," said one senior employee. "An 'average' man can compensate by working a lot of overtime, but many women don't have the time. Also, a lot of 'average' men have had good mentors, whereas the women haven't."

Nevertheless, as attitudes improve, more women are staying beyond entry levels and reaching the age where they can no longer put off having children if they want to have any. The women having babies now are confident that maternity leaves will not harm their career progression. They are less certain about the impact of working part-time. The company's handbook on the flexible work options says that staff working 80% of a normal schedule should progress at a normal rate, whereas those working less than 80% can expect some delay.

Even those working a four-day week find that it is difficult to control the time pressures, and that their day off is not always respected. One part-time employee who worked for a female partner said that, when staff had wanted to schedule a meeting for her day off, the partner suggested scheduling it on a Sunday. She got startled looks from the other staff, but it made the point that asking the part-timer to come in on her day off was no different than asking them to come in on theirs.

Many of the part-time work arrangements are structured to take the seasonal nature of the work into account. One woman who worked in the tax practice worked three days a week for most of the year, but agreed to work five days a week during March and April. "The people I worked for were not very happy with the arrangement. . . . I ended up working seven days a week in March and April." She has since transferred to another area where the part-time arrangement was better accepted.

Many support staff have also negotiated part-time work, but the formal policies supporting flexible working arrangements do not yet apply to them. One woman who was thinking of asking for a four-day week said, "The hardest part is the lack of human resources policies. It is not always clear what is available to you, as support staff. The amount of support you get depends a lot on who you work for".

The firm seems to have a traditional view of the role of support staff, even to the point of some managers still using secretaries to run personal errands for them. Support staff feel that they are expected to put in long hours and there is little recognition that they, too, have personal lives. As a result of concerns such as these, the Women's Initiatives Program has expanded its mandate to address the needs of support staff.

On the positive side, if they can find the time to take on more responsibility, the opportunities for them are increasing. As the focus for professional staff has changed from overtime or total hours to *chargeable* hours, there is a growing need for support staff to do administrative and technical work.

"You have to *ask* for promotions, and they seem surprised when you do," said one woman who had moved from secretarial work by taking on a lot of the jobs that used to be done by the professional staff. However the transition is helped by the firm's strong support for education and training. Finding the time to get to the courses may be a challenge, but rarely are staff refused permission to take courses that are in any way related to their work or professional development.

It is too soon to say what impact the Women's Initiatives Program at Price Waterhouse will have, but the senior management seems genuinely committed to it. Most of the female professional staff are optimistic, and the support staff hope that it will have spill-over benefits for them.

Price Waterhouse
Suite 3300, Box 190, 1 First Canadian Place, Toronto, ON, M5X 1H7
Telephone: (416) 863-1133

	Total	No. of Women	% Women
Full-time employees	2,328	1,177	51%
Part-time employees	53	48	91%
Board members	12	1	8%

Job category (figures based on full-time employees, unless noted otherwise):[a]

Upper level managers	277[b]	10	4%
Middle or other managers	546	200	37%
Professionals	648	331	51%
Semi-professionals & technicians	22	12	55%
Supervisors	26	24	92%
Foremen/women	1	0	0%
Clerical workers	423	394	93%
Sales workers	0	0	0%
Service workers	2	1	50%
Skilled crafts & trades workers	0	0	0%
Semi-skilled manual workers	0	0	0%
Other manual workers	12	7	58%

Percentage of full-time employees considered upper level managers:	11.90%
Top-up of U.I.C. during maternity leave:	good
On-site daycare centre?	no
Child/elder care referral service?	yes
Employment equity rep. reports to CEO/President?	yes
Target numbers for women in management?	yes
Pay equity policy?	yes
Employment equity policy?	yes
Mentoring program?	no

Noteworthy benefits:
- free tax advice
- paternity and adoption leaves can be up to one year (same as maternirty leaves)
- maternity, paternity and adoption leaves can be self-funded through a re-allocation of salary for six months before and after the leave period

Part-time employee benefits:
- full benefits if work 21+ hours/week

Notes: (a) in addition to numbers shown below, 337 employees, of which 179 (53%) were women, had been hired since the last job category analysis was done

(b) partners

Tory Tory DesLauriers & Binnington

Tory Tory Deslauriers & Binnington is one of Canada's major law firms. Specializing in business law, its clients include Petro-Canada, Abitibi Price and the Bank of Nova Scotia. Toronto-based, it is affiliated with Desjardins Ducharme Stein Monast of Montreal and Quebec City, and Lawson Lundell Lawson & McIntosh of Vancouver. Through an international partnership, it also has offices in England and Hong Kong.

In November, 1993, 16 out of 25 articling students, 45 of 101 "associates" (lawyers who are not partners) and 20 out of 101 partners at Tory's were women. These numbers put it far ahead of most law firms in terms of the recruitment and promotion of female legal talent.

On the non-legal side the numbers are even more impressive. Tory's was the first and is still the only major law firm to have a female general manager. Staff feel that her presence over the past eight years has had a major impact in creating a flexible, supportive and effective working environment. Women also head most of the other support functions, including the positions of Controller, Marketing Director, Records Manager and Coordinator of Professional Development.

How did the firm achieve these impressive numbers? "This is really an exceptional firm in terms of its attitude towards women," said one lawyer. Its relative youth helps. The firm was founded in the mid-fifties, and has grown rapidly in recent years, so it is not tradition-bound. Many of the lawyers and partners are young, often with professional spouses and young children of their own, and they tend to be understanding and flexible when it comes to the needs of working parents.

In a ground-breaking move, Tory's advertised in 1992 for lawyers who wanted to work part-time. The response was phenomenal. Many of the 200 applicants were talented female lawyers who wanted balance in their lives. "At first," explained the woman responsible for the ad, "it was assumed that the jobs couldn't be done part-time." In particular, it was assumed that work in litigation was incompatible with part-time hours. There are now 10 lawyers working part-time or flexible hours; three of them in litigation.

The nature of the arrangement varies, depending on the practice and the needs of the individual. "You have to be flexible in your definition of part-time," said one lawyer. One woman in the corporate practice works round the clock for weeks in a row when she's in the middle of a transaction, but is able to take the summer off to be with her children.

Others aim to work a limited number of days per week, but recognize that the exact number of hours will not always be predictable. Still others have targeted a number of billable hours for the year that is lower than the standard for full-time lawyers.

Of course, the standard definition of "full-time" for lawyers means tremendously long hours. One bright, single woman who came to the firm as a result of the "part-time" ad works about nine hours a day, five days a week, but is happy with the relative balance this has brought into her life. In her previous job, she found that her entire life revolved around the firm. "I wanted to do volunteer work, and to take some courses," she said.

Men are also starting to be attracted to the possibility of working fewer hours. The firm's first male part-time lawyer started in January, 1994. Explained the firm's recruiter, "We don't want to lose good people."

The firm has no official policy of encouraging the recruitment and promotion of women but, as an associate pointed out, "You need a proactive attitude for it to work and to get good women". That attitude is seen in things like the ad for part-time lawyers and in smaller things, like holding a computer training session outside normal hours to accommodate a part-time lawyer with young children.

One reason lawyers have traditionally been reluctant to consider working shorter hours was because the number of hours billed each year is a significant element in deciding who gets partnership status. Tory's has dealt with this issue in two ways. First, it is in the process of developing a part-time partnership policy, although the concept is still under active debate. In the meantime, though, one woman who was full-time when she became a partner now works three days a week. In January, 1994, the firm added its first part-time partner who had never worked full-time for the firm. She started at Tory's as a part-time associate, and was later promoted.

Second, the firm tries to minimize the status differences between partners and associates. "We share information well with associates, and we pay well", explained a partner. "It is becoming much more accepted to carve out another niche that isn't a partnership track." An associate agreed. "Partnership is not the be-all and end-all as long as the firm doesn't treat partners and associates differently." She nodded as the controller commented, "This firm goes to great lengths to try *not* to distinguish between partners and associates".

That egalitarian attitude extends to non-legal staff. "We are all part of the same machine," explained the supervisor of food services. Another staff member, who started as a clerk five years ago and is now involved in marketing the firm, said, "The attitude now is we work *with* them, not *for* them". In fact, new lawyers often depend on the good will of the legal secretaries, who tend to know more about the administrative workings of the legal system than the lawyers themselves. The younger lawyers in particular, said one former secretary, "truly recognize that secretaries are professionals in our own right". A receptionist, who had been out of the workforce for 30 years before joining Tory's, added that receptionists too were "treated very respectfully".

The recognition of support staff as part of the team also shows in the firm's cutting-edge approach to technology. "We are industry leaders when it comes to technology," said a computer trainer, who had started as a contract secretary, but was given the opportunity to shift into computer training based on her experience, despite a lack of formal qualifications.

The firm also shows its commitment to the team approach by giving all employees bonuses in good years, by having (and listening to) a staff relations committee composed of representatives of all areas of the firm, and by giving all staff access to many of the perks available, like free tickets to baseball games or other events when the tickets are not being used by clients, a free buffet lunch available to employees who cannot afford the time for a full lunch break, and a full, cooked dinner for those working late. Unlike many firms, it also has a pool of night secretaries, so it is rare for secretaries to have to work very late. If they do, the firm unhesitatingly pays for a taxi home, as it does for staff to get home from events like the Christmas party.

Benefits are generous. Many, like the meal services and an on-site dry-cleaner, are designed to minimize the amount of time employees need to spend out of the office attending to personal errands. Others, such as an employee assistance program and a child and elder care referral service, tend to their emotional well-being.

Vacation policies are also generous, and include days off for religious holidays, three 'personal days' (one for family emergencies, one for moving, and one floater) and extra time when it is needed. For example, one woman was granted extra vacation time to go see her ailing father in Malaysia; another was given a five-week leave of absence to accompany her daughter to Romania to adopt a baby and then encouraged to take two more weeks off upon her return to recover from the trip and help the new family adjust.

For those who are particularly healthy and have not had special needs for days off, the firm gives a half-day off for every three absence-free months.

The flexibility also extends to hours. People can generally adapt their starting and ending times to their own needs, and when children are sick the firm is accommodating about giving the needed time off. Said one secretary, "I like that I can be honest about the fact that I'm not coming in because my child is sick, or for other personal reasons" rather than having to pretend that the secretary herself is sick. But it works both ways. "I can, if necessary, come in late, but when needed, I will leave late."

Two receptionists job-share. The others all work a compressed work week, doing 35 hours in four days. This lowered turnover dramatically. One receptionist commented that she appreciates having a day during the week to run personal errands and to visit with her 97-year old mother.

The firm also places a priority on staff development and education. One woman went back to university to study human resources after having spent nearly a decade at Tory's as a legal secretary. She worked part-time for the firm while she was in school, and then returned as a supervisor of human resources. She noted, "There are limited opportunities in the firm regarding a career path for non-lawyers, but employees who are interested in any area are given numerous opportunities to branch out and learn". A marketing assistant, who had been a hairdresser before she joined the firm as a records management clerk, said "the sky's the limit" as far as developing oneself and taking on more responsibility and challenge within a job.

The one weak spot that emerged in interviews is internal communication. The size of the firm and its rapid growth have made it difficult to keep up with the task of keeping everybody well-informed. Morale is sometimes undermined by information spreading as rumours rather than timely facts. The firm is now addressing this problem. Everyone is now linked by electronic mail, and a new electronic staff directory includes pictures of each employee, to help make the link between names and faces. Voice mail has also improved communication. As well, staff at all levels feel that misunderstandings can be dealt with by going directly to the source, and will be resolved quickly.

In summing up what makes this firm special, an articling student said she had chosen to work at Tory's because she had been impressed by the people she met in her interviews. "This firm places a premium on people being nice to each other."

Tory Tory DesLauriers & Binnington
P.O. Box 270, Toronto Dominion Centre, Toronto, ON, M5K 1N2
Telephone: (416) 865-0040

	Total	No. of Women	% Women
Full-time employees	559	372	66%
Part-time employees	28	28	100%
Board members	7[a]	1	14%

Job category (figures based on full-time employees, unless noted otherwise):[b]

Upper level managers	102[c]	20	19%
Middle or other managers	8[d]	6	75%
Professionals	112[e]	51	45%
Semi-professionals & technicians	58[f]	50	86%
Supervisors	15	11	73%
Foremen/women	0	0	0%
Clerical workers	269	256	95%
Sales workers	0	0	0%
Service workers	30	7	23%
Skilled crafts & trades workers	0	0	0%
Semi-skilled manual workers	0	0	0%
Other manual workers	0	0	0%

Percentage of full-time employees considered upper level managers:	13.40%
Top-up of U.I.C. during maternity leave:	varies[h]
On-site daycare centre?	no
Child/elder care referral service?	yes
Employment equity rep. reports to CEO/President?	no
Target numbers for women in management?	no
Pay equity policy?	yes
Employment equity policy?	no
Mentoring program?	yes

Noteworthy benefits:
- travel assistance and subsidized fitness club memberships
- legal fee waivers or discounts on some legal work

Part-time employee benefits:
- part-time professional staff receive full benefits
- non-professional staff working 30+ hours/week get full benefits
- non-professional staff working 20-29 hours get half their benefits paid for

Notes:
(a) executive committee
(b) includes part-time staff
(c) includes 101 parners, 19 of whom (19%) are women
(d) non-legal managers
(e) includes 106 associates, 45 of whom (42%) are women
(f) articling students and para-legal staff
(g) secretarial, administrative and technical support
(h) generous: legal staff; good: managers and para-legals; none: support staff

RETAIL

Ben Moss Jewellers

Ben Moss Jewellers is a family-owned chain of 26 jewellery stores, headquartered in Winnipeg. The company was founded in 1910. The stores are located in British Columbia, Alberta, Saskatchewan, Manitoba and Ontario.

"Two weeks after I started I went to an awards ceremony for the company's top producers," said one eight-year employee of Ben Moss Jewellers. "I worked very hard to get on that list, and every year I have been." What she and others particularly like about the company is the autonomy it gives its employees. "I'm paid to do my job and free to do it my own way," said another employee. "They trust us."

Working in a family-owned business can be difficult for people wanting to advance, but employees do not feel that the family ownership at Ben Moss causes problems. Four members of the executive are family members, including the President, Brent Trepel, and the Chairman and CEO, Sidney Trepel, but whenever possible the company promotes from within. Employees are convinced that they can go as far as they want to go.

One assistant store manager appreciated that the company recognized her ability and let her rise quickly, even though she only had a Grade 11 education and had spent many years at home with her children before entering the workforce. She was also pleased that it respected the limits she places on her career progression. "I prefer being an assistant manager because I like to sell and to be involved. I don't want the bottom-line responsibility of budgeting," she said. But should the time come when she changes her mind, the opportunity to go further in management is there. "They don't push me," she said, "but they do offer me the position every time a manager leaves."

Retail sales is a mixed blessing for mothers. It can be a convenient way to work part-time, but, particularly for those in management, there are inevitably evening and weekend hours. The jewellery business also has strong seasonal fluctuations. "I worked seven days a week, 12 hours a day, for six weeks during the Christmas season," said one successful saleswoman.

Pay for the sales staff is a combination of base salary and commission, and employees believe it is comparable to that at other companies in the retail industry.

Like many small organizations, Ben Moss does not offer much in the way of formal policies aimed at making women's lives easier, but the company is reluctant to let talented people get away. One mother of three young children quit the company after ten years "because I was tired of retail hours. Within a year they approached me to come back and work [in the head office]". The new position gave her more regular hours, but less flexibility in scheduling them. When it is absolutely necessary to book something like a child's doctor's appointment during the day, she will do so, but "as a mom I try not to let personal things interfere. I believe when you are at work, you are at work".

The distribution of women throughout the company and the comments of employees both suggest that, with the current management, there is no need for a formal employment equity policy for women at the firm. Women represent 60% of the full-time employees and almost that number of the senior mangers (54%). Eighty-three percent of the middle managers are women. Said one employee, "As long as you are well-suited to your job it doesn't matter whether you are a man or a woman". Ben Moss Jewellers offers a close, family atmosphere and promotional opportunities for anyone wanting to work in retail sales.

Ben Moss Jewellers
225 Garry Street, Winnipeg, MB, R3C 1H1
Telephone: (204) 947-6682

	Total	No. of Women	% Women
Full-time employees	142	85	60%
Part-time employees	62	41	66%
Board members	7	2	29%

Job category (figures based on full-time employees, unless noted otherwise):[a]

Upper level managers	37	20	54%
Middle or other managers	18	15	83%
Professionals	0	0	0%
Semi-professionals & technicians	0	0	0%
Supervisors	0	0	0%
Foremen/women	0	0	0%
Clerical workers	24	24	100%
Sales workers	125	67	54%
Service workers	0	0	0%
Skilled crafts & trades workers	0	0	0%
Semi-skilled manual workers	0	0	0%
Other manual workers	0	0	0%

Percentage of full-time employees considered upper level managers:	26.06%
Top-up of U.I.C. during maternity leave:	none
On-site daycare centre?	no
Child/elder care referral service?	no
Employment equity rep. reports to CEO/President?	yes
Target numbers for women in management?	no
Pay equity policy?	no
Employment equity policy?	no
Mentoring program?	no

Noteworthy benefits:
- 25% discount on jewellery prices
- no pension plan, but have a group RRSP

Part-time employee benefits:
- full benefits if work 30+ hours/week; otherwise, no benefits

Notes: (a) breakdown of numbers by job category includes both full-time and part-time staff

Lenscrafters

Lenscrafters opened its first store in the U.S.A. in 1983 and expanded into Canada five years later. There are now 60 stores in Canada, in every province from B.C. to Quebec. The Canadian head office is in Etobicoke, Ontario.

Mission and value statements are all the rage these days, but Lenscrafters is one company where the "core values" really are core. One woman, who had consulted to Lenscrafters before deciding to join the company, said, "I knew the things that I was looking for in an organization and I was watching to see whether Lenscrafters walked their talk. The Core Values impressed me very much . . . but it is easy to write something down; it is something else entirely to live up to it. In my position I got to see people from all over the company, and I saw that the things on the mission statement existed, and existed uniformly".

Some of the ten core values came through repeatedly in the interviews, specifically:

- nurturing individuals;
- building on people's strengths;
- accepting and learning from mistakes;
- focusing on winning, not individual scoring;
- thinking and acting like a long-term owner;
- demanding highest possible quality; and
- having fun.

All new staff are indoctrinated in the values during a two-day orientation session, which is reinforced for head office staff by a quarterly "core value day" during which a department hosts an event that illustrates one of the values. ("Having fun" is the most popular value to celebrate on core value day, but activities are not always purely social. They have included, for example, closing the office for a day to do volunteer work at a food bank.)

What has an even bigger impact on fostering the values is the way the company is structured. Staff are not on commission, which experienced retail sales staff felt made a tremendous difference in encouraging quality service and teamwork. Bonuses are granted to stores that perform well, and split among all the employees based on the number of hours each worked during the campaign period. Outstanding performers within stores that earn bonuses can also get individual rewards.

The values of quality and fun are combined in a "Lab Olympics" in which laboratory staff from across Canada and the U.S. compete by demonstrating their skill and speed at grinding lenses.

Good internal communication helps maintain the team spirit. Retail organizations are often sharply divided between head office staff and front-line employees. Lenscrafters has all head office staff spend time in a store shortly after joining. It also runs an "Adopt-A-Store" program, whereby each employee in the head office (except members of the executive) develops a one-on-one relationship with a store. Employees phone their "adopted" store regularly, swap photos, and do whatever else seems appropriate to keep the relationship alive. This regular communication helps head office staff understand the pressures faced by store staff, and gives the latter a personal contact at head office so that they will not hesitate to call if they have a problem or question.

Employees can air opinions in peer reviews and in a detailed bi-annual survey coordinated by an outside firm. Participation in the survey is voluntary, but staff clearly feel that it is important: 93% of Canadian employees participated in the 1992 survey. Each store gets a breakdown of its own results as well as the overall data, and makes recommendations as to what it can do to improve things in its area and what the head office could do to improve things that are beyond the control of individual stores. Based on the input, the company then devises and publicizes an overall action plan.

Neither the survey results nor the focus group interviews conducted for this book identified gender as an issue of concern to staff. "Everybody is treated fairly, equally," said a lab technician. "There is no difference between men and women in this organization," said a salesperson.

The company is still growing, so there are many opportunities for advancement. One young woman decided, after having had a baby, that she needed more money, so she told management that she wanted to become a store manager. Within six months she was an assistant manager and was well on her way to becoming a manager. The company has a well developed training program and staff feel that all bright, hard-working people who want to get into management or into a different part of the operation can do so simply by letting their goals be known.

Most jobs are posted nation-wide, and, according to Elaine Martin, Director of Human Resources, "It is interesting how often we are surprised by who applies". The company tries to accommodate staff who want to move to a new location. On the flip-side, employees who turn down a transfer are not penalized. "Many times people have rejected moves," said one manager, "but they are back on the list for the next opportunity that comes up. We understand that not everybody can move."

The company has few formal policies on things like maternity leaves or flexible working arrangements, but as long as it maintains its current management style they are not needed. Store staff work on shifts, but commented that there was a lot of flexibility in changing schedules. Both store and head office staff noted the company's flexibility in meeting individual needs. "It's a give-and-take relationship," said one woman who commutes a long distance and has also agreed to let one of her employees work on an unusual schedule so that the employee can spend extra time with her father. Another staff member switched from full-time to part-time work while going to school; yet another experimented with both full-time and part-time work after giving birth to twins.

The hours are long, particularly in head office, but staff are so excited by their work that the topic of hours came up only as an afterthought, when an employee who had moved to Canada from the American operation commented on the longer hours in the Canadian office. "The hours are long and the expectations are high, maybe too high," said one manager, "but we all know that effort will pay off, and whenever there is a personal need to be met the company is accommodating." Said another, "I need to be in an organization that pushes people to the limit . . . but I'm afraid that we are going to burn out really good talent".

For the moment Lenscrafters seems to be avoiding burn-out, perhaps because " 'Having fun' is taken seriously here". The organization is young, dynamic, and not afraid to spoof the very gender issues that might cause outrage among less satisfied employees. A group of Canadian senior managers was going to the American head office to attend an awards celebration. The men asked the women who would be attending to rent tuxedos for them. Instead of grumbling about being asked to do this menial chore, the women rented tuxedos for themselves too. They made their point, which has now been immortalized in a group photo proudly displayed in the Lenscrafters head office.

Lenscrafters
21 Four Seasons Place, #230, Etobicoke, ON, M9B 6J8
Telephone: (416) 620-5425

	Total	No. of Women	% Women
Full-time employees	558	288	52%
Part-time employees	357	232	65%
Board members	9	3	33%

Job category (figures based on full-time employees, unless noted otherwise):

	Total	No. of Women	% Women
Upper level managers	9	3	33%
Middle or other managers	76	38	50%
Professionals	0	0	0%
Semi-professionals & technicians	102	60	59%
Supervisors	64	26	41%
Foremen/women	64	15	23%
Clerical workers	40	39	97%
Sales workers	95	60	63%
Service workers	7	7	100%
Skilled crafts & trades workers	0	0	0%
Semi-skilled manual workers	101	40	40%
Other manual workers	0	0	0%

Percentage of full-time employees considered upper level managers:	1.61%
Top-up of U.I.C. during maternity leave:	none
On-site daycare centre?	no
Child/elder care referral service?	no
Employment equity rep. reports to CEO/President?	yes
Target numbers for women in management?	no
Pay equity policy?	yes
Employment equity policy?	no
Mentoring program?	no

Noteworthy benefits:
- one free pair of glasses every year; 50% discount on glasses for family members

Part-time employee benefits:
- full benefits if work 25+ hours/week, except that vacation time is pro-rated, and get three days sick leave instead of five
- if work less than 25 hours, are considered casual and do not qualify for most benefits

TRANSPORTATION

Toronto Transit Commission

The Toronto Transit Commission (TTC) is one of the largest public transit companies in the world, carrying some 400 million passengers a year. It operates buses, streetcars, subway lines and a rapid transit line. Approximately 80% of the employees are unionized.

It is hard to imagine that the first female bus driver at the TTC was hired less than 20 years ago. "When I applied," she explained, "I didn't realize there weren't any female bus drivers; I just needed a job". She got the job, and worked her way through driving jobs and into management. When she looks at the organization now she sees one that has improved by leaps and bounds in some areas, but still has a long way to go in others.

In fact, there had been female streetcar drivers and other women in non-traditional jobs at the TTC during the Second World War but, as in so many organizations, those jobs were reclaimed by men after the war. As recently as 1979 only five per cent of the TTC's workforce, or 459 employees, were women. That number had increased to 1150, or 11% of the workforce, by 1993, but in many ways the TTC is still in the early stages of becoming a good employer for women. The transportation industry is still heavily male-dominated and change does not happen overnight. Nevertheless, the TTC seems serious about encouraging more women to work there and it is doing many of the right things to try to attract and support them through the difficult early stages.

It recently produced a recruiting video aimed at women, which points out both positive and negative aspects of joining the TTC in a non-traditional area. On the positive side, pay and benefits are good and there are over 1,500 different kinds of jobs to choose from, so there are many interesting opportunities. On the other hand, shift-work can last for several years before an employee has enough seniority to be able to work days and avoid weekends, and the attitudes of co-workers, many of whom resist the idea of women in non-traditional jobs, can be frustrating.

"The shift work is hard," said a single mother of two young children. "I have a babysitter who comes in till 3:30 a.m., and she'll take the kids if they are sick." There have also been concerns about the safety of women working nights but the women point out that the work can be equally dangerous for men. The TTC offers self-defence courses for women, and, as one inspector noted, "It may actually be easier for me to haul drunks off the streetcars at night because I'm a woman; women are more likely to make peace than get into a confrontation".

When it comes to attitudes, management openly admits that there are problems but it is doing what it can to improve them. In the meantime, as one woman in the video explains, "I only have to work with these people; I don't have to socialize with them."

This refreshingly open approach to recruiting has led to the hiring of a group of self-confident, unflappable women in non-traditional jobs. One woman, who started as a sweeper on night shifts and now supervises a group of very traditional men, said, "I've realized I have to be aggressive to be accepted. I've been called a bitch. Yah, I'm a bitch: deal with it!" Apparently they did, because a few months into the job she had reached the point where mutual respect had developed and she was enjoying the work. "It is the most positive environment I've been in," she said, noting that management has been particularly supportive. "When I'm challenged, management will back me up."

Women in maintenance and operations, or those considering entering those fields, have access to a Career Counselling Centre for career advice and moral support. The counselling centre also gives advice on resume writing and interview techniques to help people succeed when they apply for internal job postings.

Supervisory, management and professional women get moral support, advice and networking opportunities through the TTC Women's Network. That group holds about four luncheon meetings a year at which guest speakers cover topics such as financial planning, safety and security, and stress reduction.

Part of the difficulty in changing attitudes throughout the organization is its para-military approach to management. "We are treated like kids in school here," said one driver. "You've been bad; go to the principal's office." Said another, "In my area they call you by badge number, not name". It seems that there is support for women at the most senior levels and at the junior levels (once the women have proven themselves to their co-workers) but there is still a lot of resentment from the ranks in between. Said one driver, "The drivers are great, the inspectors are okay, the supervisors — I stay out of their way".

Managers and supervisors are now being sent on a four-day residential program called HART, which stands for Hillcrest Area Rapid Transit, a fictitious transit organization. The course is a simulation in which they must manage situations that cover a range of equal opportunity issues.

Participants write a personal contract at the end of the course, outlining actions they will take to encourage equal opportunities in their area. Three months later they attend a half-day follow-up session where they can discuss progress and problems. On-going follow-up and support are provided through a regular newsletter, an annual one-day conference, and continuing contact with the Equal Opportunity Department.

Roughly half the 1,000 or so eligible managers and supervisors have attended the course since it was first offered in 1990. Attendance is not mandatory but is strongly encouraged. Employees whose supervisors had been on the program felt that it had made a big difference.

The TTC does a lot of in-house training, so in 1993 it also ran a seminar for its 70 to 80 trainers on designing and delivering bias-free training.

Flexible hours, reduced work weeks, part-time work and telecommuting are available to non-union employees but are not common. One woman finally got permission to work part-time after a year and a half of trying. Another felt that the TTC has been reluctant to let employees know that part-time work is an option. The TTC's Equal Opportunities Directorate did a study of work and family issues in 1993 and hopes to implement new policies soon.

One indication of the importance senior management is placing on equity issues is the recent decision to incorporate equal opportunity policies and practices into the criteria examined by internal auditors when they audit a department's operations.

For the moment, the women most likely to be happy at the TTC are those who are tough enough to be path-breakers. For them, and the women to follow them, the TTC offers great potential.

Toronto Transit Commission
1900 Yonge Street, Toronto, ON, M4S 1Z2
Telephone: (416) 393-4000

	Total	No. of Women	% Women
Full-time employees	10,068	1,140	11%
Part-time employees	12	10	83%
Board members	7	2	29%

Job category (figures based on full-time employees, unless noted otherwise):

	Total	No. of Women	% Women
Upper level managers	7	0	0%
Middle or other managers	363	62	17%
Professionals	173	36	21%
Semi-professionals & technicians	146	9	6%
Supervisors	167	42	25%
Foremen/women	514	35	7%
Clerical workers	1,279	482	38%
Sales workers	0	0	0%
Service workers	375	40	11%
Skilled crafts & trades workers	889	16	2%
Semi-skilled manual workers	5,323	340	6%
Other manual workers	832	62	7%

Percentage of full-time employees considered upper level managers:	0.07%
Top-up of U.I.C. during maternity leave:	none
On-site daycare centre?	no
Child/elder care referral service?	no
Employment equity rep. reports to CEO/President?	no
Target numbers for women in management?	no
Pay equity policy?	yes
Employment equity policy?	yes
Mentoring program?	no

Noteworthy benefits:
- self-funded leave plan

Part-time employee benefits:
- same benefit package, but must pay 50% of the premiums

VIA Rail

VIA Rail is the Crown corporation responsible for providing national passenger train service. It runs trains in many regions of the country, and has offices in Halifax, Montreal, Toronto, Winnipeg and Vancouver. Approximately 80% of the employees are unionized.

"Things are really starting to move for women," said a ten-year VIA employee. "Before it was more of an obligation imposed by government rather than a true desire to improve, but within the past few years it seems to be sincere."

Overall, VIA seems open to new ideas and reasonable in its approach to human resources. Employees who had worked elsewhere felt that it was less tradition-bound than other railways because of its relative youth (VIA was incorporated in 1977). Women did not perceive a glass ceiling although, as one woman pointed out, "A railway is a railway. It is male-oriented, and women are mainly in the traditional female areas".

Women have made strong inroads in management and professional jobs but their progress has been limited in part by a lack of operational experience. Women working in non-traditional areas still meet with scepticism, but most have managed to prove themselves and become accepted. A woman who was sent to handle the human resources issues on a maintenance project was baffled by the jargon the men were using. "I asked them what it meant. They handed me a thick maintenance manual and said, 'Read it.' So I did. I read the whole thing that weekend and returned Monday morning with 15 questions. They hadn't expected that. From then on, I had their respect."

Another woman, who did a six-month stint as a supervisor in a railway station during the mid-eighties, found that there was a lot of resistance then but believed that women are accepted in the stations now. "It is the clients who are unhappy about having a woman in charge of a station now, not the staff," explained another. "The employees like having female supervisors because we listen to them, we are more diplomatic; gentler. They prefer our management style." Nevertheless, even staff with male bosses felt that VIA employees were generally listened to and treated with respect.

Pregnancy and maternity leaves are not considered a problem by most managers. VIA allows 41 weeks of maternity-related leave with all benefits continuing at company expense. It also provides full salary during the two-week qualification period for unemployment insurance (paid once the employee has been back at work for four weeks) and tops up the remaining 15 weeks of unemployment insurance payments to 70% or 95% of the employee's normal salary (the amount depends on the position and length of service).

Management women have a lot of flexibility as to when and where they get their work done, so they have few problems taking time off to deal with sick children or other personal matters. "They expect you to get the task done however you feel works best for you," said one manager.

The situation is trickier for many non-management staff, especially those who work outside the office environment. Many end up pretending to be sick themselves because VIA does not have a policy allowing employees to use some of their own sick time to deal with family needs. In many of the unionized jobs the company has to hire a replacement to cover for employees who call in sick, so the collective agreements do not provide for pay during the first three days of a sick leave. As a result, those employees have no financial coverage if they need to take time off to deal with a family emergency.

Child care is a particular challenge for parents working in the stations, as their schedules can change from month to month. They cope as best they can by trading shifts with other staff. The difficulty juggling schedules has led to an increasing number of female employees asking to switch to part-time work so that they can work a fixed schedule.

Head office staff benefit from a day care centre shared with other employers in the Place Ville Marie complex in downtown Montreal, although there is a waiting list to get in.

Most employees, including managers, find that their work can be contained to about eight hours a day. Many of them had worked long hours at various stages of their careers, but did not feel the need to do so indefinitely. One manager, who had been promoted just after a maternity leave, felt that she had become better at managing her time since having the baby. Another noted that in her, male-dominated, area of the company, "The boys do stick around till all hours, but it is more like socializing, so I stopped. It was not very productive".

Some parts of the corporation have adopted flexible hours or compressed work weeks, such as a 10-hour day, four-day week, or summer hours where staff can work longer to get one day off every two weeks or a half-day every week. Other types of alternative working arrangements are still rare.

Job-sharing and part-time work are not well accepted. One woman who had joined the company part-time in the mid-eighties found that she was constantly working overtime. "After two years they told me that I had a choice of going full-time or nothing, so I took full-time." Once she had switched to full-time status she found that she got to work on more interesting projects. Others commented that there is a lot of resistance to job sharing, and that when the staff was being cut, "job-shares were the first ones to go".

Funding cutbacks have meant that there is little opportunity for movement these days, so staff would like the company to introduce job exchanges. "After six or seven years in the same job," said one, "you need stimulation." Even so, she and the others interviewed felt that VIA was one of the best places to work in the transportation industry, and that it was serious about being a good employer for women.

VIA Rail
2 Place Ville Marie, P.O. Box 8116, Station A, Montreal, PQ, H3C 3N3
Telephone: (514) 871-6000

	Total	No. of Women	% Women
Full-time employees	4,326	803	19%
Part-time employees	177	80	45%
Board members	14	1	7%

Job category (figures based on full-time employees, unless noted otherwise):

	Total	No. of Women	% Women
Upper level managers	7	2	29%
Middle or other managers	474	121	26%
Professionals	148	47	32%
Semi-professionals & technicians	34	7	21%
Supervisors	69	8	12%
Foremen/women	53	1	2%
Clerical workers	483	233	48%
Sales workers	469	187	40%
Service workers	868	143	16%
Skilled crafts & trades workers	1,150	16	1%
Semi-skilled manual workers	381	20	5%
Other manual workers	190	18	9%

Percentage of full-time employees considered upper level managers:	0.16%
Top-up of U.I.C. during maternity leave:	generous
On-site daycare centre?	yes
Child/elder care referral service?	no
Employment equity rep. reports to CEO/President?	no
Target numbers for women in management?	no
Pay equity policy?	yes
Employment equity policy?	yes
Mentoring program?	no

Noteworthy benefits:
 • free rail pass
Part-time employee benefits:
 • pro-rated

Part III:
The Best of
The Best

The Top Ten

Ten of the organizations in this book stand out as being particularly good places to work. They had satisfied employees, advancement opportunities, and helpful policies and practices. They are (in alphabetical order):

- American Express
- Bank of Montreal
- Canadian Satellite Communications (Cancom)
- City of Toronto
- Credit Valley Hospital
- Mount Sinai Hospital
- North York Board of Education
- St. Elizabeth Visiting Nurses Association of Ontario
- Tory Tory DesLauriers and Binnington
- VanCity (Vancouver City Savings Credit Union)

What do they have in common? A genuine focus on people, both their employees and their customers. It's not a coincidence that they are all service providers; it was much harder to find employers with a strong people orientation in the goods producing and handling industries.

As you saw in Part II, the focus on people means that all their employees, male and female, are valued, and the organizations are alert to avoid policies or practices that cause needless stress. They are merit-oriented places where productive workers do well.

There are also big differences among the top ten. American Express and Credit Valley Hospital would appeal to people with hard-driving, entrepreneurial personalities, but not to those who want to have active personal lives. The North York Board of Education and the City of Toronto have long-standing, well entrenched systems to further the advancement of women within their organizations. The Bank of Montreal and law firm Tory Tory DesLauriers & Binnington have a more recent interest in making their organizations good places for women, but are taking a serious and creative approach. Cancom, Mount Sinai Hospital, St. Elizabeth Visiting Nurses Association, and VanCity stand out particularly because of the satisfaction and commitment of their employees.

Best for the Advancement of Women

American Express
Ben Moss Jewellers
City of Toronto
Credit Valley Hospital
The Gazette
Mount Sinai Hospital
North York Board of Education
St. Elizabeth Visiting Nurses Association

Best for Supportive Policies

Bank of Montreal
CIBC
City of Toronto
Credit Valley Hospital
Manulife Financial
Municipality of Metropolitan Toronto
Union Gas
VanCity

Best in the Eyes of Their Employees

Bank of Montreal
Ben Moss Jewellers
Cancom
Co-operative Trust
Credit Valley Hospital
Freda's Originals
Lenscrafters
Merck Frosst Canada
Municipality of Metropolitan Toronto
Mount Sinai Hospital
Mutual Group
North York Board of Education
The Rider Group
Tory Tory DesLauriers & Binnington
VanCity

Mentoring Programs

Bank of Montreal
Calgary Herald
Freda's Originals
North York Board of Education
St. Elizabeth Visiting Nurses Association
Tory Tory DesLauriers & Binnington

Organizations in Which the Person Responsible for Employment Equity Reports to CEO/President

American Express
Avon Canada Inc.
Bank of Montreal
Ben Moss Jewellers
Calgary Board of Education
Cancom
Co-operative Trust
Cott Corporation
Freda's Originals
Lenscrafters
Manpower Temporary Services (Toronto) Ltd.
North York Board of Education
Ontario Provincial Police
Pan Pacific Hotel
Petro-Canada
Price Waterhouse
St. Elizabeth Visiting Nurses Association
VanCity
Wood Gundy

On-site Day Care Centres

Calgary Herald
City of Montreal
City of Toronto
Loto-Québec
Maritime Life Assurance Co.
Merck Frosst Canada Inc.
Municipality of Metropolitan Toronto
Mount Sinai Hospital
Mutual Group
Ontario Hydro
Petro-Canada
VIA Rail
York University

Child and Elder Care Referral Services

American Express
Bank of Montreal
BC TEL
Canadian Broadcasting Corporation
CIBC
Canada Mortgage and Housing Corporation
Credit Valley Hospital
Manulife Financial
Merck Frosst Canada Inc.
Municipality of Metropolitan Toronto
North York Board of Education
Pan Pacific Hotel
Petro-Canada
Price Waterhouse
Tory Tory DesLauriers & Binnington
VanCity

Flexible Benefits Packages

Flexible benefits packages let employees choose from a menu of different benefits and levels of coverage. Usually such packages have a basic level of coverage which is extended to all full-time employees. A formula is used to decide how many extra credits each employee is entitled to. The credits can be used by each employee to pay for the benefits that seem most useful to her (or him). If an employee has left-over credits, some employers refund their value by adding it to the employee's pay. If the employee has used all her (or his) credits, but wants higher levels of coverage, such coverage can usually be bought by the employee and paid for through payroll deductions.

American Express
BC TEL
Mutual Group
NOVA Corporation of Alberta

Part IV:
Advice to Employees and Job Hunters

Advice to Employees and Job Hunters

1. *Do not be timid in discussing pay.* One female vice-president commented, "Most of the women I've interviewed are very timid when talking about pay. I've always been paid the same as a man because I've demanded it." Try to find out what men in comparable positions in your industry earn. Don't under-sell yourself.

2. *Think about benefits when assessing an offer of work.* Benefits are notoriously difficult to compare, but they can add 20 to 50% to the value of your salary. Think about which benefits are most important to you; you may even be able to negotiate some of them, such as vacation time.

3. *Demand the resources you need to get your job done effectively.* If at all possible, negotiate for adequate support staff and facilities before accepting a new position. If you get promoted, but are not given adequate support to do your job, you're likely to fail.

4. *Learn to delegate.* Women often trap themselves with an over-developed sense of responsibility. If you start doing other peoples' work for them, you will not be able to get your own job done efficiently and effectively. Accept that the way somebody else does the work may not be exactly the way you would. Ask yourself if the difference is really important enough to justify the time of doing or re-doing it yourself.

5. *Don't get bogged down in detail.* Details are important, but they are also time-consuming. For each project or activity, decide which details are crucial to the final outcome and don't worry too much about the others.

6. *If you are thinking of taking an extended leave, working part-time or job-sharing, assess the financial impact before making your proposal.* Many employers that top-up unemployment insurance benefits earned during a maternity leave do not hand over the money until the employee has been back at work for some time. Find out what the provisions are in your organization. If you want to work on an alternative working arrangement, find out what will happen to your benefits, not just your salary. You may be able to negotiate full coverage.

7. *Assess the career impact of working on an alternative working arrangement (AWA).* Will you be considered for other positions while you are working on an AWA? Will you still have access to

interesting, career-enhancing work? Is that important to you? Will you still have access to support services and facilities? If you plan to work from home, how will you ensure that you are not forgotten? How will you be perceived if you later decide to return to a regular working arrangement? You cannot have definite answers to these questions in advance, but talking to other women in your organization who have done what you hope to do will help. You may also want to chat with managers and supervisors about their attitudes towards women who work on such arrangements. (See Appendix A for more advantages and drawbacks to AWAs).

8. *Prove yourself first.* You can afford to take bigger risks once you have established a reputation for being a top performer. Those risks can be anything from working part-time for a few years to allowing your "feminine" side to show in a male-dominated organization.

9. *Network, and find mentors.* It's difficult to find time for networking, but it is important. You can learn a lot during a casual lunch-time conversation. If you have limited time for networking, concentrate on finding mentors. Don't be shy about asking senior people for advice: most people love to share their wisdom, as long as you ask them at a time when they have a few spare moments to talk.

10. *Learn to negotiate.* You don't have to accept situations in which you are unhappy, but if you want to change them you must know how to negotiate. Read books on negotiating skills. Those skills apply to every interpersonal relationship.

Part V:
Advice to Employers

Why Should Employers Care?

It's clear that we still have a long way to go before most Canadian employers accommodate the needs of women so that women can be as productive and successful as men.

Should women be accommodated? There's no consensus on this question, even among women themselves. If a woman chooses to have a child or trains to be a typist rather than an electrician why should the employer bear any costs for those decisions?

The employers in this book concluded that the costs of doing nothing were higher than the costs of being accommodating. The benefits of becoming a better employer for women show up in several ways:

1. *Best brains*: Women make up nearly half the Canadian workforce and their share of the workforce is projected to keep increasing for the next several years.[1] Declining birth rates over the past three decades are shrinking the labour pool from which employers can draw (even though it may not feel that way to the thousands of employees who lost their jobs during the recession of the early nineties). The Conference Board of Canada predicts that the percentage of people aged 15 to 54 will continue to decline until at least the year 2036.[2]

   Organizations that are not good places for women to work will lose access to some of the best minds in an increasingly competitive market for them. They will have trouble recruiting talented women and keeping them. One study found that 37% of women had quit a job because of child care problems, for example.[3] That's hardly surprising when you consider that, in 1992, 64% of married women with children under 16 had jobs, up from 49% in 1981.[4] Even most women with pre-school aged children have paid employment: 57% of those with children under age three (up from 40% in 1981) and 62% of those with children aged three to five (up from 46% in 1981).[5]

   The number of employees with responsibility for aging parents is also increasing. In one recent survey 46% of respondents said they were involved in elder care, 26% of them combining it with child care responsibilities.[6] The percentage of the population aged 65 and

---

1 Statistics Canada, Labour Force Annual Averages, 1993, Catalogue #71-220.
2 Paris, Helene, "The Corporate Response to Workers with Family Responsibilities", The Conference Board of Canada, 1989.
3 Fernandez, John, A.T. & T., 1987/88 study on 30 major companies with over 30,000 employees.
4 Statistics Canada, "A Portrait of Families in Canada", publication number 89-523E.
5 As above.
6 The Canadian Aging Research Network, "Work & Family, the Survey", March 1993.

over is expected to nearly double to almost 25% of the total population by the year 2036.[7] The proportion of senior citizens who are over age 80, and more likely to have major care needs, is also expected to increase during the next few decades.[8]

Even employees with no child or elder care responsibilities are less loyal to their employers than they used to be, and are demanding an increasing amount of flexibility and autonomy in their work. They too are looking for balance between their work and personal lives. In a survey of business and professional employees, 52.2% said they would consider a new, less demanding job in order to preserve their family and personal lives.[9]

2. *Marketing advantage:* Organizations that are now including a more diverse group of people in their decision making processes find it easier to develop innovative solutions to problems. Noted CIBC President, John Hunkin, "We realized that if we could get it right we'd have a great competitive advantage.'"[10] Added Rob Cummings, the CIBC's Senior Vice-President, Personal and Commercial Bank, "To have only men in senior roles diminishes a company's understanding of the marketplace and itself".[11]

Better representation of women can also help an organization sell its products and services. Employment equity laws require action from companies wanting to do business with government. Even when dealing with the private sector, firms like Price Waterhouse have noticed that potential customers are starting to ask what they are doing for women. Clients want to see women at the negotiating table doing more than serving coffee.

One company has gone a step further. It markets a mutual fund that only invests in companies that it considers good for women.[12] It looks at similar criteria to those used for this book in deciding who qualifies. Of course, the companies chosen also have to be solid investment prospects.

3. *Productivity increase:* Most women (like most men) work because

---

[7] Paris, Helene, as cited earlier.
[8] Monica Townson & Associates Inc., "Leave for Employees with Family Responsibilities", Women's Bureau, Labour Canada, 1993, p. 9, and Paris, Helene, as cited earlier.
[9] Le Magazine Affaires Plus, cited in "Canadian Families", The Vanier Institute of the Family, 1994.
[10] "Smashing the glass ceiling: bank sees benefit in promoting women to top ranks", Financial Post, v.87(19), May 8/10, 1993, p. 24.
[11] As above.
[12] Women's Equity Mutual Fund, offered by Pro-Conscience Funds Inc., San Francisco, California.

they have to in order to support themselves and their families. The number of Canadian families living below the poverty line would more than double if the mother were to quit her job[13]. A few statistics highlight the impact of the struggle to balance work and family responsibilities on productivity:

- Absenteeism for personal or family reasons doubled between 1982 and 1992.[14]
- Most Canadian employers attribute at least a quarter of their problems with employee stress and absenteeism to work and family conflicts.[15]
- 63.3% of readers surveyed by a business magazine said they would compromise their career advancement in order to devote more time to their personal or family lives.[16]
- In an American study of the impact of child care concerns, 42% of women and 31% of men reported missing work due to child-care-related problems.[17]
- In the same survey, 54% of women and 27% of men reported stress on the job, and 42% of women and 32% of men reported a negative effect on their work performance.

The employers in this book are convinced that productivity was not harmed as they became better places for women to work. Many believe it improved. In one of the few attempts to measure productivity separately from factors like reduced absenteeism and turnover, the Bank of Montreal tested the output levels of translators before and after they were allowed to work from home. It found that in every case the number of pages translated had either stayed the same or increased.

Some Employers Just Don't Get It

Most Canadian workplaces are still set up for the "traditional" family, with a working father and a stay-at-home mother. In 1958, 87% of Canadian families fit that mold.[18] Estimates of how many still do range

---

[13] National Council of Welfare, "The Poverty Profile", 1994.

[14] Higgins,C., Duxbury, L., and Lee, C., "Balancing Work and Family: A Study of Canadian Private Sector Employees", December 1992.

[15] Paris, Helene, as cited earlier.

[16] Le Magazine Affaires Plus, as cited earlier.

[17] Fernandez, John, AT&T study, as cited earlier.

[18] Liberman, Karen, in speech to "The Flexible Workplace" conference, The Canadian Institute, October 27 & 28, 1992.

from 12% to 27%.[19] Organizations where most senior executives are still in traditional families are particularly reluctant to change the way they have always operated. They don't understand the need.

Women commented repeatedly in interviews that their organizations had improved when they got new senior managers who had wives with careers of their own, or when the boss got divorced and suddenly had a greater child care load.

In fact, the marital arrangements of management men seem to be more relevant than their age in determining whether employers are good for women. Women with young male co-workers, in communities where most of the wives stay at home, find the men every bit as resistant to new types of working arrangements as older men living in traditional families.

Many employers have odd perceptions of how well women are doing in their organizations. Several employers overlooked a shortage of women in upper level management when they completed the survey for this book, commenting "We do not have any areas in which women are under-represented." Even in organizations that have long had a female-dominated workforce, most of those answering do not seem to think that the proportion of women in senior management should be about the same as it is in the employer's workforce as a whole, or even in mid-management.

Interviews with employees who have quit their jobs can be an important source of information about an organization's weaknesses. Surprisingly, many employers don't conduct routine exit interviews. It's true that not all employees will open up and state their real reasons for leaving. However, if many women choose not to return after a maternity leave or quit shortly after returning, interviewing them could be a good way to find out why. It's best to have an outsider do the interviews and give the employer a summary report once the numbers are large enough to provide anonymity. This is similar to the general statistical reporting provided by many employee assistance programs.

When Price Waterhouse wanted to find out why its first try at work and family policies had not improved its female retention rates, it hired outsiders to interview high-potential women who had left the firm. The information gathered during the interviews helped the firm plan further improvements.

---

[19] Lero, D. and Johnson, K., "Integrating Work and Family Responsibilities: A Review of Workplace Policies and Programs in Canada", Population Studies Division, (Ottawa: Statistics Canada, 1990), p. 10., and Liberman, Karen, as cited earlier.

Advice to Employers

1. *Knowledge is power — so empowering your staff means keeping them as knowledgeable as possible.* Well-informed employees make better decisions and are more motivated. It may sound obvious, but it's a lesson many employers have trouble learning.

2. *Don't waste your clerical talent.* Think carefully before hiring for the sake of a university degree. Will that degree really lead to better performance than you could get by developing a staff member who already knows your business and is eager to learn and do more?

3. *If you fire somebody for sexual harassment, acknowledge it.* Letting employees know that strong action has been taken when necessary is the most powerful way to signal that staff should neither harass nor accept harassment.

4. *Interview all departing staff.* If possible, hire an outside firm to conduct exit interviews and have it bring problems to your attention. Keep statistics on why people leave. Look beyond the obvious. If many women left after having had babies, don't just accept that each one wanted to have more time for her family or left for "better opportunities". Ask yourself why so many consider those options "better".

5. *If you are serious about alternative working arrangements, do the following:*
   - develop user-friendly guidebooks for employees and supervisors about your rules, how to make a proposal, and what factors to think about in making the decision;
   - train your human resources staff to help employees and their supervisors reach an agreement, and let all employees know that such a service is available;
   - adapt your other systems to cope with AWAs. Think, for example, about how you track employee numbers, whether management pay is based partly on the number of *full-time* employees supervised, whether budgets specify a maximum number of bodies rather than full-time equivalents that may work in a department, and how factors like pensions and merit increases are affected if an employee switches to job-sharing or a reduced work week. (See Appendix A for information about AWAs.)

6. *Advertise part-time and job-sharing positions internally.* Don't limit job-sharing to people who can find their own partners.

Advertising such positions also signals that you accept alternative working arrangements as part of the mainstream.

7. ***Don't insist that people return to full-time work before even applying for a promotion.*** Let them apply and then: (a) make the case to you about how the new position could be done part-time or with job-sharing, or (b) consider switching to full-time work in order to take the new job.

8. ***Keep in touch with women on maternity leaves.*** Some may want to do some work while on leave, others may not. Most women, though, don't want to feel that the employer has forgotten that they exist. They want to know what changes are happening in their absence. Most importantly, be sure to discuss options with them as long in advance as possible if it looks like their jobs will be eliminated or restructured in their absence.

9. ***When planning child care assistance, think about who you are trying to help and find out what they need most.*** If your goal is to get management and professional women back to work quickly, an on-site day care centre with a large infant care program may be your best bet. If you are more concerned about clerical workers, financial help to offset the costs of child care could be more useful. If you have many shift workers with young children, try to schedule shifts long in advance and consider changing systems that require frequent rotations between night-time and day-time work.

10. ***Most important: Demonstrate commitment, right from the top.***

Appendices

Appendix A

A Guide to Alternative Working Arrangements

This appendix contains the following sections:
* *The Jargon*, definitions of the terms commonly used when people talk about alternative working arrangements;
* *Pros and Cons of Alternative Working Arrangements;*
* *How Common are Alternative Working Arrangements.*

The Jargon

Alternative working arrangements (AWAs): include flextime, job-sharing, compressed work weeks, reduced work-weeks (sometimes called permanent or continuous part-time), and telecommuting (sometimes called telework or flexiplace).

Compressed work week: Employees work a standard number of hours each week, but in fewer, longer days (e.g. working four, 10-hour days instead of five, eight-hour days). Generally, the hours are agreed to between individual employees and their immediate supervisors, but in some cases an entire department will agree to work on the same compressed work week schedule.

Continuous part-time: See reduced work week.

Flexiplace or (flexplace): See telecommuting.

Flextime (or flexible hours): Employees work a standard length day or week, but with flexible starting and ending times. Employees are usually expected to be present during core hours (typically 10:00 a.m. to 3:00 p.m.). In some organizations, they must start and end at the same time every day. In others, they can vary their times, as long as they are available during core hours.

Job sharing: Two employees share the same job, usually with each working 50% of the time and earning half the pay and benefits. Typical arrangements include: partners alternate working three days one week and two the next; each partner works $2^1/_2$ days every week; each works three days every week, with one day of overlap to exchange information.

Permanent part-time: See reduced work week.

Reduced work week: Employees work fewer hours each week than is standard. Many, for example, work three or four-day weeks, with each day being the standard length. Another, less common, option is to work a shorter day, five days a week.

Telecommuting (or telework): Doing some or all of the job from a location other than the company's office. The work is usually done from the employee's home, but sometimes from telecommuter centres that have facilities like photocopiers (see, for example, Bell Canada). Also called flexiplace or flexplace.

Pros and Cons of Alternative Working Arrangements

Compressed work week

Advantages for employees:	*Advantages for employers:*
• allows free time during the week to attend to personal errands, take courses, spend time with children, or just relax • may normally have worked 10 hours a day anyway — this way get compensatory time off • some employees work more effectively on a compressed schedule	• satisfied employees • may be more efficient, depending on the nature of the operation • cost savings possible, especially if an entire department is on the same schedule (so, for example, the facility can be closed one day a week)
Drawbacks for employees:	*Drawbacks for employers:*
• may become over-tired during regular, long shifts • may be less efficient toward the end of a long day than toward the end of a $7\frac{1}{2}$ or 8-hour day • may need to come in during time off for meetings or to get extra work done • if an entire department is on a compressed work week, individual employees may be unhappy with the arrangement	• may be a challenge to coordinate varying employee schedules • employees on a regular schedule may believe that they work more than those on the compressed schedule (especially if most employees routinely work over-time)

Flextime (flexible hours)

Advantages for employees:	*Advantages for employers:*
• easier to attend to personal errands, medical appointments, courses, etc. • can arrange to be at work during the employee's most productive times of day • no feelings of guilt associated with "sneaking off" to attend to a personal errand, a child's school concert, etc. • avoid the worst of commuter traffic	• satisfied employees • employees may be more productive, as they are working during their most effective times • less tardiness and absenteeism (employees can take the time they need to attend to personal errands, and then return to work, rather than pretend to be sick, thus taking the full day off) • can be a way to provide coverage of telephones, etc., for more hours each day without having to pay for over-time work
Drawbacks for employees:	*Drawbacks for employers:*
• those who start and leave work early (or late) may find that they are perceived as slackers by those who stay later (or start earlier) • may have to come in earlier or stay later than scheduled to attend meetings • people who start early often find themselves staying later than they are supposed to	• a challenge to coordinate varying employee schedules • employees on a regular schedule may resent seeing those on the flexible schedule arrive "late" or leave "early"

Job sharing

Advantages for employees:	*Advantages for employers:*
• allows days off to attend to personal errands, spend time with children, take courses, or relax	• able to attract and retain good employees who are unable or unwilling to work full-time
• many believe that they bring greater energy and productivity to their jobs than they did on a full-time schedule	• increased productivity possible because: (a) each partner may bring greater energy to the job than she (or he) could sustain during a full-time work schedule, (b) "two heads are better than one" when it comes to creativity and problem-solving, (c) minimal absenteeism, because employees have days off to attend to personal errands, and the job-sharing partners normally replace each other during vacations and other absences
• allows employees to keep work-related skills current and earn some income during periods of their lives when full-time work is not desired or possible	
• shift workers may be able to share shifts in a way that makes it easier to arrange for child care (e.g. by working all days or all nights for a month at a time, instead of switching every few days)	• cost savings possible from reduced absenteeism and possible reductions in benefit payments
Drawbacks for employees:	*Drawbacks for employers:*
• reduced income and benefits	• managers have more people to supervise — communication and performance evaluations may both be more difficult with a job-sharing team than with one employee
• may be seen as less committed to their careers	
• may be difficult/frustrating to coordinate work with job-sharing partner	
• may limit career advancement, especially for job-sharing employees who want to continue to work part-time	• costs may be higher if: (a) overlapping time is scheduled to ensure effective communication, and/or (b) full benefits are paid to each partner
• may have to find last-minute child care in order to cover for an absent job-share partner	

Reduced work week

Advantages for employees:	*Advantages for employers:*
• allows days off to attend to personal errands, take courses, spend time with children, or relax • many believe that they bring greater energy and productivity to their jobs than they did on a full-time schedule • allows employees to keep work-related skills current and earn some income during periods of their lives when they can't or don't want to work full-time • lower child or elder care costs (such costs may be eliminated entirely if spouses work complementary schedules)	• able to attract and retain good employees who are unable or unwilling to work full-time • increased productivity possible from employees who bring greater energy to the job than they could sustain during a full-time work schedule • reduced absenteeism, because employees have days off to attend to personal errands and may experience fewer stress-related illnesses • save money by allocating employee resources more efficiently (may be able to hire part-timers to cover specific busy periods or to do jobs that do not require a full-time employee). May also be a reduction in benefit payments
Drawbacks for employees:	*Drawbacks for employers:*
• reduced income and possible loss of benefits • may limit career advancement (often seen as less committed to their careers, may miss important networking opportunities) • many end up working more hours than they are supposed to, often coming in for meetings or doing telephone consultations on their days off • may feel less a part of the team	• a challenge to coordinate varying employee schedules • may be resentment from employees working on a standard schedule, who tend to forget that part-time colleagues are only paid a partial salary

Telecommuting (telework)

Advantages for employees:	*Advantages for employers:*
• increased productivity due to fewer interruptions • eliminates daily commuting time • cost savings (travel, clothing, food, before- and after-school care for children) • reduced child and elder care-related stress, as employees are more accessible to their dependents and their dependents' care-givers • can get some housework done during "coffee breaks" and other down times • more comfortable clothing and working environment • avoids office politics	• satisfied employees • may cut costs for office space • employees may be more productive, due to fewer interruptions • forces managers to evaluate staff on productivity rather than time spent • able to recruit from a broader talent pool (e.g. workers who are not located near the employer's facilities, some disabled workers, people who want to work from home for child or elder care-related reasons)
Drawbacks for employees:	*Drawbacks for employers:*
• loneliness, isolation • may be difficult to separate family and work life: work may impinge on personal or family time; noise and interruptions from family may impinge on work time • takes discipline and self-motivation • may have extra expenses, such as the purchase of computer equipment, special insurance to cover business use of household items, possibly an extra telephone line, higher utilities costs • may not have a suitable space in which to work • may not qualify for workers' compensation should an accident occur while working at home • career progress may be harmed by lack of visibility, lack of networking, and poor understanding of office politics • may lose access to the services of support staff	• must learn new skills to manage employees who are off-site • some employees not effective/productive if working from home • may be complaints from those still on-site about having a greater burden for dealing with emergencies, customer calls, and other office-centred activities • extra costs associated with providing the equipment necessary for employees to work from home

How Common Are Alternative Working Arrangements?

Even when there are official policies allowing AWAs, not all employees can use them. A 1988 survey done for the Conference Board of Canada found that in only a minority of companies were AWAs available to all types of workers.[1] For example, only 17.4% of companies saying they allowed job-sharing made it available to all categories of workers. Surveys have found that the arrangement available most commonly to Canadian workers is flextime. Nearly half the companies surveyed by the Conference Board said they allowed flextime, either formally or informally. Yet only a third of those companies said it was available to workers in all job classifications.

Even employees in jobs that have access to AWAs still invariably need their supervisors' approval to use them. This discretion makes it impossible to get a realistic estimate of how many employees really have access to AWAs. Probably the best indication comes from the views of the employees themselves. A 1992 study showed only 17.5% of employees using flextime but 75% saying they would like to.[2]

---

[1] Paris, Helene, "The Corporate Response to Workers with Family Responsibilities", The Conference Board of Canada, 1989.

[2] Higgins, C., Duxbury,L., and Lee, C., "Balancing Work and Family: A study of Canadian private sector employees", National Centre for Management Research and Development, The University of Western Ontario, 1992.

Appendix B
Summary of Maternity and Child Care Leave Legislation

Jurisdiction	*Maternity Leave*	*Child Care (Parental) Leave*
Federal	17 weeks	24 weeks (shared or taken by one parent)
Alberta	18 weeks	no provision
B.C.	18 weeks	12 weeks for each parent (maximum allowed for combined maternity/parental = 32 weeks)
Manitoba	17 weeks	17 weeks for each parent
New Brunswick	17 weeks	12 weeks (shared or taken by one parent)
Newfoundland	17 weeks	12 weeks for each parent
Nova Scotia	17 weeks	17 weeks for each parent
Ontario	17 weeks	18 weeks for each parent
P.E.I.	17 weeks	17 weeks for each parent
Quebec	18 weeks	34 weeks for each parent
Saskatchewan	18 weeks	no provision (although do have 6 weeks paternity leave)
N.W.T.	17 weeks	12 weeks for each parent
Yukon	17 weeks	no provision

Source: Family-Related Leave and Benefits, Human Resources and Labour Canada, published 1993.

Appendix C
More About How the Best Were Chosen

Approximately 730 organizations were sent an eight-page survey for this book. They had to have at least 50 employees to qualify. The first 500 surveys were sent to the chief executive officers of the companies listed by the Financial Post as the largest companies in Canada. The rest were sent to employers uncovered through research or those that contacted me after they heard about the book. I also followed up with human resources staff at some of the top 500 that were reportedly doing good things for women but had not responded to the initial survey.

One hundred and thirty-two organizations replied. Since these were self-selected employers that perceived themselves as being better than average for women, readers should be wary of drawing statistical conclusions from the data in the book about the "typical" Canadian employer.

I selected 70 of those that replied for follow-up interviews. Focus groups were held in 60 of the organizations. In most cases two groups of 10 to 15 women each were interviewed. One group consisted of management women; the other comprised non-management women. They held various types and levels of jobs, and had different lengths of service with the organization. Some had children, others did not. Sometimes, such as at the universities and school boards, more groups were held as the employees did not break logically into single management and non-management groups. On rare occasions only one focus group was held.

Women at the other 10 organizations were interviewed by telephone. In those cases the employer provided a list of at least 20 women (usually more) who worked in different types and levels of jobs. I interviewed a selection of the women whose names were provided.

It was not feasible to interview a statistically significant, random sample of women in each organization. Instead, I had to rely on the employers to invite a well-balanced selection of women to participate. Some did choose a truly random sample. One, for example, went through the company telephone directory inviting every fifth woman on the list. Smaller employers often invited all female employees to attend. Others undoubtedly chose women who they thought would say good things. To try to counteract that bias effect, I told the employers and each group that if I only heard positive comments I'd be suspicious. I found that typically the first one or two women to speak would be restrained, but the third or fourth would say something negative or controversial that got everybody talking. At that point even the original speakers would often revise what they had said.

Sometimes complaints were clearly personal gripes that had little to do with the overall organizational culture. At other times, I checked odd-sounding statements with human resources staff for clarification. Even within the best of organizations there will always be dissatisfied employees and occasional unjust decisions.

There are also difficulties comparing the data provided on the numbers of women at various levels in each organization. The survey used the same job categories that are used in the federal employment equity legislation. However not all employers are federally regulated, and even those that are interpret the job categories differently. The government suggests which job titles should go into each category, but even job titles can be inappropriate to compare. Wood Gundy, for example, has 372 people called vice-presidents, or 23% of its total staff of 1,592. Co-operative Trust, which is also in the financial services sector, has four vice-presidents, or 2% of its total staff of 195.

Also, as noted by an article in the Financial Post Magazine, many women in senior management are in the "pink-collar ghettos" of human resources and public relations, although I believe this is starting to change.[1] Employers included in this book were asked to specify which positions were held by women in upper management. If they had only one woman in upper management she usually was in either human resources or public relations. If they had more than one, senior women were likely to be in core business areas too.

Despite the weaknesses in both the numbers and the selection of women to interview, I found that the interviews were always consistent with what the employee distribution numbers suggested. Interviews at organizations with few women in senior management invariably leaned toward the negative.

Polices, however, had little correlation with the interviews. Some organizations had many supportive policies on the books, but no senior management commitment to them. The reverse was often true in small organizations. They had no or few formal policies, but a lot of senior management commitment to being a good employer for women.

---

[1] Financial Post Magazine, "The Boys Club," September, 1993, p. 18.

Index of Employers

SUGGESTIONS

Do you know of other good employers for women in Canada? Do you have any comments or suggestions for a second edition? Have you found any mistakes that we should know about? If so, please fill in this form or send a separate letter to:

Frank Communications
253 College Street, Suite 200, Toronto, Ontario, M5T 1R5
Fax: (416) 591-7202

Recommended employer: _____

Address: _____

Contact name: _____

Contact's title: _____

Telephone #: (_____) _____ Fax #: (_____) _____

Why do you think this employer would qualify as one of the best for women?

_____

_____

_____

_____

_____

_____

Other comments or suggestions: _____

_____

_____

_____

_____

Note from the author: I'd like to know more about you. If you have a moment, and want to help, please complete and send in the reader survey on the back of this page. Thanks!

READER SURVEY

I read this book because I am:
- ☐ interested in the topic
- ☐ unhappy with my work situation
- ☐ job-hunting
- ☐ responsible for HR/employment equity in my organization
- ☐ other? _____

I heard about this book:
- ☐ from a friend/colleague/counsellor
- ☐ saw it in a bookstore
- ☐ saw an advertisement for it
- ☐ saw an article or heard an interview about it
- ☐ other? _____

I am: ☐ female ☐ male

I have: ☐ a full-time job ☐ a part-time job ☐ no paid job

My spouse lives with me, and has:
☐ a full-time job ☐ a part-time job ☐ no paid job

I/we look after ____ child(ren) aged _____ and ____ elderly parent(s) or others who live with me/us.

I work as a: _____
(e.g. secretary, lawyer, clerk, mid-manager, ...)

The other people who do the kind of work I do in my organization are:
☐ mostly women ☐ mostly men ☐ pretty evenly mixed

In its treatment of women, I think my employer is:
☐ excellent ☐ above average ☐ average
☐ below average, but trying to improve ☐ awful
(If excellent, or above average, please fill in the suggestion form).

What I liked about the book:

_____

_____

_____

_____

What I did not like, or think could be improved in the next edition:

_____

_____

_____

_____

Please mail to: Frank Communications, 253 College Street, Suite 200, Toronto, ON, M5T 1R5 or fax to: (416) 591-7202.
Thanks for your help!

WANT YOUR OWN COPY?

Please send _____ copies of *Canada's Best Employers for Women: A Guide for Job Hunters, Employees and Employers* to:

Name: _____

Address: _____

_____

City & Province: _____, _____

Postal Code: _____

Cost per book:	$17.95
Postage and handling costs:	$ 3.50
GST (7%, at time of printing):	$ 1.50
Total cost per book:	$22.95
Multiply by number of copies ordered	× _____ copies
TOTAL ENCLOSED:	$_____

Mail copy of order form with cheque or money order payable to Frank Communications to:

Frank Communications
253 College Street, Suite 200
Toronto, Ontario
M5T 1R5

Most orders are shipped immediately, but please allow 4-6 weeks for delivery.

Note from the author: I'd like to know more about you. If you have a moment, and want to help, please complete and enclose a copy of the reader survey.

GIVE A GIFT TO FRIENDS OR COLLEAGUES

Please send a copy of *Canada's Best Employers for Women: A Guide for Job Hunters, Employees and Employers* to each of the people listed below.

Send to:

Name: _____

Address: _____

City & Province: _____, _____

Postal Code: _____

Send to:

Name: _____

Address: _____

City & Province: _____, _____

Postal Code: _____

Send to:

Name: _____

Address: _____

City & Province: _____, _____

Postal Code: _____

Ordered by: (name) _____

    Telephone (_____) _____ / Fax (_____) _____ .
    (Important in case there is a problem filling your order.)

[   ] Please enclose a card with each book, saying the book is a gift from (name, if different from above): _____.

Cost per book:	$17.95
Postage and handling costs:	$ 3.50
GST (7%, at time of printing):	$ 1.50
Total cost per book:	$22.95
Multiply by number of copies ordered	× _____ copies
TOTAL ENCLOSED:	$ ____

Mail copy of order form with cheque or money order payable to Frank Communications to:

    Frank Communications
    253 College Street, Suite 200
    Toronto, Ontario
    M5T 1R5

Most orders are shipped immediately, but please allow four to six weeks for delivery.

Note from the author: I'd like to know more about you. If you have a moment, and want to help, please complete and enclose a copy of the reader survey.